SOU'

REAPPRAISALS IN OVERSEAS HISTORY

COMPARATIVE STUDIES IN OVERSEAS HISTORY

general editor

H. L. WESSELING

PUBLICATIONS OF THE LEIDEN CENTRE
FOR THE HISTORY OF EUROPEAN EXPANSION

Vol. I – H.L. WESSELING (ed.), *Expansion and Reaction.*

Essays on European Expansion and Reactions in Asia and Africa, by F. Braudel, H. Brunschwig, S.N. Eisenstadt, J.C. Heesterman, J.L. Miège, R. Robinson, I. Schöffer, H.L. Wesseling, and E. Zürcher.

Vol. II – P.C. EMMER and H.L. WESSELING (eds.), *Reappraisals in Overseas History.*

Essays on Post-war Historiography about European Expansion, by C. Bayly, H. Bley, L. Blussé, H. Brunschwig, A. Hopkins, J.L. Miège, N. Steensgaard, J. Stengers, H.L. Wesseling, and G. Winius.

Vol. III – L. BLUSSÉ and F. GAASTRA (eds.), *Companies and Trade.*

Essays on Overseas Trading Companies during the *Ancien Régime,* by P. Boulle, K.N. Chaudhuri, P.C. Emmer, O. Feldbaek, E. Kato, P.W. Klein, D. Lombard, O. Prakash, E. Schmitt, N. Steensgaard, and G.D. Winius.

(forthcoming)

Subsequent volumes will deal with Racism and Colonialism, Colonial Cities, and the Theory and Practice of Imperialism.

REAPPRAISALS IN OVERSEAS HISTORY

edited by

P.C. EMMER and H.L. WESSELING

Essays on Post-War Historiography about European Expansion by C.A. BAYLY, H. BLEY, L. BLUSSÉ, H. BRUNSCHWIG, A.G. HOPKINS, J.L. MIÈGE, N. STEENSGAARD, J. STENGERS, H.L. WESSELING, and G.D. WINIUS.

LEIDEN UNIVERSITY PRESS
1979

The distribution of this book is handled by the following team of publishers:

for the United States and Canada

Kluwer Boston, Inc.
160 Old Derby Street
Hingham, MA 02043
USA

for all other countries

Kluwer Academic Publishers Group
Distribution Center
P.O. Box 322
3300 AH Dordrecht
The Netherlands

Library of Congress Cataloging in Publication Data CIP

Main entry under title:

Reappraisals in overseas history

(Comparative studies in overseas history; v. 2)
Bibliography: p.
Includes index.
1. Europe – Foreign relations – 1945 – Historiography.
2. Imperialism – Historiography.
I. Bayly, Christopher Alan. II. Emmer, P.C.
III. Wesseling, H.L. IV. Series.
D1058.R38 325'.34'09 79-11994

ISBN 90-6021-444-7 (hard cover)
ISBN 90-6021-447-1 (paperback)

PRINTED IN THE NETHERLANDS

CONTENTS

EDITORIAL NOTE

The Editors received assistance from Frank Perlin, M.A., in particular with regard to the contributions by Brunschwig, Miège and Stengers, which had to be translated from French.

PART I

INTRODUCTION

1. WHAT IS OVERSEAS HISTORY? SOME REFLECTIONS ON A COLLOQUIUM AND A PROBLEM

by

H.L. WESSELING and P.C. EMMER

I

Expansion and Reaction, volume I of our *Comparative Studies in Overseas History,* was devoted to a critical discussion of the concept "the expansion of Europe." For this second volume, consisting of essays on historical writing, a more practical approach has been chosen. The purpose is to use a history of historiography to illustrate the problems which have concerned the historians of the non-Western world since 1945 as well as the changes that have taken place in this field.

In the first volume we posed the question: does the history of European expansion in fact exist; should it not instead be incorporated in the national and regional histories of the areas it affected? This volume confirms that overseas history does indeed exist. In most European countries – and they are the primary concern in this volume – as well as in Japan, there are schools, centres, journals, etc. for *Überseegeschichte, Histoire d'Outre-Mer* or *Estudias Ultramarinas.* In short, overseas history is alive and well.

Nevertheless a problem does arise here, namely what exactly is overseas history? The first observation to be made in this respect is that overseas history is not the same as the history of European expansion. In *Expansion and Reaction,* we described the history of European expansion as "the history of the encounters between diverse systems of civilization, their influence on one another and the gradual growth towards a global, universal system of civilization."[1] But overseas history is a much broader concept. Overseas history deals not only with the encounters between Europeans and non-Europeans, but also with the economic, social, political and cultural systems of the non-Europeans themselves. In many respects the

[1] H.L. Wesseling (ed.), *Expansion and Reaction; Essays on European Expansion and Reaction in Asia and Africa* (The Hague 1978), p. 4.

phrase overseas history is an unfortunate one. It resembles a somewhat clumsy attempt to replace the term 'colonial history,' which has unpleasant political connotations, by another, more neutral term. While this change of names may eliminate the feeling that the non-European past is to be regarded from the comfort of the colonial hammock – in reality overseas history continues of course to be a Western concept. Indeed just the use of the word 'overseas' implies that the histories of Asia, Africa and America are to be tossed into one heap, whereas in fact the only characteristic they have in common is that they are not European history.

There are two reasons for retaining the concept of 'overseas history' for the time being. In the first place it is an established branch of science. The field of overseas history developed gradually out of the practice of West European history – not from the illusion that the object of this speciality would form a geographic or cultural unit. Quite simply, the Western historian encountered a degree of similarity in the nature of the source material for non-European history. The sources available either were created by Europeans or originated in Africa, Asia or America itself. Both types of sources have contributed towards the development of this speciality. The sources bequeathed by the Europeans are characterized by a certain uniformity because they cover predominantly the history of the large overseas trading companies as well as the colonial administrative apparatus. These sources refer continuously to the contacts between people or groups of people from two or more cultural circles. The sources originating in Asia, Africa or America differ entirely from most of the Western historical material. The techniques which the scholars of the non-Western world must use to understand and analyse these latter sources are widely divergent but have in common that they all add an extra dimension to the investigation: the overseas historian who happens to be a European must be capable not only of shifting in time but also of entering a culture other than his own.

The second factor which adds a coherence to overseas history is social rather than scientific in nature. In the world today, the 'Third World' is an important subject in politics and the social sciences. However the references of this concept are not geographical but economic. It includes all countries with a national income which is low and/or very unevenly distributed among the population. Since in practice this means almost all of the countries outside of the European and North American continents, the concepts 'history of the Third World' and 'overseas history' overlap to a large extent. Thus it appears that the term 'overseas history' is not only a functional concept for the practice of history but it also a useful tool for investigating the historical background of the problems of the 'Third World'. As a result the term 'overseas history' will remain in use for some time, through lack of a better alternative.

The second question conjured up by the title of this volume involves the concept 'reappraisals'. Is there a need for a survey of the studies of overseas history since 1945? The answer is not difficult. Since World War II almost all branches within the field of history have undergone revolutionary changes. Various surveys have described new insights developed with respect to political, economic, social, and even Church history. The essays collected in this volume examine the influence which these changes within the science of history have had on the practice of non-Western history.

But history does not take place within a vacuum. In addition to the internal, scientific changes within the profession, the major political and social upheavals since World War II have also exerted an influence on the hypotheses and approaches of historians. In this connection, the very first factor to be considered is the process of decolonisation, a process which has only recently reached completion – more or less. This explains why the contributing authors were asked whether this exogenous factor was important to the development of non-Western history. To what extent are the historians of the ex-mother countries influenced by this pursuit of independence and how did decolonisation and the new nationalism affect the historians in the developing countries themselves?

The purpose of the essays in this volume is therefore to show what has been written about the history of the Third World since 1945 and to determine the characteristic features as well as the most striking gaps in this historiography. The choice of subjects was not based on a geographic division of the 'Third World' into Asia, Africa and Latin America. Overseas history is in fact still largely dominated by Western historians. For this reason a division based on the '(ex-)mother country' instead of the '(ex-)colony' was preferred. Obviously limitations had to be applied here. In view of the quantity and diversity of English and French studies of overseas history, selection was necessary. Instead of a more or less complete but unavoidably superficial bibliographic survey, it seemed to us in these two cases that an analysis in depth of a few of the most important historiographic problems and trends would be more worth while. To represent English historiography we chose for obvious reasons India and, in the second place, West Africa. This latter region seemed to be the most interesting of the English African empire because of the prolonged contacts with the West.

Moreover the important English economic-history school concentrated mainly on this area and, finally, through this choice, a significant comparison with French historiography becomes possible.[2]

Southern Africa appeared to be too specific, too *sui generis,* for our purposes, while Australia and New Zealand – not to mention North America – were certainly overseas territories at one time but are not of course part of the Third World today. For France, North Africa was as obvious a choice as India was for English historiography. French historiography on black Africa seemed and still seems – in spite of the critical tone of Brunschwig's essay – to be important enough, also from a comparative point of view, to warrant a separate contribution. For the essay on historiography in Scandinavia, the Iberian peninsula, German-speaking Central Europe, the Netherlands and Belgium, the authors were not restricted by geographical boundaries since the total yield in the field of overseas history is relatively low in these countries. Latin America should also be mentioned at this point. This continent has been independent for more than 150 years and has developed its own historical tradition, separate from that of Portugal and Spain. Although most of the authors also take the new historical activities in the former colonies into consideration, historical writings in the Portuguese and Spanish-speaking countries of the Americas are not discussed. In order to do so, a separate contribution would be necessary which is unfortunately absent here.[3] The authors of the essays in this volume apologize for these *lacunae* and refer the reader to the selective bibliography included in this volume.

In conclusion – an observation: in spite of the many gaps this collection is a first attempt to prepare an inventory of the field of overseas historiography. In the past, volumes of essays have been published concentrating on the history of overseas colonies of one (ex-)imperium or one period out of the common past of Western

[2] For English Africa, see as a supplement to Hopkins' essay: Christopher Fyfe (ed.), *African Studies since 1945* (London, 1976) with contributions by Shula Marks, Thomas Hodgkin and T.O. Ranger.

[3] For Latin America, see in particular: Woodrow Boraf, "Latin American History in World Perspective" in Charles P. Delzell (ed.), *The Future of History: Essays in the Vanderbilt University Symposium* (Nashville, Tennessee, 1977), 151-172 and Charles C. Griffin (ed.), *Latin America. A Guide to the Historical Literature*. University of Texas Press (Austin/London, 1971).

colonization.[4] One could conclude from this that the scholars of overseas history do not engage in introspection and self-reflection. This is a rather striking phenomenon because the European historiographic tradition since the nineteenth century, shows that the practical investigation of history always has been accompanied by reflections on the historical method and the historian's task. This is particularly characteristic of the important German historical school.

Lately, however, Western historiography has been plagued increasingly by doubts about the scientific value of the historical method and scepticism concerning the social relevance of the practice of history. In the Third World the situation seems to be quite different. Methodological discussions on 'oral history', 'ethnohistory', etc. do take place but – probably in reaction to the functionalistic and a-historical approach in anthropology – history appears to be flourishing rather than waning. In addition the social relevance of historical research is easily recognized. Historical analyses of traditional societies are presumed to contribute directly to an understanding of many of the problems relevant today. Vindication of a distinctive national past plays an important role in the process of nation-building in young states. Whether the study of history in the Third World will as a result obviously differ in character – at least temporarily – from that practiced for instance in Europe is a question which is not answered in this book but is raised by some of the authors, e.g. Brunschwig and Stengers.

II

In terms of historiography, India is without doubt the most important area in the Third World. Before 1945, many surveys of the history of India had already appeared, in which the coming of the British and the period of colonisation were the center of the analysis. The colonised were of little interest. As Bayly writes ". . . the people of India emerged simply as stage rabble, to be speedily defeated and

[4] For essays on the countries which used to belong to the British Empire, see Robin W. Winks (ed.), *The Historiography of the British Empire-Commonwealth* (North Carolina, 1966).
For essays on specific periods of overseas history, see Rudolf von Albertini (ed.), *Moderne Kolonialgeschichte* (Cologne/Berlin, 1970) and Clive Rewey and A.G. Hopkins (eds.), *The Imperial Impact; Studies in the Economic History of Africa and India* (London, 1978).

pacified."[5] In the historiography after 1945, the author recognizes two important invigorating impulses: the influence of American historians with their high regards for cultural anthropology, and the studies produced by Indian historians themselves. In fact Bayly is the only author who devotes a large portion of his essay to history written by scholars from the Third World. It is striking here that initially Indian historians made no attempt to introduce a truly new approach. Bayly points out that the main aim of the history departments of the various universities in India seemed to be, in the first instance, to produce a mirror-image of English colonialism as described in European historiography, without taking on new issues. Under the influence of growing nationalism, they rebelled against colonial domination but *in historicis* that meant only a change in evaluation, not in subject. Only recently have Indian historians turned towards their own past: the 'British Raj' has been replaced by the 'Indian Village'. However once again these new trends within India correspond to changes in English and American historical studies on India.

English historiography on Africa is much younger than that on India. Africa was, of course, colonised later than India but this fact alone still cannot explain entirely the enormous difference in interest. According to Hopkins, historians did not begin to study Africa until after World War II, whereas India was a subject of historical research long before this. Probably this discrepancy can be attributed to the fact that already the first contacts with Asia so stimulated Europeans that they were inspired to further exploration and study; in contrast the first quick encounters with Africa were such that for three centuries this continent was regarded as inaccessible and uninteresting. The interest in Africa's past developed during the period of decolonization in the nineteen fifties. Probably this explains why Hopkins devotes so much attention to political and economic developments. Plans, calculations and ideas about the development of the Third World appear to have imparted more direction to the study of Africa's past than any other factor. In this connection, Hopkins places considerable emphasis on the reversal from liberal optimism concerning the development of the Third World – prevalent in the period 1950-1960 – to a radical pessimism which dominated – after 1960 – the models of development of the political economy. It should be noted here that this reversal also penetrated into the historiography of Asia and Central and South America. Furthermore Hopkins points out that as a

[5] See page 22.

eedingly important for the future prospects of university duates in England itself. In the new Departments of History in ica, African history became an important subject, but the chers were trained in the (ex-)mother country. There too the v curricula were set up. This was possible because of the high ree of autonomy which forms the basis of higher education in gland and makes the introduction of new subjects possible. As a ılt of the centralism of French universities such innovations are ch more difficult in France, which could explain the lethargic ction in that country to the demand for scholars of African tory for the francophone universities in Africa. In France itself prospects for the future are indeed restricted. In this connection ınschwig points out that there are only a limited number of chairs African history.

The importance of the supply-and-demand factor could also be strated by the development of African studies in North America. the United States (and also in the Caribbean) interest in Africa is ıted to the emancipation of the black population in North and ıtral America. In their search for an identity, the American cks see Africa as the country from which they originated. The cks reached the university in the mid-nineteen fifties and the tory curriculum was adapted – slowly at first but later in an celerated tempo – to this new group of 'clients', to the benefit the practice of African history.

Miège's essay supports Brunschwig's views on the significance of titutionalisation, although in a reverse sense. He describes how, hin the framework of the decentralisation of research institutions France, several 'centres of excellence' were established far from is. As a result, a number of universities in Southern France now ve not only extensive archives at their disposal, including the hives of the North African administrations, but also university irs and libraries for Maghrib studies.

While there exists, in any case, an important overseas histori- raphy in England and France, despite all the differences and ances in appraisal, this applies to a much lesser extent for the naining countries in Europe considered in this volume. The blication of books and articles is without a doubt meager, at st when one takes into account the fact that Spain, Portugal d the Netherlands administered large areas outside of Europe er extended periods and have retained a gigantic paper legacy.

In his contribution, Winius notes that as far as overseas history the Iberian peninsula is concerned, historians do pay attention to s subject but ignore new theories and international developments.

result of the practice of African history, a relativ technique has grown into an important historica interview. The scarcity of written sources in la and the lack of books written by Europeans ab this continent forced the historian to come to tradition which exists among many of the Af registration and analysis of African oral history be inconceivable without close co-operation wit The use of the special technique of oral history operation with anthropology as an auxiliary scie of African history into a separate branch. Withi seas history as a whole, an analysis of Africa's pa better than any other the distinctive nature of Western history. Hopkins supports this by ment historiography of Africa the emphasis is on the h region, a specific tribe. Contacts with Europ several interesting topics, but they form only African history.

How can this historiography at the level of th dynasty be reconciled with the desire for a trul ography; this problem is considered by Brunsch tone of Brunschwig's contribution is somber, bec the number and the quality of the African histori a great deal to be desired, the works cited in h here too the history of Africa itself is the central relationship between Africa and Europe. Accordi there are still too many 'blank spaces' in the h French Africa; moreover the scholars of this speci in debate. According to Brunschwig this can be at extent to the inadequate institutionalisation of French institutes of higher learning.

Brunschwig's somber commentary can, howe somewhat by considering the study of history i with anthropology. In this latter field, the Fren world-wide reputation, especially of course Lév regard to Africa – also Claude Meillassoux and both of whom have published studies with an obvi And yet the nucleus of Brunschwig's argument historical writings – stands, when one compares essay with those in Hopkins' contribution. T relatively speaking, in Black Africa exhibited by t Americans can be attributed to two factors. The many new English-speaking universities in decolo

The Spanish and Portuguese colleagues often still practice true 'colonial' history with an obviously triumphal description of the European performance, as was common in Western Europe up to World War II. In fact Winius states that Iberian historiography as a whole shows signs of falling behind and becoming isolated. He attributes this partially to the prolonged dictatorial regimes in Spain and Portugal during this century, but also signalizes a difference in mental outlook between Iberian historians and their colleagues from Western Europe. Although the general situation cannot be considered impressive, several valuable detail studies are mentioned in this essay. As for the ex-colonies, they did not receive a new historical impulse during this period. In fact most of these areas were already independent long ago, and the Spanish overseas territories as well as Brazil have built up their own historical tradition, as mentioned previously. Since Angola and Mozambique have only been independent for a few years, they have not had the time to train their own historians.

Stengers observes in his essay that up to 1960 the history of Africa as written in Belgium was highly similar to that produced in Spain and Portugal. In Belgium too overseas history was dominated by a triumphal undertone with respect to the Belgian activities in the Congo. This is fairly surprising because the Belgian historians were far less isolated than the Iberian and their work can in general certainly withstand the scrutiny of international critics. Probably this lag in the practice of African history in Belgium can be related to the relatively late decolonisation. Stengers also mentions the stimulating influence of English and American scholars of African history on the historiography of the Congo, an element which also emerges in the historiography of Iberian expansion. As in Angola and Mozambique, historiography does not yet play an important role: the tradition of the university of Zaire is as yet still too short for Zairian historians to have already been able to create their own account of the history of the Congo. Because Stengers' essay is purposely limited to the Congo, one could mistakenly presume that Belgian overseas historians were concerned only with Africa. The inaccuracy of such an assumption is proven by the well-known studies of Verlinden, Stols and Everaert on the sixteenth century, a period in which the Flemish contributed significantly to the establishment of the Spanish and Portuguese empires.

The theory that a relationship exists between the time of decolonisation and innovations in overseas historiography cannot be confirmed by the Dutch case. The independence of the Dutch East Indies occurred fairly soon after the end of World War II and led to sharp conflicts between the Netherlands and Indonesia. In the Netherlands, the abrupt termination of the band with the 'girdle of emeralds' did not, however, result in a modern critical approach to the colonial past while at the same time the pre-war Orientalistic approach came to an abrupt end. Thus in the Netherlands a sort of historical vacuum developed: the history of Indonesia became a voluntarily imposed taboo among Dutch historians. There is an enormous discrepancy between this disinterest and the immense and valuable archives which are stored in Holland. Most of these refer to Indonesia, but there is also material on West and South Africa, the Middle East, and on South, Central and North America.

In his contribution Wesseling maintains that in the Netherlands the trauma of Indonesian independence has now been absorbed and that a growing number of young historians is making use of the abundant material in the archives in an attempt to fit Dutch overseas expansion into the international framework. Wesseling's survey demonstrates quite clearly just how unbalanced the basic structure of Dutch overseas historiography really is: there are a few excellent Dutch studies dating partly from before World War II as well as several important publications from the period immediately afterwards and then . . . nothing. A substructure of detail studies is entirely lacking and the elimination of this has only recently been undertaken.

To conclude this summary, the essays on Scandinavia and on German-speaking Central Europe should be mentioned. The contributions of Steensgaard and Bley reveal a common trait: in Scandinavian and Germanic overseas historiography, the colonial past of the countries themselves plays only a subordinate role. The modern involvement of the social sciences in development and underdevelopment is considered much more important. Nevertheless in both of these linguistically defined areas, good studies have been published on the history of the Danish, Swedish and German ex-colonies.

According to Steensgaard, the limited number of historical studies on Asia, Africa and America is a direct result of the small size of the historical world in the Nordic countries. There are many more professional historians in West and East Germany, Austria and Switzerland than in Scandinavia and as a direct correlate, the number of publications on overseas history is also much larger. According to Bley, however, German-speaking historians are not immediately interested in the Third World *an sich* nor in the history of European expansion and the reactions to it. The German historical tradition is much more interested in the problems of *Universal-*

geschichte and the world beyond Europe is considered from this point of view. In addition in both East and West Germany there are many historically inclined political scientists and anthropologists who look to the non-European past for the key to explain current problems of development and underdevelopment.

Blussé's essay does not quite fall within the scope of this volume. It could be described as a first modest attempt to do full justice to the non-European point of view. We have already mentioned the development of national historiographic traditions in Australia, New Zealand and the Americas, which do not fall within the context of this volume. In Indonesia, Indochina and Africa on the other hand, the national historiography has not yet developed sufficiently in breadth and depth, despite several exceedingly valuable studies, to justify separate treatment. And finally, Bayly incorporated Indian historiography in his paper in a most elegant fashion. We feel that it would also be interesting to include a separate paper on the historiography within an Asian country. In spite of the distinctiveness of the once "closed country", the questions treated here are of general significance. How was European expansion regarded from the other side and what was the influence of the science of history in Europe on historiography outside Europe? In his essay on this subject, Blussé shows that European expansion also made a deep impression in Asia. One result on the positive side was that Japanese historians investigated the effects of European expansion within their own country. These studies incidentally were carried out within familiar frames of reference because the Japanese adopted to a large extent Western methods of historical research. But the study of European expansion also had a negative side: the Japanese attempted to find herein legitimation for their own urge for expansion as it was manifested between the two World Wars. However, Japan's interest in the European phase in its own history is not typical of Third World historiography. Historical events in this country contrast sharply with those in the countries in Asia, Africa and America which were colonised by the Europeans. On the other hand it still was Japan that was able to develop its own version of its reaction to European expansion. In most of the colonised countries, the practice of history is dominated by the West and there is no question of a really autochtonous tradition. All of the authors dealing with historiography in these regions point out that a separate non-Western variant of history does not exist. Europe and North America are the leaders in determining the objects, methods and techniques of 'overseas' history.

III

Before returning to the question posed at the beginning, namely does overseas history possess a character and a quality of its own, it is useful to note whether this collection of essays has yielded any specific subjects which serve as the central themes of overseas history. This appears indeed to be the case. As far as European expansion is concerned, these subjects are 1. the history of geography and anthropology; 2. the voyages of discovery; 3. the first contacts with non-Europeans; 4. the overseas trading companies; 5. the Colonial Offices; 6. colonial civil servants; 7. missionary activities; 8. colonial armies and colonial wars; 9. colonial lobbies; and 10. colonialist/imperialist ideologies.

On the non-Western side one can mention 1. the chronology and structure of the precolonial African, American and Asian territories; 2. the comparison between the demographic, social and economic developments before and after contact with the West; 3. nationalism; 4. the transfer of power; 5. the role of collaborators; and 6. protest movements as well as revolutions, uprisings and other forms of resistance.

Little can be deduced however from these essays about the distinctive nature of overseas history. The papers reveal instead that in this respect overseas history exhibits a certain ambiguity. The history of European expansion in the traditional sense, i.e. of the activities of Europeans overseas, demands little in the way of special skills and can be investigated successfully by an 'ordinary' historian. But if the goal is instead a history of expansion and reaction, then a different historical approach is required. This approach not only demands several specific technical skills, such as mastery of the interview technique or some fluency in a strange and difficult language, but also produces its own methodological problems resulting in a fundamental difference from the practice of European history. The same applies to the study of pre-colonial overseas history. If this is true, we are facing a major problem, viz. whether the well known disparity of power also exists *in historicis*. Many authors have shown how the science of history as practiced in the West has continued to dominate the historiography of the overseas world, even after decolonization. However it remains to be seen whether this is only a transient phenomenon, the aftermath of the colonial period and the result of a temporary gap. It may be more closely related to the Western concept of history itself.

The science of history as it is practiced in Europe today – and which developed from the legacy of the Greeks via innovations during the sixteenth and seventeenth centuries into a professional science in the nineteenth century – is characterized by two approaches. On the one hand the synchronic approach which concentrates mainly on comphrehension of time periods in their uniqueness. In this case historical understanding is directed towards acquiring an insight into the relationships between political, economic, social and cultural phenomena in a specific period. The historian attempts to explain the behaviour of people within the mental framework of their times and their culture. In essence this approach is an inheritance of German historicism which focusses on *Verstehen* instead of explaining, as indicated by Ranke's famous motto: "Jede Epoche ist unmittelbar zu Gott". The second, possibly even more important, tradition is the diachronic approach, i.e. listing series of dated events which are noted and described as unique singular facts but which only acquire significance and meaning within a chronological sequence and causal relationship. This historical approach was, and usually, is referred to pejoratively by *Annales* historians as 'event history'. However, even if it is not the ultimate answer, 'event history' is not only the correlate but also the substratum of structural history. It is justifiable to ask whether it is possible for other cultures, far less engrossed with problems of chronology but also with far fewer written or otherwise dated sources, to practice history according to this 'event' model. Although non-Western history may encompass as many events, it certainly has fewer sources at its disposal. In such a case the structure-directed approach is not so much the consumation of the event-directed approach – it is the only possible choice. In short, one is not seduced by structural history but condemned to it.[6]

This may be the most important problem of overseas history. It is in any event more important than the problem of the evaluation and appreciation of European expansion, which because of their different pasts Europeans and non-Europeans could be expected to view differently. In this respect, however, it appears that there is no longer a marked distinction between the aimers and the targets of the cannons. As far as the evaluation of the negative and positive aspects of European expansion is concerned, the two groups of

[6] See Henri Brunschwig, "Une Histoire de l'Afrique noire est-elle possible?" in *Mélanges en l'honneur de Fernand Braudel* (Toulouse, 1973) Vol. I, 75-87 and Henri Moniot "L'Histoire des peuples sans histoire" in Jacques le Goff and Pierre Nora (eds.), *Faire de l'histoire. Vol. I: Nouveaux Problèmes* (Paris, 1974), 106-123.

historians are equally divided. If for instance we look at the well-known question of the "development of underdevelopment", it appears that although the hypothesis originated in a circle of Latin American economists, it was enthusiastically adopted by Western sociologists and historians who proceeded to enhance and develop it.[7] A Dutch historian, for instance Van Leur, is found to be more sceptical about the role of the West than a historian from India, such as Rajan.[8] The Belgian King Baudouin and the former premier of the Congo, Lumumba, disagreed radically in their appreciation of the Belgian colonial administration but they were equally emphatic about its pronounced influence. Historians today are more likely to agree on appreciation but disagree on the lasting influence of the Belgian presence in the Congo.[9]

Does this mean that there are no differences between Western and non-Western scholars of overseas history, that they are in other words interchangeable? This is not a new question. The most extreme answer holds that African history can only be practiced by blacks. This would rob history of its scientific pretensions, which are after all based on the interchangeability of its scholars. Of course the Indian or Indonesian historian is by birth, breeding and education much more familiar with his own culture and society than the European. But this is not a fundamental difference. Sociologists and anthropologists must overcome the same problem. *Mutatis mutandis* it also applies to the European delving into very ancient periods of European history. The most important instrument for an intersubjective approach to overseas history will probably be found in the development of a common apparatus of concepts. In addition to theoretical analyses, comparative studies can also be very useful in this respect. Does something like a colonial city, with its own function and position, exist irrespective of differences in time and place? Does the South American concept of *dependencia* also function in Africa? Can the concept of 'dual economy' as encountered in Indonesian historiography also be applied to the Caribbean? What are the similarities among the large trading com-

[7] Immanuel Wallerstein and Terence K. Hopkins "Patterns of Development of the Modern World-System; Research Proposal" *Review* 1/2 (1977), pp. 111-145. Catherine Coquery-Vidrovitch (ed.), *Connaissance du tiers monde* (Paris, n.d.). Rudolf von Albertini, *Europäische Kolonialherrschaft, 1880-1940* (Zürich, 1976), pp. 8-13.

[8] M.S. Rajan "The Impact of British Rule in India", *Journal of Contemporary History*, Vol. IV, No. 1 (1968), pp. 89-102.
For Van Leur, see page 131.

[9] For Baudouin and Lumumba, see page 171.

panies in Asia and the Atlantic and what was their function during a specific phase of the capitalistic system? Is there a connection between racism and colonialism?[10] These are questions which shall be considered in future volumes of our *Comparative Studies.*

[10] See Rudolf von Albertini, "Einleitung" in Rudolf von Albertini (ed.), *Moderne Kolonialgeschichte* (Cologne/Berlin, 1970), pp. 11-38.

PART II

THE GREAT COLONIAL POWERS

2. ENGLISH-LANGUAGE HISTORIOGRAPHY ON BRITISH EXPANSION IN INDIA AND INDIAN REACTIONS SINCE 1945[1]

by

C.A. BAYLY

I. GENERAL TRENDS

The critical period of change in the post-war historiography of British expansion in the Indian subcontinent came in the years 1958-62. New life was given to the study of the impact of ideas on imperial practice by the publication of E.T. Stokes, *The English Utilitarians in India,* and the work of a number of young American scholars, notably B.S. Cohn and R.E. Frykenberg, was beginning to appear at conferences and in learned journals. At the same time, stock-taking of Britain's imperial past gave rise to a new historical interest in the nature of Empire. Since Robinson and Gallagher's *Africa and the Victorians* (1959) concluded that African Partition was 'a giant footnote to the conquest of India,' it was only a matter of time before younger scholars would turn, or be directed to the text. text.

The Centres of Study

Changes in public policy reinforced this interest. In America, the increase in foreign aid and involvement in the Third World left its legacy in a number of overseas study programmes and a readiness among the major foundations (Ford, Rockefeller, etc.) to fund historical and anthropological work on India. In Britain, government money was directed to a number of South and East Asian Centres and new scholarly journals emerged. In India, the anniversary of the Rebellion of 1857 and the decennial celebrations of Independence centred attention for a more detached appraisal of the country's colonial past, though one which was to be increasingly conducted in

[1] No attempt is made to deal with all important literature in the field. I have merely tried to sketch what I see as the main trends in two or three areas which I know better. More comprehensive and specialised articles are listed hereafter.

a Marxist idiom. Finally, in the Australian National University a flourishing research seminar in Indian studies began to meet in 1960.

The years between 1945 and this turning point are more difficult to characterise. Some lines of thought which were evident before the Second World War continued, while the economic and political preoccupation of post-War Asia with development had begun to impinge on the historian's consciousness. Interest in the earliest days of British expansion in India and in the East India Company had been well established before the War. The study of the rise of the Company, and the early revenue and judicial arrangements in India had been a staple of the old imperial training boards in Britain. The dissolving empire had been fascinated by its own origins, and studies of this sort were felt to be edifying for the last generation of Civilians and for the public alike. There was a brief period after the demission of empire and before the onset of nostalgia, inquisitiveness and guilt, when it appeared that modern Indian history might virtually disappear from history syllabuses. During these years, the London School of Oriental and African Studies, C.C. Davies at Oxford and Percival Spear at Cambridge kept the subject alive. Their interests and expertise with the India Office Records left an indelible stamp on the subject. But as to the content of university courses themselves, a preoccupation with constitutional and institutional history was evident. The tradition of Stubbs', *Select Charters* and Pollock and Maitland's, *History of English Law* was still too strong in the history faculties of major British Universities. Overseas history, as a *parvenu,* was still obliged to validate itself through a minute analysis of the lapidary prose of India's law-givers and proconsuls. The people of India often emerged simply as a stage rabble, to be speedily defeated and pacified.[2]

In America, Indian studies remained largely indological and were represented, for instance, in the work of Norman O. Brown and his pupils at Philadelphia. Elsewhere there was a little interest in India as part of the British Commonwealth, an institution that appeared unduly significant to Americans as their new geopolitical responsibilities began to weigh with them. The richest vein of all was that of Holden Furber, whose *John Company at Work* (1948) was a book greatly in advance of its time. Whereas most British and Indian historians were still concentrated on the strategic and institutional imperatives of empire, Furber vastly enlarged our understanding of

[2] This is far from a caricature. The only Indian history taught at Oxford in the early 1960s was a paper on 'Britain and India in the time of Warren Hastings', and the only set book for the Indian side was Grant Duff's *History of the Marattas* (London, 1826).

the economic forces which drove European capital into the country trade of north India. Ultimately, his work was to provide the basis for an interpretation of British expansion which modifed the crude argument that it was an engrossment of industrial raw materials, and yet gave due weight to changes in the world economy and the commerical underswell of British advance.[3] Later historians have shown how the economic expansion of private traders and the Company's own trading problems created many of the political crises with Indian states which provided the centrepiece of previous interpretations.[4] But another rich vein of pre-War scholarship was completely lost. Herman Goetz's questioning of the cultural decadence of India during the 18th century was never developed in political or social history.[5] It is only in the last decade that a group of 'young and youngish' American historians have begun to question and refine the whole argument of decline and anarchy in the Indian political system which was the other main pillar of the strategic explanation of British expansion.[6] Above all, what is most striking is the lack of a sociological perspective in English or American studies of India at this time. There was nothing comparable to the work which had been done for Indonesia in the 1930s by J.C. Van Leur and B.S. Schrieke. The reason for this lies partly in the disapproval with which British academic circles regarded anthropology until very recently. Yet this cannot provide a complete explanation. In Africa, a historical anthropology had begun to emerge from the work of M. Fortes, E.P. Evans-Pritchard and others before the War. Most probably, this laggardliness represented a long gestation. It was not until the publication of E. Leach's, *Political Systems of Highland Burma* that British and American anthropologists began themselves to reinstate history as a relevant discipline and move beyond small, pre-literate communities.

[3] Notably represented by P.J. Marshall, *East India Fortunes: the British in Bengal* (Oxford 1976), 'Economic and political expansion: the case of Oudh' *MAS*, 9, 3 (1975); see also S. Bhattacharya, *The East India Company and the Economy of Bengal* (London 1954); J. Nicholl, unpublished Ph.D., University of Cambridge, 1976.

[4] E.g., C.C. Davies, *Warren Hastings and Oudh* (London 1939); Percival Spear, *The Twilight of the Moghuls* (Cambridge, 1951) pioneered an approach that dealt more deeply with the Indian side.

[5] H. Goetz, *The Crisis of Indian Civilisation in the 18th and early 19th centuries* (Calcutta 1938).

[6] M.N. Pearson, 'Political Participation in Moghul India', *IESHR*, 9, 2, 1973 deals with new writing on the late Moghul and emergent regional states; S. Gordon is beginning to extend our knowledge of the Mahrattas, see his 'Slow conquest: the Mahrattas and Malwa' in *MAS*, 11, 1 (1977).

In Indian universities, the period before 1965 was characterised by a conflict between ideology and institutional affiliations. There was certainly a splendid early literature of trenchant criticism of colonialism and British expansion represented by the work of Naoroji and by B.D. Basu's, *The Rise of the Christian Power in India* (Calcutta, 1934). Yet the sources which Indian historians of India used, such as the National Archives and the India Office Library, fostered an interpretation which was often no more than a mirror image of British historiography. The dispute was not about the underlying causes of British conquest, or about the meaning of that conquest, but tended instead to resolve around rival interpretations of the motives of Clive and Warren Hastings and the incidence of atrocities against Indians. Even broader disputes, about the fate of hand-loom weavers or of landed proprietors under the British, were documented by reference to the same sources. British historians elaborated one office memorandum thrown up by contemporary officialdom, while Indians relied on another, and opposing view. The archival remains of Holt Mackenzie were weighed against the bureaucratic ashes of Lord Moira. Undoubtedly the connection of many Indian academics with British universities, and in particular with SOAS, heightened those tensions. They were trained in a tradition which scholarship and patriotism alike demanded they modify. Yet there was no coherent general interpretation of much of their modern history to which to turn, outside the popular works of J. Nehru and the trans-Himalayan rumblings of Marx and Lenin. In these circumstances, it is not surprising that the most creative school of Indian historiography was that of Aligarh Muslim University which concentrated its efforts on the Moghul period. Here the documentation was available in India; Indians had an enormous advantage in technique, while European historical scholarship had made almost no progress since the later works of W.H. Moreland. Outside Aligarh, N.K. Sinha also presided over a flourishing school of modern Indian history in Calcutta. Here again vast materials were at hand, while Bengalis had a sophisticated tradition of both Marxist and non-Marxist radicalism and anti-colonialism. The conflict between ideology, training and documentation was not so acute.

The Topics Studied

Within the last decade, our understanding of the expansion of European commercial activity in coastal south Asia before 1750 has been considerably extended. The lines of debate are similar to those that have been raised in a more general context by Meilink-

Roelofsz[7] and N. Steensgaard,[8] among others. Indian historians, notably Ashin[9] and Arun Das Gupta[9] have shown that 'medieval' Indian trade linking the sub-continent with the Persian Gulf and South East Asia was much more than a luxury trade. Bulk trades in calicoes and cheap cottons existed alongside the trade in spices and precious artifacts. Sixteenth and seventeenth century Gujerat must have been one of the most thriving commerical economies in Asia at this time. By the same token, the view of Portuguese power and activity has also been modified. M.N. Pearson has sought to show how the Portuguese enforced their unsteady grip on Gujerati seaborne trade through the pass (*cartaz*) system.[10] He emphasises that the answers must be found not only in the small technological advantages of the Europeans, but also in the nature of the indigenous states. Moghul princes did not regard the sea as 'their element' and so long as they continued to receive remittances from land tax and tolls, they were prepared to allow the Portuguese a share. This finding is an interesting complement to that of Ashin Das Gupta who has shown that the decline of Muslim and Hindu Gujerati trade and shipping in Surat after 1700 was, in part, connected with the increasing demands the merchant community sustained from the declining Moghul nobility when their other landed sources of wealth fell off during the Mahratta Wars.[11] Thus the tightening stranglehold which the Europeans (in this case the English) imposed on Indian international trade was closely connected with the internal conditions of late Moghul India.

Was Portuguese trade in coastal India predominantly 'tribute taking' rather than a commerical enterprise along Dutch or English lines? The answer is still in doubt. Pearson has shown convincingly that the Portuguese politics of Diu, Daman and Goa were maintained by the taxation of other traders. But many historians recognise the importance of private Portuguese trade. Tightly organised Dutch East India Company activity in Coromandel in the late 17th century was perhaps quite different from the Portuguese private interests sheltered under a tottering, 'tribute-taking' state structure.[12]

[7] M.A.P. Meilink-Roelofsz, *Asian Trade and European Influence in the Indonesian Archipelago between 1500 and about 1630* (The Hague 1962).

[8] N. Steensgaard, *Carracks, Caravans and Companies. The Structural Crisis in European-Asian Trade in the Early 17th Century* (Scandinavian Institute of Asian Studies 1973).

[9] A. Das Gupta, *Malabar in Asian Trade* (Cambridge 1968).

[10] M.N. Pearson, *Rulers and Merchants in Gujarat* (Berkeley 1974).

[11] A. Das Gupta, MS on Surat 1700-1740 in the author's possession.

[12] T. Raychaudhuri, *Jan Company in Coromandel* (s'Gravenhage 1962).

But there are distinct parallels to the later in 18th century Bengal where the English Company also acted as an umbrella for an expanding private trade. European maritime capitalism in Asia grew up alongside and never finally eliminated the conquistador aspect of colonial relations. Our conclusions must, however, remain tentative until the publication of K.N. Chaudhuri's major work on the English East India Company.

Finally, our understanding of the impact of European activities on the peoples of coastal India during this period is beginning to develop. Portuguese policies of physically concentrating and converting fisherman peoples such as the Paravas of South India and the Karavas of Sri Lanka anticipated the type of changed definition of caste and community which arose from colonial administrative policies in later centuries. The rise of 'comprador' groups such as the Weavers of Calcutta or the Parsis of Bombay through opportunities in European commerce began quite early.

The 18th century historiography on British expansion has been less affected by the recent alarums and excursions which have shaken other parts of the field. It has tended to develop slowly along the lines laid down by Holden Furber and P. Spear. A broad consensus has emerged about the relationship between economic and political advance. Scholars have demonstrated the slow build-up of European corporate and private capital in the sea-borne trade of south and east Asia. There was general agreement that specific military factors, and the 'regionalisation' of power within the late Moghul Empire provided the conditions for the emergence of the British East India Company as the dominant power within the coastal states. The further expansion of British financial and economic power into the Indian hinterland during the later 18th century is thought to have caused instability in inland régimes. But historians agreed that the political crises which led to the extention of formal Empire were also brought about by strategic fears and the pressure of the system of the Company's subsidiary alliances on weak agrarian states. The examples where it could be satisfactorily proved that British traders actually pushed the officials of the East Indian Company to territorial aggrandisement are exceptions rather than the rule.[13] Thus an approach appears to be emerging which is similar in many respects to the dominant interpretation of the expansion of Europe into north-east Africa in the mid-19th century.[14] In both cases the

[13] Pamela Nightingale, *Trade and Empire in Western India* (Cambridge 1972).

[14] Compare, for instance, R. Owen, *Cotton and the Egyptian Economy.* (Oxford 1966), with Robinson and Gallagher, *Africa and the Victorians*; William Roger Lewis, *Imperialism. The Robinson and Gallagher Controversy* (New York 1976).

historiography reflects the need to take into account European commercial expansion, and also the particular motivations of the actors as they appear in official papers. In the Indian case, historians are interested in charting the commercial and political changes with greater precision rather than fashioning any new, monolithic theories. P.J. Marshall has documented in detail the movements of British private capital within the Bengal trading system.[15] Scholars of the indigenous régimes have attempted to display more precisely the effects of British commercial and financial pressures on the agrarian systems of the local states.[16] The networks of indigenous traders and financiers are also now receiving attention, as they provided the capital and market information for the commerical invasion of the interior.[17]

British expansion, of course, was not simply a geographical expansion, but a penetration of the Indian social system. In an agrarian society, the emphasis has naturally fallen on the origin and results of British land-revenue policy, for this was the point where the state was thought to bear most directly on the countryside. Here, in the immediate post-war years, the great tradition of 19th century official studies was considerably elaborated from the Calcutta and London papers of the Company.[18] Works on the central organisation of the East India Company and on the Permanent Settlement of the revenues of Bengal developed themes inherited from Hunter and Baden-Powell. But in both the 'imperial' and 'nationalist' interpretation, the land-systems introduced by the British were credited with an considerable impact. They either

[15] *East India Fortunes, op. cit.*

[16] E.g., R. Barnett, 'The emergence of Avadh as an autonomous political system', unpubl. Ph.D. dissertation, University of California 1976; Karen Leonard, 'The Kayasthas of Hyderabad' Ph.D. diss.; University of California, 1972. P.B. Calkins, 'Formation of a regionally orientated ruling group in Bengal', *JAS*, 29, 1969-70; A.M. Khan, *The Transition in Bengal* (Cambridge, 1972); J. Richards, *Moghul Administration in Golconda* (Oxford 1975).

[17] E.g., T. Timberg, 'A North Indian Firm seen through its business records', *IESHR*, 8, 3, 1971; 'Thee types of the Marwari firm' *IESHR*, 10, 1, 1973; K.P. Mishra, *Benares in Transition* (Delhi 1975); C.A. Bayly, 'Indian Traders in a traditional setting', in A.G. Hopkins and C. Dewey (eds.) *The Impact of Imperialism* (Athlone 1977): Gotam Bhadra, 'Some aspects of the social position and functions of merchants at Murshidabad, 1965-93', Indian History Congress, Chandigarh, 1973; G.T. Kulkarni of Deccan College, Pune, is also working on the rôle of traders and financiers under the Mahrattas. See his 'Banking in the Eighteenth Century', *Artha Vijana*, vol. V/2 (1973).

[18] S. Gopal, *The Permanent Settlement and its effects* (London 1954); C.H. Phillips. *The East India Company* (Manchester 1940); P. Spear, *Twilight of the Moghuls* (Cambridge 1951).

dislocated society causing Holt Mackenzie's 'melancholy revolution' in landed property, or they provided peace, stability and growth. The change of direction in the late '50s and early '60s broadened the approach in two ways. First, there was a new interest in the content of the ideas of the administrators themselves; second, there arose a consuming desire to document the local effects of those measures from the wealth of provincial and district records.

The new interest in ideology was influential, but in a curiously indirect manner. Stokes' work and that of Guha (1962)[19] were parts of a growing attempt to end the historiographical isolation of Indian studies. Indian issues had once been central to the concerns of late-Victorian ethnologists or political theorists, providing raw material for debates on 'Aryanism' and the 'village community'. But India appeared to shrink in relevance in the late imperial period. Even Marxists accorded it little attention. Lenin's failure to find a 'national bourgeoisie' there moved the centre of interest elsewhere, though J. Nehru and M.N. Roy tried hard to put India's problems in an international framework. The *English Utilitarians,* however, tried to demonstrate the impact of early Victorian political theories on the governance of India and detected the subtle reasoning of Ricardo and James Mill behind the heavy handed land-revenue assessments which the British laid on their Indian peasantry throughout the 19th century. Guha broke behind the truism that Cornwallis's settlement of the land revenue of Bengal represented the working-out of English models of aristocratic landlordism and claimed to find a tradition running back to 'les Physiocrats' informing the British decision to replace Moghul fiscal lordships with a landed gentry. It has proved easy enough to refute such arguments on the influence of theory on practice. Many authors have pointed out that immediate practical issues – the need to raise revenue for war, local political considerations, or the prejudices of 'the men on the spot' – were more important than broad policy worked out in the reflective atmosphere of Calcutta or London.[20] There remains a nagging feeling that the rôle of ideas cannot be so easily dismissed, and the debate has shown signs of life again recently. At the broadest level, the minimal rôle of the state in India after the 1830s, by comparison, say, with the culture system of Dutch Java seemed only to be partly explained by the different economic facts of the

[19] *A rule of Property for Bengal* (The Hague 1963).

[20] Especially, A Siddiqi, *Agrarian change in a North Indian State* (Oxford 1973); J. Rosselli 'Theory and Practice in North India', *IESHR,* 8, 2, 1971; Imtiaz Ahmed, *Land Revenue Policy in North India: The Ceded and Conquered Provinces* (*1801-33*), (Calcutta 1967).

two colonies. The very early and crushing victory of laissez-faire ideas in British ruling and commercial circles also appears to have been significant. And in the case of the policy of the individual district officer, we are brought face to face with the fundamental historical problem of the importance of ideology in motivation. As in the case of the relationship between nationalist or imperialist ideas and practice, it is all too easy to relegate ideas to the rôle of an outward dressing, or at best an *ex post facto* legitimation for policies dictated by material necessity. Yet at the very least, when actions took place within a context of debate, decisions on land-revenue and settlement had to be seen to be compatible with one or other set of economic ideas.[21] The time appears right to open up these issues again with the more sophisticated approaches that are now available to the historian of ideas.

The broad view of Indian rural history taken by Stokes, Guha and later Metcalf, paradoxically, turned scholars in Britain, Australia and India towards the study of the localities. The revolt of 1857, for instance, seemed to be a good historical testing-ground for measurement of Britain's effect on Indian rural society. Detailed analysis seemed to show that far from a revolt of the commercialised middle peasantry, the locus of revolt was often the traditional closed peasant corporation or traditional raj which had hardly been touched by cash cropping or government.[22] The revolt became a rebellion of expansion, a traditional resistance movement, rather than a revolt of settlement against the agents of the market economy. A strong division continued to exist between those scholars who emphasised continuity in rural society and those who saw change and the emergence of a rich peasant class,[23] but they had begun to develop tools for the detailed analysis of Indian rural organisation. At the same time a new generation of American scholars of Indian society were also moving in the same direction. Their work was first widely presented at a congress in Michigan in 1962. The book that emerged from this meeting, *Land Control and Social Structure in Indian History* (1969) is possibly the most influential volume published on British India in the post-war years.

[21] E.T. Stokes, 'The Land Revenue system of the North-Western Provinces and Bombay Deccan; ideology and the official mind' in C.H. Philips and D. Wainwright (eds) *Indian Society and the Beginnings of Modernisation* (SOAS, London 1976).

[22] E. Stokes, 'The First Century of British Colonial Rule in India', *Past and Present,* no. 58, 1973; T.R. Metcalf, *The Aftermath of Revolt* (Berkeley 1966).

[23] See, e.g., R. Kumar, 'The Rise of the Rich Peasant in Western India' in D.A. Low (ed.), *Soundings in Modern South Asian History,* (London 1968); N. Charlesworth 'Rich Peasants and Poor Peasants in Western India', (SSRC Conference paper, Cambridge 1975); cf. paper by P.J. Musgrave, *ibid.*

The American Impact

The move of American historical-anthropologists into the Indian field in the 1960s was a momentous event and one which had profound consequences. Its origins are themselves an interesting case study in historiographical change. America's position after the end of the War, and the wartime experience of many young Americans stimulated a new interest in the problems of the Third World. Kennedy's Peace Corps provided a later, second generation of students whose fascination with India was prior to and withstood archival mumification. At the same time, earlier contacts persisted. Many of the new American historians of India had missionary connections; others came to India through an interest in Britain. On the intellectual side, this was pre-eminently the phase when the influence of social anthropology was brought to bear on historiography. But the dominant anthropological approach was still the 'empirical' anglo-American village study tradition which had arisen in British Africa and Polynesia during the 1930s. Cohn's seminal papers on Benares in the 19th century have echoes of Evans-Pritchard and Fortes' *African Political Systems* (1942), while Frykenberg's work on village strength in south India took historians into areas where they had never yet trod, even in the more developed field of European studies. Older ethnographical traditions were also evoked. As befits a republican intelligentsia in the pre-Vietnam era, treatment of the 19th century colonial officers was self-confidently objective. The old Civilians, it was said, often misunderstood, or misrepresented the nature of Indian society because of their political or racial prejudices. Nonetheless, many of the leading ideas of this new generation were derived from those of the amateur ethnographers and settlement officers of a century before. In a sense this was inevitable. Training in anthropology made it possible for them to recognise the features of caste, 'caste dominance', lineage and clan, of which earlier historians had been blissfully unaware, but they were still bound by sources derived from the colonial archives. Only much more recently was a conscious movement initiated to break these bounds.

The great boon which the American historians of this generation conferred upon the subject was a move away from an exclusive concentration on British land-revenue policy, and the minute chronicling of debates about settlements. Instead, Indian society was to be seen in terms of the control of land, as a hierarchy of social groups who had rights and power over the produce of the villages. The introduction of the anthropological concept of a dominant caste group, locally controlling land, made the interpretation of 18th and 19th century rural history much richer. The rise to power of an 18th century Raja of Benares, for instance, could now be seen as a series of events by which a dominant lineage of Bhumihar Brahmins achieved land control around the city by warring against earlier local magnates.[24] Previously these events had been chronicled as if the most appropriate comparison had been with the gyrations of feudatories in early medieval Europe. The introduction of the idea that economic systems were 'embedded' in social structures which is associated with Karl Polyani and G. Dalton was much less abrasive than in contemporary African studies. But it was at least admitted that 'landownership' might have a wholly different meaning in Indian society from that which it had in Europe.[25] The emphasis on different 'levels' of Indian rural society (another adaptation of *African Political Systems*) meant that a much clearer grasp of the supposed pre-colonial anarchy in Indian society was now possible. If the land-controllers in local situations remained virtually identical throughout the period, how anarchical could the anarchy really have been? Most significantly, this new approach threw considerable doubt on the degree of real change initiated by the British in India, and on the nature of European expansion. Previously, the concentration on administrative and constitutional history had reinforced the view that the colonial rulers had vastly affected Indian society, either by destroying the landed classes and 'deindustrialisation' as the nationalists insisted, or by the introduction of the benefits of western society in the 'imperialist' formulation. Now it was admitted that British policy may have been declaratory rather than effectual, and that its effects may never have percolated to the villagers or small towns. What mattered more was persistence or change in dominant land-controllers, and British revenue systems were too dependant on the knowledge of local men to have much effect here.

Thus the works of the 'land-control' phase purported to show what was happening 'on the ground' or 'at the grass roots'. The leading idea was that events writ large in the textbooks, such as the creation of a market in land by colonial rule, or the Ryotwari or Zamindari settlements, had little impact on local society. This worked on its own dynamics and was isolated by poor communications and the inherent strength of its social structures from outside influences. One danger, however, in this style of study was the

[24] B.S. Cohn in *Land Control, op. cit.*; see also his 'Political Systems in 18th century India; the Benares Region', *Journal of the American Oriental Society*, 82 (1959).

[25] W.C. Neale in *Land Control,* op. cit.

temptation to overgeneralisation from unrepresentative cases. Thus it is not clear how far Frykenberg's autonomous villages in Guntur District were representative of south India as a whole. Equally, the close, 'tribal' Rajput communities which Cohn and later R. Fox studied were to some extent exceptional and village or brotherhood strength to repel outside penetration may have been less elsewhere in north India.[26] The outcome of renewed debates over the generality of these cases is of importance to the whole field. Despite their rather limited geographical range the studies of Cohn and Frykenberg were the main supports of a view still generally held, which argues for continuity and downgrades the impact of imperialism and British expansion.

Another problem with this work was its tendency to a very static analysis of social structures. Thus, rather than isolating the main elements of historical change, it tended to set up a series of 'snapshots' of social organisation with little account of the transition between one and the next. This is again manifest in Cohn's seminal work. Here we are given a series of descriptions of land control and agrarian structures under the Moghuls, Rajas of Benares and the British. The argument for continuity turns on the ability of elements dispossessed in the formal workings of the revenue-system and the 'market in land' to maintain their influence and control. This survival is the result of a postulated expansion of agricultural output and growing commerce which made it possible for new controllers to arise without the displacement of existing ones. Yet the vital context within which this model of continuity works – the growth of output and commercial farming which accompanied the beginnings of British rule – is merely noted in passing. What might have happened to the 'dispossessed' where new resources were not available remains unconsidered even today. Thus the grave fault of most local studies, including the Cambridge studies of political history, is this tendency to treat localities as objects of study rather than as examples of the working out of general changes against the background of particular conditions.

Influence of Anthropology

During the 1960s and '70s anthropologists continued to explore lines which were suggestive and important for historians. F.G. Bailey's work on highland Orissa[27] dealt with the expansion of the

[26] R. Fox, *Kin, Clan Raja and Rule* (Berkeley 1970). cf. B.B. Chaudhuri, 'The Land Market in Eastern India', *IESHR*, 12, 1, 2, 1975; E.T. Stokes. 'Pax Britannica and Agrarian Society in North India', *MAS*, 9, 4 (1975).

[27] *Caste and the Economic Frontier* (Manchester 1959).

market into non-commercial villages and showed how new avenues for ritual and social mobility were created. His work seemed to elucidate the final stages of a change which was occurring throughout the north Indian plains in the 19th century. Later, the focus of interest shifted to the mobility of castes and communities. An important work here was R. Hardgrave's, *The Nadars of Tamilnadu*[28] which showed how a low caste of agriculturalists engaged in the manufacture of an alcoholic drink based on palm juice raised themselves ritually and politically in 19th century south India. Hardgrave was criticised for the assumption that the Nadars were ever a coherent political or social community, but his work provided the starting point for more complex studies of small communities in India.[29] Another focus of interest was the rôle of caste as a set of face-to-face, local relationships. The ritual patron-client ties of the villages (the *jajmani* system) were investigated in the countryside[30] and in its modified urban form.[31] These studies complicated historians' views of social organisation in 19th and 20th century India, emphasising the persistence of links of patronage across the bounds of class and caste.

Towards the end of the 1960s the focus in anthropological studies changed perceptibly. Following the publication of Louis Dumont's, *Homo Hierarchicus* (1966), village field work took on a less empirical and more theoretical direction. Organising cultural ideas, it was now thought, should be recovered from literary and religious sources and then tested against the empirical village data. The new trend was evident in the recent work of Brenda Breck[32] and D.F. Pocock.[33] As we shall see, it was to become more influential in historical circles in the course of the last two years.

Economic History

The 'break towards the localities' in the early 1960s was also evident in the more rigorous economic history. The work of Morris

[28] *The Nadars of Tamilnadu. The Political Culture of a Community in change.* Berkeley 1969).

[29] E.g., the largely unpublished work of F. Conlon on the Saraswat Brahmins; T. Timberg on Marwaris (above) and I. Carroll on the Kayasths, see her 'Origin of the Kayasth Temperance Movement, *IESHR*, 11, 4 (1974).

[30] Jan Breman, *Patronage and Exploitation. Changing agrarian Relations in Gujarat, India.* (Berkeley 1974).

[31] L. Hazlehurst, *Entrepreneurship and the Merchant Castes in a Punjabi City*, (Duke University, N.C. 1966).

[32] *Peasant Society in Konku. A Study of Right and Left Subcastes in South India* (Vancouver 1972).

[33] *Kanbi and Pattidar. A study of the Pattidar Community of Gujarat* (Oxford 1972).

D. Morris on industrial labour (1965)[34] and of Dharma Kumar on rural labour (1965)[35] demonstrated the value of testing general hypotheses in particular areas, and also of the use of analytical ideas from outside the discipline. For our purposes the importance of both these works, and of recent ones in the same mould (e.g. McAlpin, 1973)[36] is that they once again downgrade the rôle of imperialism as either an institutional or as an economic force in Indian society. The British, it is implied, were much less important than long-term trends in Indian economic organisation such as the restricted market, population pressure, poor technology, etc., in determining the form of the Indian economy in the 19th century. It is in this area of debate that Indian historians of India have made their most positive contribution in recent years. Since Naoroji the impact of imperialism has been a major historical concern for Indians, but interest in economic history has also been stimulated by the need to put debates about present-day planning into an historical framework. The Delhi University, Delhi School of Economics and more recently, Jawaharlal Nehru University, have developed respected scholarly traditions in this field. Funds for research have also been available through institutions such as the Indian Statistical Institute and the Indian Institute of Management, Calcutta, since it is believed that the disposition of scarce resources to scholars can better be justified in areas with an apparent relevance to economic planning. On the whole, Indian historians have joined other critics in rejecting the views of Morris. They continue to assert the destructive rôle of imperialism, but their approach has become more sophisticated. Recently, attention has concentrated less on the supposed destruction of India's handloom-weaving industrial base by the Company than on restraints to growth imposed by colonial institutions. The dominance of British capital in the banks of the colonial coastal enclaves, the limited links between the enclaves and the hinterland, and the dire effects of British legal, development and revenue policies on agricultural growth in this hinterland have all received study.[37] Very recently, however, attention has moved again to structural features. It has been suggested that technological changes in the mid-19th century

[34] *The Emergence of an Industrial Labour Force in India: A study of the Bombay Cotton Mills* (Berkeley 1965).

[35] *Land and Caste in South India* (Cambridge 1965).

[36] 'The Impact of Railroads on prices and consumption in India', University of Wisconsin, Ph.D. Thesis, 1973.

[37] A.K. Bagchi, *Private Investment in India, 1900-39* (Cambridge 1972), reviewed by Morris, *MAS*, 8, 4 (1974); E. Whitcombe, *Agrarian Conditions in Northern India*, I, *The U.P. under British rule, 1860-1960* (Berkeley 1972).

in the trade between India and the rest of the world sealed India's 'dependence' within the colonial world system.[38] Indian merchants, who competed fairly well until this point, simply did not have the knowledge, technique or access to world-wide shipping freightage or insurance facilities to compete in the world market, so that the profits from the big mark-ups in jute, cotton etc., went to foreigners. Curiously, Morris' own recent work leaves room for this more restricted interpretation of the growing commercial impact of imperialism.[39] Entrepreneurs are, he writes, bound by their own particular and local readings of profit and profitability which depend largely on sources of information. Indians failed to compete in the colonial enclave economies (particularly Bengal) because they did not have sufficient information. It is ironic that Morris' new relativist approach to the perceptions of entrepreneurs also leaves room for the reappearance of the other great bogey of colonial economic history-values, and in particular Hindu pre-industrial values. Morris, along with Milton Singer[40] for the anthropologists, attempted to lay the ghost of Weber by showing that Indians could and did adapt their religious and ritual behaviour to commercial and even industrial activity. But 'values' albeit specific and local ones connected with family, status and security, are now allowed as affecting the commercial judgements of Indian merchants. Values are dead. Long live values!

Similar trends are apparent in recent studies of Indian rural society. Here the apogee of local studies was fairly recently reached with the publication of Tom. G. Kessinger's, *Vilyatpur* (Berkeley, 1974).[41] This work brought together the techniques of family reconstitution pioneered in European history with new and much more precise evidence derived from the most basic level of administrative records. Kessinger used the material left by the administration's

[38] E.g., Amales Tripathi, 'Indo-British Trade between 1833 and '47 and the commercial crisis of 1847-8', *Indian Historical Review,* 1, 2 (1975), K.N. Chauduri, *Economic Development under the East India Company* (Cambridge 1974); D.K. Basu, 'The British and the Banian in Calcutta', *Bengal Past and Present* (July-December 1973); M. Vicziany, 'The Structure of the Bombay Cotton Trade, 1840-70' paper presented to SSRC Conference, Cambridge, 1975.

[39] 'Values as an Obstacle to Growth' in South Asia, *Journal of Economic History,* 27 (1968) cf; his 'Entrepreneurship in South Asia: the Rashomon Effect', paper presented to conference on colonial port cities in Asia, Santa Cruz, Calif., 1976.

[40] *When a Great Tradition Modernises* (Philadelphia 1973).

[41] See also his, 'History and anthropology; the study of economic and social change in rural India, *The Journal of Interdisciplinary History,* 3 (1972) and 'Historical Materials on rural India', *IESHR,* 7 (1970).

village record keepers, but was able to aggregate it in wholly new ways. Stratification in the Punjab village which he studied derived primarily from cycles of demographic change within family and lineage groups and successful access to bye-employment. Here he echoed Chayanov and Shanin's work on rural Russia. Imperialism, exploitation, and 'values' were implicitly much less important. But the successful use of local records raised as many problems as it answered. Recently, Kessinger himself has criticised what he regards as an 'over-behaviourist' approach, asserting that peasant society should be seen in terms of peasant values. At the same time, others have noted that the Indian rural communities so far studied were relatively homogeneous, powerful and favoured. In poorer Bengali society, by contrast, the dominance of rural local-controllers (both *zamindar* and *jotedar*) was reinforced by imperial revenue, administrative and possibly commercial policies.[42] Scholars are increasingly nagged by the thought that here also the local persistence of élites is not necessarily an argument for the continuity of the pre-colonial situation. It could equally well apply to a situation of stagnation – an 'equilibrium-trap', where the outer-world was held steady by the impact of colonial trade and cash-cropping, and the inner world by the effects of revenue policies. Imperialism is dead. Long live Imperialism!

What we have seen in recent studies of this first phase of European expansion into Indian society is a retreat into the 'locality' which contained the seeds of its own antithesis. By examining the nature of social and economic changes in particular areas, scholars have been forced to ask questions again about the nature of these processes and the conceptual framework within which they might be set. This evolution is also very apparent, as we shall see, in studies of the nationalist response to British expansion and imperialism. But it seems to be part of a wider trend; part perhaps of a need to try to put together a critique and analysis of the modern social order from the fragmented specialisms of the first post-war years. The search for order and context is superior to the doctrine of any particular ideology. Neo-Marxists, Neo-Weberians, and even geopoliticians of the old Halford Mackinder type feel the same pressures. The mood is summed up by Immanuel Wallerstein, an anthropologist of Africa who is now in the process of becoming a grand theorist.

> It was a false perspective to take a unit like a 'tribe' and to seek to analyse its gyrations without reference to the fact that in a colonial situation, the governing institutions of a tribe, far from being sovereign, were closely circumscribed

[42] R.K. and R. Ray, 'The Dynamics of Continuity in rural Bengal' *IESHR*, 10, 2 (1973).

by the laws (and customs) of the larger entity of which they were indissolubly part, the colony.[43]

II. INDIAN REACTIONS

Studies of Indian reactions to the expansion of Europe have until recently been confined to a limited political realm. Works have appeared which link the emergence of new regional cultures in Bengal and elsewhere to British efforts to westernise and define the civilisation of their subjects. Scholarship of the revivalist Hindu Arya Samaj,[44] and Muslim reactions from the holy war (*jihad*) to the political association, is flourishing.[45] But in part at least this is because the colonial rulers' fears of militant political challenges from this quarter generated literature and controversy. Little truly-historical literature on changes in social organisation or religious practice among Hindus is yet available.

The Nationalist Phase

For the first fifteen years after Independence, studies of Indian nationalism were themselves cast largely in the mould of the biography of the 'great man' – the leader taken out of context of his followers. During the early 1960s, however, a new focus emerged centred on the study of Indian élites, their interplay with each other and with the colonial government. The perception behind this approach was the very evident domination which limited social groups appear to have established over the activities of the Indian National Congress, the new English press and the formal political associations which emerged in the later 19th century. Attention was given to the *bhadralog* (gentry-*literati*) of Bengal, to the powerful Chitpavan Brahmins of western India, to the Tamil and Telegu Brahmin élite of southern India, and so on.[46] There was a very close

[43] Immanuel Wallerstein, *The Modern World System* (New York 1974) introduction.

[44] K.W. Jones, *Arya Dharm. Hindu Consciousness in 19th Century North India* (Berkeley 1976).

[45] See P. Hardy, *The Muslims of British India* (Cambridge 1973), bibliography.

[46] E. Irschick, *Politics and Social Conflict in South India* (Berkeley 1969); J. Broomfield, *Elite Conflict in a Plural Society* (Berkeley 1968); A. Seal, *The Emergence of Indian Nationalism* (Cambridge 1968); Gordon Johnson, *Provincial Politics and Indian Nationalism* (Cambridge 1973); N.G. Barrier, 'The Arya Samaj and Congress politics in the Punjab' *JAS*, 26 (1966); M. Patterson, 'Chitpavan Brahmin family histories', in, M. Singer and B.S. Cohn (eds.), *Structure and Change in Indian society* (Chicago 1968); B.S. Cohn, 'The Recruitment of Elites under British rule in India' in A. Tuden and S. Plotnikov, (eds.), *Studies in Social Stratification* (Philadelphia 1966).

connection between this insight and the type of sources which began to be exploited during these years. Congress delegate lists, official sources and the anglicised press carefully listed 'caste', profession and place of residence of those who attended the early Congress meetings. Once categories had been generated out of these sources, attention turned to how they could be defined and what was their motivation in politics.

Anil Seal, for instance, appears to have understood these social groupings as whole 'castes' which had taken advantage of the opportunities offered by English education and the professions. Here he showed his reliance on the official censuses and views of the British civilians that the Indians they dealt with could best be seen as 'castes'. To John Broomfield, the *bhadralog* who took such a prominent part in early nationalist Bengal, were a 'status group' in the Weberian sense. To S.N. Mukherjee, working on an earlier period, the *bhadralog* was essentially a class defined by its relationship to British commercial institutions and the govermental apparatus that this required.[47]

Another area of concern was the motivation of these variously defined groups in politics which at this time was seen in terms of agitation and compromise with the colonial government through formal political institutions and the press. For most authors, the early phase of Indian nationalism could be seen in terms of élite conflict of various degrees of subtlety, and occasional obeisance was made to Pareto. In the simplest statement, English-educated élites were felt to struggle for the limited educational facilities and appointments offered by the colonial rulers and the new professions. The struggle for increased power and position was in large part what nationalism was about, but since the jobs and resources were limited and new groups were being educated, conflict between élites developed, and this sometimes deepened into communal conflict. The classic and baldest case is Seal's analysis of the manner in which conflict between a rising élite of Hindu Kayasthas (the clerical caste) and the traditionally dominant Muslim service people of upper India broadened out into a conflict between political parties based largely on religion. Since the Congress in northern India was supposed to be very much a preserve of Kayasths, the Muslims led by Sir Sayyid Ahmed Khan staged a 'breakaway' which ultimately led to the foundation of separate Muslim political institutions.[48] As many commentators have pointed out, Seal left

[47] S.N. Mukherjee, 'Caste, Class and Politics in Calcutta. 1818-38' in E. Leach and S.N. Mukherjee, *Elites in South Asia* (Cambridge 1968).
[48] Seal, *The Emergence, op. cit.*

little room for ideas or even for other types of political and social activity in his interpretation. A much less bald description of élite conflict was given by Eugene F. Irschick and Broomfield, who gave weight to Tamil literary revivalism and Bengali cultural nationalism respectively in their works. For Broomfield, nationalism was not merely the 'container' for the material grievances of each élite, 'each élite . . . developed a nationalism as a means of political fulfilment *and* as a further expression of its identity'.[49]

Broomfield's work went further, for he tried to extend his analysis to encompass the general political changes which appeared to have occurred in Indian nationalism after 1918 with a theory of the rise of 'counter-élites'. These groups, he thought, were the up-and-coming politicians of the coastal provinces and also the local élites or newly educated classes of inland India and hitherto backward parts of the country. These 'counter-élites', the followers of a more advanced form of nationalism during the Gandhian period, were expressing wider grievances and could also broaden the appeal of nationalism as they were not too closely identified with privileged Indian public men or with the material benefits of British rule. It had long been apparent that the years 1918-21 represented something of a turning point in the history of Indian nationalism. This view had been neatly summarised by Gopal Krishna who demonstrated the great increase in formal membership at this time and also the reorganisation of Congress along linguistic boundaries.[50] But the broad distinction between 'élite' and 'mass' movements was proving as suspect to historians of India as it was to those of Africa. Broomfield suggested how the appearance of a new radicalism in 1920 could still be consonant with the continuing rôle of the *bhadralog* in the politics of Calcutta, and he was thus able to blunt this sharp distinction.

It is not clear how Seal's analysis of élite conflict would have attempted to encompass the historical developments of 1918-47. But judging by the work of some of his pupils and related attempts to deal with the decolonisation of Africa, it would have emphasised the continued manipulation of 'collaborating élites'.[51] The Imperial government had co-opted one élite after another and seen it subverted by the extended appeal of a nationalism based upon material

[49] J. Broomfield, 'The Indian Elites: A theory of Indian History', *IESHR*, 3, 2 (1966).

[50] 'The Development of the Indian National Congress as a Mass organisation', *JAS*, 25 (1966).

[51] J. Brown, Gandhi's Rise to Power (Cambridge 1972); R. Robinson in W.R. Lewis, *Imperialism, op. cit.*

grievance. When the last collaborating élites, the Princes, the landlords and the conservative Muslims, were clearly incapable of holding the country for the British, it was time for them 'to pack their bags and leave'.

This concentration on English-speaking élites as the beneficiaries and ultimate challengers of the British Raj was not only apparent in Indian studies. It was perhaps connected with the contemporary preoccupations of the world of the 1950s, where the political descendants of the early anglophone and francophone élites, the Nehrus, Nkrumas and Diems, were seen grappling with the constitutional and social problems left to them by the colonial powers. In the Indian case, it also sprang from the opening up of new source materials. With cheaper air travel and larger grants from expanding educational institutions, European and American scholars first began to go to India in numbers. The most exciting and accessible sources they encountered were the political files (Home Politics, Home Police, Home Public) of the National Archives of India and the private papers of some English-speaking nationalists. The political files were replete with an almost paranoid documentation of the daily meetings and speeches of those whom the British saw as dissidents. The letters of Indian leaders set out the growing attempts to cobble together a continental alliance between like-minded men, while the English language press showed them in action, calling public meetings and voicing their regional and local complaints. This type of material was ideal fodder for the microfilm camera which had become a major tool of the streamlined historian of the 1950s. Great quantities of files and newspapers were filmed through the offices of complaisant Indian organisations and conveyed like a Nabob's loot back to the vaults of the American South Asian Microfilm Project, the Centre of South Asian Studies in Cambridge and the Australian National University. The accessibility of basic material in these libraries, the great financial investment and the natural caution of research students have combined to perpetuate much work of the 'élite conflict' type, though interest has moved elsewhere. Trends in historiography may be started by ideas, but they are maintained, and even fossilized by institutions.

The élite line of argument was the first attempt to broaden the study of Indian reactions to imperialism away from policy and the hagiography of great men to encompass regions and social formations. It marked the emergence of modern Indian political history as a (more or less) respectable discipline. Its drawbacks were clear, not least to its authors. Obviously an interpretation which stresses the rôle of élites and government policy will arise from an investigation of the written remains of those élites and of the imperial government. Economic change, local issues, indigenous movements of revival and change, and the history of the 'masses' would *a priori* be underplayed. Refinements and refutations have therefore come thick and fast. One line taken, particularly in India, is that the work of the early '60s encourages anti-national tendencies and will downgrade nationalism to a 'struggle for the loaves and fishes of office'. A more reasoned version of this criticism insists that nationalist ideas cannot be related to social formations (whether castes, élites or classes) with any degree of accuracy. What we have is an 'intelligentsia', an 'establishment' or a 'radical party', and it is ideas or cultural perceptions rather than Bengal's plural society which determined the course of politics.[52] These critics have not been able to grapple with the problem that particular sets of ideas seem to emanate from or appeal to certain groups of people and not to others, and that we therefore need an external explanation of historical change beyond and outside the ideas themselves. But clearly, we are at the root of a major difficulty. How can we blend together the rôle of interest and ideology; how can we comprehend the evident historical rôle of special groups and the dynamics of privilege with an appreciation of what people themselves think about what they are doing? One fruitful approach which has been applied to communal and religious change in India is that of Karl Deutsch.[53] Privileged groups select from their historical experience certain symbols which can be used to communicate with non-élites and mobilise them to political action. Ideas as well as interests are thus brought into play. So the privileged Muslim service groups of upper India selected and employed the symbols of the Urdu language and the *Khilafat* to mobilise popular Muslim feeling against the British.[54] The difficulty with this refinement is that it is still not clear how far the élite itself is a free agent, and how far an existing feeling of community, or the *virtú* of the symbol itself, forces its hand. If it could be shown how the actions of the élite themselves must be consonant with certain codes of behaviour and how these codes of behaviour are selected and passed on through education, we might be

[52] S. Sarkar, *The Swadeshi Movement* (Calcutta 1974); L. Gordon, *Bengal: The Nationalist Movement,* (Berkeley 1975).

[53] K. Deutsch, *Nationalism and Social Communication. An Enquiry into the Foundations of Nationalism* (Cambridge, Mass. 1973); Paul Brass, *Religion, Language and Politics in North India* (Cambridge 1974); for a similar approach, R. Cashman, *The Myth of the Lokmanya. Tilak and Mass Politics in Maharashtra* (Berkeley 1975).

[54] Brass, *Religion, Language, op. cit.*

nearer to resolving the issue of interest and ideology in a manner which incorporates both.

Local Studies

Differences of opinion over the rôle of the élites will doubtless persist. In the late 1960s and early 1970s, however, a new style of approach to imperialism and nationalism emerged. This was an emphasis on local studies and on the study of regional political *structures*. It was partly a development of and partly a reaction against the élite studies. Clearly, scholars were influenced by the trend which we have observed in theories of British impact on Indian rural society. The work of Frykenberg and Cohn seemed to offer examples of the manner in which local studies could refine and render more precise our understanding of nationalism and imperialism in Indian society. Influences from outside the field also contributed to this shift of emphasis. Local history had long since lost its stigma of antiquarianism in both Britain and Europe. Studies of the French Revolution, the rise of Fascism, electoral and political change in modern England, had all benefited from the sharply different view from the parish pump. This approach was thought to be overdue in Indian studies, where no attempt had been made for the later imperial period to map out a 'structure of politics', or attend to the different levels of political organisation, so that the élites of earlier studies seemed to be writing, agitating and 'collaborating' in a vacuum. Some of the works which attempted to fill this gap were associated with Cambridge,[55] but there were parallel developments elsewhere.[56] In addition to new ideas, new sources were now proposed. Historians could go outside the National Archives of India to a variety of local records: family histories and even vernacular local newspapers. In the mid-1960s historians began to move timorously outside the bounds of the

[55] For a succinct, if exaggerated demonstration of the difference between this approach and the 'élite' studies, see D. Washbrook, review of J. Brown in *MAS*, 7, 1 (1973), and *Provincial Politics: The Madras Presidency, 1870-1920* (Cambridge 1976); C.J. Baker, *The Politics of South India, 1920-37* (Cambridge 1976); C.A. Bayly, *The Local Roots of Indian Politics. Allahabad 1880-1920* (Oxford 1975); F.C.R. Robinson, *Separatism among Indian Muslims* (Cambridge 1974); B.R. Tomlinson, *Congress and the Raj, 1929-47* (London 1976); Seal, *et. al.* in *MAS*, 7, 3 (1973).

[56] J. Masselos, 'Bombay City politics, 1870-90', *South Asia*, I, I (1973); M. Roberts 'Problems of Social Stratification and the demarcation of national and local élites in British Ceylon', *JAS*, 33 (1974); J. Leonard, 'Urban Government under the Raj', *MAS*, 7, 2 (1973); J. Mcguire, 'The Social basis of Hindu political leadership in Calcutta', SOAS seminar, December (1975).

major cities, only to meet anthropologists moving back into the cities with the message that village studies were dying. In the event, these new local works also came to rely heavily on the old staples of English newspapers and imperial, or at best regional, records. When the records of Dustypore municipality, local schools and political organisations were discovered they were found to have an irritating tendency to deal with matters such as drains and slaughter-houses which even the most devoted local historian could not turn into an appetising meal for his colleagues.

In the 'new' Cambridge formulation, three or more levels of politics were described. At the local level, a variety of 'big men', controllers or patrons were isolated. These men, who controlled land or credit or access to employment, headed patron-client systems composed of extended families and direct economic and ritual dependants. They subsisted in an uneasy alliance with yet more parochial figures such as 'village bosses', 'neighbourhood leaders' and leaders of artisan guilds in city quarters. The local magnates were thought to be linked to the provincial and imperial levels of politics through their informal connections with publicists and a variety of interest groups for social, economic and political reform which were largely, though not exclusively, drawn from the westernised professional classes. Politics was mainly about the flow of resources within this total structure of Indian political society which was conceived of as an accommodation between a fragile imperial control and local patterns of power and influence. Caste was relegated to a much less important rôle than it had held in the élite conflict studies; it was seen as a source of sentiment and organisation capable of direction by both patrons and publicists, but not as the basic dimension of political organisation. A further important modification to the earlier view was that actual access to power rather than social or educational dominance was seen to be important. Thus at the local or even provincial level, the educated lawyer-politician, who was apparently the élite figure, was seen to be much less significant than the socially inferior local notable, or even the cartels of rural-controllers. As a consequence, this approach broadened the definition of politics to take account of issues of a fleeting or local nature such as bargaining for resources through municipalities and district boards, protests over the weight of land-revenue, or the problems of inferior government servants, which had been largely ignored before.

Most significantly, according to the 'new' Cambridge historians, political movements were not to be seen exclusively as products of religion, ideology or national fervour, or as expressions of restricted westernised élites. The actual meaning of these movements could only be grasped by understanding their *function* within the total structure of politics. Thus the Congress movement was from time to time a 'container' not only for the grievances and aspirations of the educated élites, but for organisations, interests and issues springing from all levels of regional and local politics. Thus when the Congress succeeded in bringing a wide range of people to its meetings, it was because magnates had helped bring in their clients, because parochial religious leaders and petty landlords could be roused to action by a whole variety of pressures from above and below passed on through a tangle of economic and political 'connections'.[57] Again, extremist and moderate factions may have been created by ideology, but their persistence and degree of success depended on a whole range of more local fears over the allocation of benefits in a poor society. In Washbrook and Baker's view the non-Brahmin movement in Madras could not be seen simply as a reflection of deep cultural cleavage in south India, for the sudden polarisation of provincial politics along communal lines was related to the complex interplay of magnate and lawyer-politician around the fount of patronage in Fort St. George.[58] Even the Khilafat Movement of 1918-22, the pre-eminent example of a Muslim ideological response in modern India, was held by Robinson to be intimately related to the constitutional and economic tensions of those years.[59] Secular politicians with immediate and short-term concerns summoned up the djinn of 'religion in danger' and mobilised the power of the *ulama* only to find that they could not easily coax it back into its bottle.

The analysis of political change in this approach is more ambiguous. Much of the argument depends on the assumption that large-scale economic change does not occur or only affects the conduct of politics very slowly. Thus the main motive force behind political change is the rôle of administration. Government, expanding in order to gain a closer, more detailed and more lucrative control of Indian society, distorts the relationship between various levels of politics and rouses discontent. So the movement of the Indian nationalist response from an élite phase to a mass phase is largely illusory. A series of agitational waves (in the 1880s, 1920s, 1930s, etc.), reflecting increased activity by government was followed by periods of quiescence when imperial concessions had extended

[57] Bayly, *Local Roots,* pp. 88-99.
[58] Washbrook, *The Emergence of Provincial Politics,* Ch. VII; Baker, *South India,* 1-84.
[59] F.C.R. Robinson, *Separatism,* pp. 257ff.

imperial control and divided its Indian opponents. Congress, it is admitted, probably involved more people from different social classes in its later agitations, but the support of the masses, or of the poorer peasantry was transitory and had little effect on the movement's social priorities. What mattered was Congress' growing rapport with urban and rural controllers, and this was fostered as much by the extention of electorates as by economic change or immiseration.

Diversification: the History of Regional Economics, Political Ideas and Culture

The reaction to this local school has been as sharp as to the earlier élite studies, though few have yet grasped how they differ. One interesting line of criticism, however, turns on the treatment of economic change, and especially on economic change in the countryside. Some parts of these works, of course, do admit that different political patterns emerged in areas of rapid economic change,[60] and there is disagreement how far the patron-client model had been modified by 1920. But should not the whole political and social structure be set within a much wider context – that of *underdevelopment*? Is not the whole magnate-client relationship, the sterile gyration of service communities around a government skimming off the surplus from a class of 'bastard' feudal landlords, a consequence of dependence within the colonial world system? The problem here is that we know so little about the internal or external economy of later British India. Was the persistence of local political élites or land-controllers in Cohn's model, really a sign of the unchanging rural scene or had the commercial and institutional changes of British rule actually restricted and frozen social change? In some areas we are just beginning to understand the relationship between economic change and the formation of politically significant classes; the realm of the urban merchant, and more significantly, of the rich peasant, for instance. The categories are crude, but the distinction between rich and middle peasant is no easier to form than it has been in the case of Mao's China or contemporary Latin America. However, it is not doubted that the crucial juncture in the history of Indian reactions to British imperialism was that between the urban politician and a small but significant class of rural people. Surveying recent literature, E. Stokes concludes that it was a dominant peasantry fortified with strong supra-village links

[60] Washbrook, 'Country Politics', *MAS,* 7, 3 (1973); Bayly, *Local Roots,* pp. 32-39, 47-51.

of clan or 'caste', rather than the middle peasant of Wolf's hypothesis, who provided the main thrust towards politics in the rural areas.[61] Over the next few years, scholars will begin to map out in detail the relationship of these groups to the expansion of the world market in India. Were the peasant magnates (*jotedars*) of Bengal or the rich farmers (*pattidars*) of Gujerat allowed their dominance over rural society by the actions of monopsonistic buyers from the colonial enclave supported by a tribute-taking political authority? Or did the particular conditions in rural society: rising population, low capital investments and technology play a greater part? The answer will obviously be a combination of both, but at least the external context within which the rural controllers and town connections operated, will have to be more seriously studied.

Another fruitful critique of the regional and local studies came largely from America and related to the rôle of ideas and spontaneous movements in politics. The patron-client model, it was argued, was too mechanistic and left too little room for radical and populist reactions, or even for altruistic pressures to social reform among the educated. Moreover, the relationship posited between ideas and political action was as crude as had been the case with the earlier élite conflict theory. E.F. Irschick, abandoning some of his earlier conclusions, suggested a useful compromise. Ideological movements had a functional rôle in politics, but that the functional use of these ideas must to some degree have depended on their appeal as ideas.[62] But this still leaves us with the grave historical, even philosophical problem which we have noted in Brass's adaptation of Deutsch. Can our analysis in any way go beyond the statements of the actors themselves? If leaders in southern India in 1916 asserted that they were attempting to break a Brahmin stranglehold on politics and administration, can an account that ascribes other motives to them have any validity unless we can prove that they were actually lying? The problem goes back to an ancient dispute in the social sciences. But it has been raised critically again by a very recent trend within studies of Europe in India which shows signs of altering dramatically the focus of debate within the field.

A new subjective account of European expansion and Indian reactions is emerging which insists that historical change must be understood primarily at the level of symbol and culture, and that the first aim of research must be to establish the 'indigenous' meaning

[61] E. Stokes, 'The return of the Peasant to South Asian Studies', *South Asia* (1977).

[62] 'Interpretations of Indian political development', *JAS*, 34, 2 (1974).

of events and institutions, before one can even begin to estimate the impact of the west. The implications to this approach are evident, though not yet spelled out, in the only major published work yet to see the light of day, R.B. Inden's, *Marriage and Rank in Bengali Society* (Berkeley, 1975). But these are still only implications. As in the case of much structuralism, or 'deep linguistics', the mystique and inwardness of debate is obstructive. Is it an attempt by the academic to re-establish his priestly status in a world where he has lost plausibility both as a teacher and a social engineer? Inden's key point, however, is that marriage exchanges (and hence much of the organisation and direction of Bengali society) derive from Bengali cultural concepts which relate to the expression of innate differences in inherited bodily substances in terms of different codes of ritual and social conduct. Attempts to explain Bengali society in terms of western concepts of class or landed aristocracy are therefore false. Inden tantalizingly implies that the effect of British rule was to encourage new educational and occupational definitions of rank which were gradually to impinge on the indigenous definitions. In this interpretation, therefore, British expansion brought about a change in Bengali values at a much deeper level, by modifying the goals of society itself. Inden himself has recently embarked upon a study of Indian kingship, but the implications of this for the study of European expansion are more apparent thus far in the work of his colleague, B.S. Cohn.

Drawing on a tradition that has influenced Clifford Geertz and found its most dramatic exponent in Marshall Sahlins, Cohn now defines culture as a set of symbols with meaning for the historical actors involved.[63] Culture and 'polity' (i.e. political structure) are interrelated, so that 'political' actions can only have meaning within their particular cultural context. We cannot simply assume, as standard studies of Indian political and social history have done, that actors are maximising money or power. By imputing to Indians universal political motivations and organising them into élites, classes or political systems, we are simply imposing our own historical and cultural experience in an area where it is inappropriate. Our only hope is to try to understand the indigenous meaning of cultural and political phenomena by studying what people said about their actions through the historical documentation. Thus the British obsession with the niceties of Moghul court ritual (the durbar system, *nazar,* ritualised gifts between superior and inferior) is not

[63] 'Honour and Honours', paper presented to the SSRC conference on Indian Social and Economic history, Cambridge (1975).

seen as empty pomp, or even as an *ex post facto* legitimation of brute imperialist power, but as an attempt to control people at the level of cultural symbols of honour and authority to which they respond. Authority, which defines political action, is no more and no less than the capacity to create honour. The British at first worked within the Moghul system of status, ranks and precedences, but they misunderstood and altered these symbols because of preconceptions drawn from their own culture. The Rebellion of 1857 is here important not as an actual rebellion, but because it involved the destruction, "desacralisation", of the imperial centre of Delhi, which had retained its ritual significance throughout the early phase of British expansion. After 1858, the British started again by using their own symbol of the Monarchy to create honour, and thus control society. Only when Gandhi provided a powerful symbolic solvent to this newly fashioned British legitimacy, did British control at the cultural and symbolic level weaken. By suggesting that the absence of revolt in British India can be explained in terms of the British control of the symbols of legitimacy, Cohn appears to be implying that the nature of the British *Raj* must be fundamentally explained in these terms.

The 'culture and authority' school, with its concern for the indigenous meaning of symbols now shows signs of becoming the dominant historical interpretation in studies of imperial India in the United States. Many students are now analysing estates, *raj* systems, imperial assemblages and temples as 'redistributional systems' of honour and social status.[64] They are generating indigenous categories of 'urbanisation', of kinship, of social status and of politics. Economic history and the activities of the European Companies are affected, since it is asserted that the market itself is no more than a cultural symbol. Thus before we can understand the impact of the west in India, we must understand the meaning of market, of supply and demand, of retail and wholesale in the Indian case. This position is much more radical than that of the Polyani school, and it has an institutional backing on a much grander scale. Grant-giving bodies have begun to proclaim that the aim of future U.S. researchers should be to elucidate the indigenous meaning of social

[64] E.g., Arjun Appadurai and Carol Breckenridge, 'The South Indian Temple; Honour, authority and redistribution', *Contributions to Indian Sociology* (Forthcoming) December (1976); N. Dirks, 'Political authority and structural change in early south Indian history', *IESHR*, 13, 2 (1976); the work of A. Oster on market and temple in Bengali culture, forthcoming; for a more orthodox approach following Dumont, see S. Barnett in the symposium on 'hierarchy', *JAS*, 36, 4 (1976).

forms previously misunderstood through cultural myopia. Moreover, this emphasis is now strong in the University of Chicago which has long commanded appointments and the content of scholarly journals in several parts of the country.

The roots of this trend are both cultural and intellectual. In the last twenty years social anthropology in the United States has switched from the 'anglo-saxon' empirical school associated with Evans-Pritchard, Radcliffe-Brown and Malinowski, to a more thorough-going neo-Weberianism, thus bringing it into line with other social sciences. The impact of structuralism with Europe and the work of L. Dumont provided exciting evidence of the possibilities of theory in Indian history and anthropology. But structuralism was too closely associated with French intellectual traditions to be thoroughly acceptable. The new and more sophisticated Marxism is still politically suspect and alien, despite the interest shown by some American historians such as Eugene Genovese. A refurbished and radical Weberianism was thus the obvious inheritor within the American academic tradition, particularly in view of its distinguished pedigree at the University of Chicago. But I take the trend to be a more general one. There appear to be parallels in the work of V. Turner on African kingship which has stimulated interest in the African meanings of power and authority and the extent to which the colonial powers were able to manipulate them. Similarly, and in a more historical context, Terence Ranger has begun to work on the expansion of Europe in Africa as a system of cultural change – as a phenomenon which must be understood not only in terms of the expansion of European economic power, but in terms of the creation of new patterns of behaviour through religious conversion, the imposition of work-discipline and the manipulation of values.[65]

There is a great excitement about much of this work and a feeling that it reaches through to new levels of explanation in the historiography of relations between the white races and the rest of the world. But it is to be hoped that it will not stunt the growth of empirical studies in the way that much of the 'break towards the locality' eschewed theory and methodology. The omens are mixed. Sometimes its proponents have indicated that they feel systems of culture and symbols to be entities in themselves, superior to and governing actual social life. In writing, however, they are more cautious, and disclaim any attempt at this stage to show how the cultural world relates to 'polity', neither claiming that it is superior

[65] T. Ranger, 'The invention of tradition in colonial Africa', *Past and Present* Conference (1977).

or prior. Thus Inden states that he is not attempting 'an objective explanation of actual social change' in much the same way as David Schneider's *American Kinship* (1972) seems to accept that 'dog' may be a cultural symbol but it is also an animal that bites. If this standpoint rather than the more radical one is maintained, it is evident that the new approach is valuable, but partial. It cannot *replace* the study of European expansion as actual social and economic change; it can only show the consequences of that expansion on the values of the imperialists and the conquered peoples. The problem from the historian's perspective is that we cannot understand why models of behaviour and values should arise and change. Why should Bengalis be constrained to act like the products of an English public school; why was the use of Gandhi's new symbols of legitimacy able to effect political change in some places and at some times and not in others? The answers to these problems, as far as we can see, must still lie in the long-term expansion and contraction of a European world-system based on resources that are commonly valued *between* cultures and on technological superiority. That the exploitation of resources and technology are in a sense themselves defined by culture cannot detract from the fact that the invention of some patterns of behaviour (the chartered company, the maxim gun, industrial capitalism) are more powerful solvents of social relations than others (the digging-stick, family firm or asagai for instance).

To the historian the roots of historiographical change may appear to be purely intellectual: the dialectic of debate within the subject. What is striking in this brief survey of recent literature on Britain and India is the extent to which external ideas and institutions have shaped our interests. National traditions of scholarship still remain strong. The questions we ask are still determined by our exposure to the social scientific and neo-Weberian traditions of the United States, or the radical empiricist and neo-Marxian traditions that have been more common in Britain and Europe, or now among the Indian intelligentsia. Institutions, the policy of monied foundations, and simple matters of access to vernacular and Indian materials have limited and fashioned the direction of our enquiries. Our poor grasp of the complex indigenous background to the expansion of Europe has reinforced the dominance of anthropology and the social sciences in the literature. From the beginning then, fundamental questions about social organisation and the nature of social description have intruded themselves into historical writing. This has proved refreshing, but it has also restricted the development of a consistent historiography. The new emphasis on culture and symbol, for instance, has directed attention away from the more empirical studies of local social structure before any degree of coherence was appreciable in these. The dominance of the social sciences has also led to a preoccupation with social *structure* at the expense of an analysis of historical *change.* Thus our literature remains fragmented not merely as between periods, regions and intellectual traditions, but also between different conceptual levels. Studies are in progress of the cultural ideals of the British and their Indian subjects. There are studies of the broader polity, economy and society of colonial India; there are also studies of the small institutions (villages, family firms, castes and clans) which functioned within this environment. The problem of how to relate these levels has now become critical. We are still not clear how, for instance, the investment decisions or cultural milieu of the small organisations affected structure and change within the total economy and society. As we have shown, the links between the world of 'objective social change' and that of cultural symbology can be grasped neither empirically or theoretically. A new attempt at integration is badly needed.

What form should a new approach take? First, the false distinction between values and interests could well be abolished. Analyses of political change, local power and patronage do not need to be couched in terms of gross machiavellianism. Local interests were important in India because they were expressions of local values as well as the objectives of power-seekers. The importance of local 'publicists' or 'bosses' in so many political movements does not really imply the victory of materialism over abstract values, merely the priority given to subsistence, the honour of family, ancestors and community, in a complex society. Equally, the cultural historian does not need to perpetrate the pointless circularity in argument which insists that all we need to know about a given set of brahmins, say, is that their behaviour can be understood in terms of Brahmin Values. To an historian it is less crucial whether in some abstract sense 'culture' encompasses what Sahlins calls 'practical reason', or *vice versa.*[66] Such a question is only possible if we adopt a static, sociological analysis of society. Social change in history seems more circular. General ideas are built up and refined because they were valuable and useful to people in the context of their daily lives. Once formulated those ideas in turn inform and even change the way they see their daily lives. A complete historical study (and

[66] M. Sahlins, *Culture and Practical Reason* (Chicago 1976).

there is no reason why all studies should be complete) would presumably need to 'close the circle', dealing with ideology and practice and the way ideas are taught and learned within the family and small group. S.J. Tambiah's study of Buddhist polity in Thailand, *World Conqueror and World Renouncer* (Cambridge, 1976), shows how these different levels of analysis can be mutually enriching. The concept of 'moral economy' which has been applied to the town mob in 18th century Europe as well as to the South-East Asian peasantry also has great potential for the Indian historian.[67] This approach seeks to show how values, economic practices and politics look from the perspective of the individual family or small community, but it can be broadened to throw light on broader formations such as class or castes. In the case of the peasant, the nature of politics, economics and ethical values are all seen to be related to the overriding need to guarantee subsistence and continuity. Values, in this approach, are not 'out there' but intimately bound up with the practice of daily life. One cannot be understood without the other. This view 'from the inside outward' could very well be applied to studies of Indian peasants, *rajas* and merchants. We could see how concepts such as caste and religion were adapted by people to their everyday lives and at what points the impact of the colonial state affected them most nearly.

LITERATURE

General

M.H. Case, *South Asian History, 1750-1950, a guide to periodicals, dissertations and newspapers* (Princeton 1966).

H.D. Sharma, S.P. Mukherji and L.M.P. Singh (eds.) *Indian Reference Sources. An annotated guide to Indian reference books* (Varanasi 1962).

M. Patterson and R. Inden, *Introduction to the Civilisation of India: South Asia, an Introductory Bibliography* (Chicago 1962).

R. Winks, *Historiography of the British Empire-Commonwealth* (Durham 1966) (R. Crane and D. Singhal).

J.P.C. Roach (ed.) *A Bibliography of Modern History* (Cambridge 1969) (K. Ballhatchet).

[67] James C. Scott *The Moral Economy of the Peasant* (Yale 1976);
JAS, Journal of Asian Studies; IESHR, Indian Economic and Social History Review; MAS, Modern Asian Studies.

Bibliographical Essays: early phase

P.J. Marshall, 'British Expansion in India', *History,* 1975.

M.N. Pearson, 'Political participation in Moghul India', *IESHR,* 9, 2 (1975).

E.T. Stokes, 'The first century of British Colonial Rule in India', *Past and Present* 58 (1973).

B.S. Cohn, *The Development and Impact of British administration in India: A bibliographical essay* (Delhi 1961).

Economic development

M.D. Morris and B. Stein, 'The Economic History of India; a bibliographical essay', *Journal of Economic History* 21, 2 (1961).

M.D. Morris, 'Towards a re-interpretation of Nineteenth-century Indian Economic History', *IESHR,* 5 (1968).

D. Kumar, 'The Economy under the Raj', *South Asian Review,* 3 (1970).

D. Kumar, 'Recent research in the economic history of modern India', *IESHR,* 9 (1972).

W.G. Macpherson, 'Economic Development in India under the British Crown, 1858-1947', in A.S. Youngson (ed.) *Economic Development in the long-run* (London 1972).

E.N. Komarov, 'Survey of Russian pre-Revolutionary and Soviet studies on the Economic History of India in the modern age', *Contributions to Indian Sociology,* I (1961).

Later imperial period

B.S. Cohn, 'Society and Social Change under the Raj', *South Asian Review,* 4 (1970).

J.B. Harrison, 'The rulers and the ruled', *South Asian Review,* 3 (1969).

R.J. Moore, 'Recent Historical Writing on the modern British Empire and Commonwealth: Later Imperial India', *Journal of Imperial and Commonwealth History* (January 1975).

S. Ray, 'Historians of the Twentieth Century: India after Independence', *Journal of Contemporary History,* 2, 1 (1967).

Topics

K. Gough, 'Indian Peasant Uprisings', *Economic and Political Weekly,* 9 (1974) (special number August 1974), f. 1391ff.

E. Stokes, 'The return of the Peasant to South Asian Studies', *South Asia* (1977).

P. Hardy, *The Muslims of British India* (Cambridge 1972), bibliog.

K. Jones (ed.) *Sources for Punjab History: a bibliographical anthology* (East Lansing 1973).

3. EUROPEAN EXPANSION INTO WEST AFRICA: A HISTORIOGRAPHICAL SURVEY OF ENGLISH-LANGUAGE PUBLICATIONS SINCE 1945

by

A.G. HOPKINS

INTRODUCTION

A survey of the kind undertaken here would not have been possible in 1945: all the relevant books available at that time could have been listed on one page. Most were general rather than specialised studies, though what they lacked in detail they often made up for in quality. The literature published in French was probably richer than that in English, for reasons which Professor Brunschwig's essay may explain. Nevertheless, the distinguished studies of McPhee, Hancock and Blake[1] can stand comparison in any company, and, as is well known, English-language studies of Africa in an allied discipline, anthropology, were both highly regarded and widely influential.

The body of literature available today is essentially the product of the last twenty years: it expanded just at the moment when decolonisation became inevitable. Colonial rule seemed to make academic study redundant, apart from ethnographic surveys. It was the collapse of imperial power and the realisation that independent Africa would become important in world affairs that spurred the study of the continent. In the 1960s economic prosperity and university expansion made it possible to mount an intensive research effort on Africa and on the Third World generally. Britain took a leading part in this boom, and so too did the major universities of West Africa, but the largest funding and the most numerous scholars in the English-speaking world were to be found in the United States. There, academic enterprise was linked, albeit indirectly, to the world role which the United States had assumed at the end of World War II. Understanding Africa became an essential preliminary

[1] Allan McPhee, *The Economic Revolution in British West Africa* (1926); W.K. Hancock, *Survey of British Commonwealth Affairs, 1918-1939,* Vol. II, part 2 (1942); and J.W. Blake, *European Beginnings in West Africa, 1451-1578* (1937).

to representing the interests of the 'Free World', once the British lion had been retired from active service.

This sudden and massive expansion of research has now, some twenty years later, generated large bibliographies, such as Duignan and Gann's *Bibliographical Guide to Colonialism in Africa* (1973), Hogg's *The African Slave Trade and its Suppression* (1973), Coquery-Vidrovitch and Moniot's *L'Afrique noire* (1974) and Halstead and Porcari's *Modern European Imperialism* (2 Vols., 1974), to list just four recent and varied examples. Allied guides include Brunschwig's regular surveys in the *Revue Historique,* abstracting journals, such as *African Abstracts* and *Historical Abstracts,* and annual lists of dissertations on Africa recorded in *International Dissertation Abstracts.* There is a wide range of scholarly journals,[2] several monograph series (now faltering but still intact),[3] and various large, multi-handed surveys of African history.[4] The university presses of Oxford and Cambridge have carried out their own amicable partition of the continent, so that the map, once painted largely red, is now coloured dark blue and light blue.[5]

A small proportion of this immense historical literature is the work of amateurs, who continue to be attracted, in the main, by the compelling horrors of the slave trade. Such studies occasionally enjoy considerable popularity, as in the recent case of Alex Haley's *Roots* (1977). However, the main trend has been towards increased professionalism, as expressed in the deployment of new techniques of historical reconstruction, such as the use of oral traditions, in frequently diverse language requirements, and in the multi-disciplinary nature of much of the historical research on the continent. Uneven though the coverage of regions and centuries is at present, Africa has acquired a historiography which it, more than any other continent, lacked. And though specialists frequently complain about a shortage of written evidence, the indications are that they are still producing more data than they are consuming. In this respect the future of the subject seems healthy. Unemployment is still a long way off.

[2] The *Journal of African History,* founded in 1960, provides a good guide to the major trends in historical research.

[3] Notably Oxford's *Studies in African Affairs,* and the *Ibadan History Series* published by Longman.

[4] Such as J.F. Ade Ajayi and Michael Crowder, eds., *History of West Africa,* Vol. I (1971, 2nd ed. 1976), Vol. II (1974).

[5] The *Cambridge History of Africa,* currently under way, is intended to span the continent; Oxford has opted for regional specialisation: *The Oxford History of South Africa,* Vol. I (1969), Vol. II (1971), and *The Oxford History of East Africa,* Vol. I (1963), Vol. II (1966).

The Two Phases

A consideration of the historiography of European expansion into West Africa cannot be detached from the broader intellectual trends which have influenced African studies as a whole during the past twenty years. A first attempt to classify this vast and diverse literature suggests that there have been two major phases, each corresponding to a *Zeitgeist* or mood which permeated research in archive and field alike. These two phases reflect scholarly reactions to economic and political changes in the world at large. The first phase, which began in the mid-1950s and lasted until the late 1960s, can be characterised as liberal optimism. The second phase, which began in the late 1960s and remains influential today, can be termed radical pessimism. Around these central tendencies clustered other lines of approach, some discordant, others harmonious, momentos of ancient ideas and precursors of new.

The liberal optimists reacted against their inheritance of imperial history and set about writing African history. They sought to show that Africans had produced great states and great leaders in the past, and could do so again if given the opportunity by colonial powers. Thus, the history of Africa written in the late 1950s and early 1960s tended to be political in orientation, to be supportive of anti-colonial movements and to provide legitimation for newly-independent states. From the outset, then, African history has served a purpose related to pressing needs of the day. This function becomes clear only when the literature is considered retrospectively: most scholars accepted then, as they do now, the priorities of the day and tried to be as objective as possible about the answers they gave to the questions they had decided to ask. The questions posed at the time of independence were testing ones: In answering them historians became entrepreneurs, creating an African past where none was thought to exist, apart from the story of Europeans in Africa. Successive editions of J.D. Fage's pioneering *Introduction to the History of West Africa* (1st ed. 1955; 4th ed. 1969) chart the expansion of historical knowledge about this part of the once 'Dark Continent'.

As historians provided histories which were functional to the requirements of the new states of Africa, so other social scientists set about solving the pressing development problems of these states. This was the time when North American influences on the Anglo-Saxon literature were particularly pronounced in matters of economic, social and political development. The achievement of political independence in tropical Africa was a time of optimism and confidence, when economists thought they could plan and deliver prosperity, when sociologists and social psychologists felt certain they could transform backward social structures and inhibiting mental attitudes, and when political scientists were convinced that the well known multi-national firm, Westminster Constitutions Ltd., could set up branches in desert and jungle. Not for the first time, missionaries descended on Africa, though the new generation possessed Ph.D.'s in development planning and held calculators in their hands. And why not? It was then orthodox to believe that spiritual welfare (or psychic income) could be correlated with material progress and quantified by means of increments in the Gross National Product.

Social scientists, like historians, were strongly influenced by events in the wider world, notably the need to win Africa to the liberal-capitalist cause at a time when the Cold War was still in its last icy stages, and when it was clear that there was going to be a contest between American and Russian informal imperialism following the collapse of the European empires in Africa. At this time, however, securing Africa for the future was an exercise which, so it was said, could be achieved without reference to its past. Indeed, economists, sociologists and political scientists were open and sometimes militant in their belief that history and historians should be kept well in the background. Thus, despite the fact that historians and social scientists were influenced by similar external circumstances, their research endeavours remained separate. The new African history was not used by social scientists; and social scientists themselves did not create any history, except by their own actions – which are now coming under historical scrutiny.

The second phase began when changes in the world outside the scholarly community began to alter the assumptions of modernisation theorists. In Africa, plans of economic development began to look more impressive on paper than in practice; closer inspection of traditional societies revealed them to be heterogeneous and also more complex than had been thought; and political instability and military rule signalled the decline and fall of the black hopes of white liberals. At first these potentially disturbing discoveries were fended off or ignored. The mechanism of cognitive dissonance was set in motion to confirm that it was not the theories that were wrong (the theories on which so much time and money had been spent), but African recalcitrance or incompetence in implementing them. Thus did disillusion come upon some of those who had begun, ten years earlier, by supporting African independence. To increasing troubles in Africa were added, in the late 1960s, serious economic problems in the advanced industrial states, leading to doubts as to whether capitalism was able to sustain its own growth, let alone transmit development to less advanced regions. In the United States, the source of so much of the developmental thinking of the first phase of liberal optimism, an additional factor, the Vietnam War, had immense domestic political and psychological repercussions, sapping confidence in American assumptions and prescriptions for the world.

The result, once again in schematic terms, was a reaction among academics against liberal-capitalist and non-historical analyses, and a shift in the direction of interpretations based on radical assumptions and making use of history, which now, indeed, is regarded as providing the key to understanding contemporary problems. Intellectually, this second historiographical phase drew most of its inspiration from the revitalised New Left, notably in France and Latin America, though there was (and still is) a renewed interest in non-Marxist institutional approaches to development problems too. The assumptions underlying the new trend, though sometimes expressed in complicated language, are comparatively simple, and are virtually the opposite of those which went before them. Underdevelopment is now seen not as an original condition, but as a created process brought about by international trading links which, far from spreading development, transmit underdevelopment, as metropolitan centres excavate the peripheries which fall under their control. The dependency thesis of André Gunder Frank is currently being applied to Africa to explain how backwardness was created from the time of the overseas slave trade onwards. African history is still supposed to be relevant, but now the purpose of historical study is to locate the roots of underdevelopment in the distant past and to change the present rather than to support it. The newly-recognised significance of history and its relation to present-day policy-making has led to a rather speedy conversion among social scientists to studies of the past, especially to economic history. A new kind of orthodoxy is beginning to emerge, in which a frequently schematic view of history is conjured up to support recommendations about current policy.

The Four "Bulges"

These broad influences make it easier to comprehend the literature on a specific subject – European expansion into West Africa. It becomes possible to show that research in this area is not merely a catalogue of increasing publications on more and more detailed topics (though this trend is certainly present), but is related to the historiographical phases outlined above. In establishing this connection, I do not wish to deny the presence of other influences, to imply that there were no contrary streams of thought, or to detract from the individuality of notable contributions to historical research. Above all, the fluctuating fortunes of the schools of thought identified here are to be seen as gradations of emphasis rather than sharp breaks with the past. The relationship is a general one and it operates in an indirect way. Nevertheless, it does provide a measure of central tendency which is essential to any historiographical analysis. I shall consider four 'bulges' in the literature which together cover the history of European expansion into West Africa: the era of the slave trade; the period of 'legitimate' commerce and informal political relations; the 'scramble' for Africa at the close of the nineteenth century; and, briefly, the era of colonial rule (c. 1900-c. 1960).

Sea-borne connections between West Africa and Europe date from the late fifteenth century, four hundred years before Africa was brought fully under European rule. For much of this period, and particularly during the eighteenth century, European relations with West Africa were dominated by the Atlantic slave trade. In the early phase of liberal optimism studies of the slave trade tended to be political in orientation, focussing on the relationship between trade and state formation and on the role of African leaders, who were regarded as archetypal resisters and as nation-builders. Thus, I.A. Akinjogbin's pioneering study, *Dahomey and its Neighbours, 1708-1818* (1967), argued that the founders of the kingdom of Dahomey consistently opposed the slave trade until external pressures forced a change of policy, and also drew parallels between Dahomey and the centralised government and standing armies that characterised the nation states of early modern Europe. In this way African participation in the Atlantic slave trade could be explained, and a historical line could be drawn through the centuries to join early state-building movements with those being undertaken in Africa at the time of independence.

In the mid-1960s liberal optimism began to be superseded by liberal realism, as the limitations of 'special' explanations of African behaviour became apparent, and as interest quickened in economic history, making use of universal neo-classical postulates and deploying, where possible, quantitative techniques. African creativity was not denied, but Africans began to be viewed as hard-headed businessmen responding willingly and rationally to the profitable opportunities provided by the slave trade. Research was undertaken on the Atlantic slave trade as a business venture,[6] and the size of the trade was estimated in Philip D. Curtin's *The Atlantic Slave Trade: a Census* (1969). Curtin's study, the first serious attempt to count the number of slaves shipped from West Africa, arrived at a figure which was roughly half the total previously guessed at and argued over for more than a century. His work has generated a great deal of further empirical and quantitative research, and has merged with a similar stream flowing from studies of slavery in the United States in the nineteenth century. Recent years have seen the appearance of a number of important studies, which together provide a reliable guide to current scholarly preoccupations: Engerman and Genovese's *Race and Slavery in the Western Hemisphere* (1975), a special issue of the *Revue française d'histoire d'outre-mer* entitled 'La traite de noirs par l'Atlantique: nouvelles approches', edited by Emmer, Mettas and Nardin (1975), and a more specialised collection of essays edited by Anstey and Hair, *Liverpool, the African Slave Trade and Abolition* (1976).[7] The slave trade has become big business again, as the new slavers busily trade numbers with each other in the academic journals. The exchange between Curtin and Inikori[8] clearly illustrates the wide-ranging and seemingly intractable problems facing scholars who elect to work in an area where statistics and morality are joined and cannot, it seems, be put asunder. The slave trade is not a subject for the faint-hearted.

Liberal realism, with its stress on dispassionate analysis, has also experienced increasing criticism recently from radical pessimists, who have sought to re-focus attention on the adverse consequences of the trade for Africa, rather than on the mechanics of business organisation or the clinical counting of heads. The popular statement of this position is Walter Rodney's book, *How Europe Underdeveloped Africa* (1972). The current revival of Marxist approaches is represented in this context by the critique of the methodology of liberal scholars expressed by Meillassoux in his review of Curtin's latest book.[9]

[6] See, for example, Henry A. Gemery and Jan S. Hogendorn, 'The Atlantic Slave Trade: a Tentative Economic Model', *Journal of African History,* XV, 2, (1974) pp. 223-46.

[7] The most recent survey is Roger Anstey, 'The Slave Trade of the Continental Powers', *Economic History Review,* XXX, 2, (1977), pp. 259-68.

[8] *Journal of African History,* XVII, 4, (1976), pp. 595-627.

[9] 'Une géographie historique de la Sénégambie', *Journal of African History,* XVIII, 3, (1977), pp. 449-52.

The second bulge in historical research relating to European expansion is located in studies of the so-called 'era of legitimate commerce', that is the period from the abolition of the Atlantic slave trade in the early part of the nineteenth century to the eve of the partition of Africa at its end. Interest in this period was encouraged in the late 1950s and the early 1960s as much by the ready availability of documentary evidence as by any clear conception of its historical significance, though the research which resulted was clearly dominated by the themes of great states, great leaders and African resistance to European encroachments. Emphasis was placed on the creativity of the African elite and on its capacity to manage state systems effectively. Detailed work of high quality was produced. Studies of the Niger Delta, the most important exporting region of West Africa in the middle years of the century, related the development of 'legitimate' trade to the rise and fall of states based on entrepôt functions, and to shifts of power among lineages within stable state strcutures.[10] Biographies of prominent African leaders rescued reputations which had been obscured during the long reign of imperial history. The creoles, conventionally regarded as tame collaborators, have been rehabilitated and presented as advocates of the revival of African culture and as the articulate founders of constitutional resistance to European rule.[11] It has been shown that representatives of church and state were men of distinction and principle.[12] This tradition of liberal, nationalist historiography was incorporated in the monographs appearing in the Ibadan History Series, published by the Longman Group (though not all the volumes conform to this image).

Liberal realism took the form of an attempt to penetrate below the elite and to deal with some of the economic problems neglected by the primarily political bias expressed in the pioneering work on this period. Latham's study of Old Calabar viewed the large African wholesalers as men of self-interest rather than as proto-nationalists.[13]

[10] See, for example, K.O. Dike, *Trade and Politics in the Niger Delta, 1830-1885* (1956), and G.I. Jones, *The Trading States of the Oil Rivers* (1963).

[11] Christopher Fyfe, *A History of Sierra Leone* (1962) and *Africanus Horton 1835-1883: West African Scientist and Patriot* (1972); J.D. Hargreaves, *A Life of Sir Samuel Lewis* (1958).

[12] J.F. Ade Ajayi, *Christian Missions in Nigeria, 1841-1891* (1965); James Bertin Webster, *The African Churches among the Yoruba, 1888-1922* (1964); E.A. Ayandele, *Holy Johnson* (1970); Obaro Ikime, *Merchant Prince of the Niger Delta* (1968).

[13] A.J.H. Latham, *Old Calabar, 1600-1891* (1973).

Neglected themes, such as the continuation of internal slavery after the abolition of the overseas slave trade, have been explored;[14] little-known adverse consequences of the new trade have been revealed;[15] and a case has been made for the historical distinctiveness of the period not in terms of trade relations, but in terms of changes in the structure of export production, which saw the widespread involvement of small cultivators in overseas trade for the first time.[16]

The radical critique of the various liberal positions has so far remained at the level of generalities about the adverse effects on West Africa of the 'distorted' development brought by increased external trade and greater specialisation. However, it is probable that more detailed studies will be undertaken from this perspective in the near future, and it is to be hoped that they will illuminate our understanding of important but at present obscure problems. At the moment, the arguments of liberals and radicals alike suffer from a shortage of information on the effects of the growth of 'legitimate' commerce on indigenous producing units, and on the welfare consequences of the expansion of foreign trading activities.

The third bulge in the literature occurs with the classic case of nineteenth-century imperialism, the partition of Africa in the last quarter of the nineteenth century. In this short period Afro-European relations, which for centuries had been on the whole informal and confined to the coast, were transformed. This was the time of inland expansion and conquest, which resulted in the creation of European colonies throughout West Africa and indeed in Africa as a whole.

In surveying the vast literature on the 'scramble' it is impossible to escape, even in West Africa, those twin Egyptian pyramids – Robinson and Gallagher. No detour is possible: these imposing edifices dominate the landscape and have to be climbed. It is unnecessary here to summarise what has long been a widely known and acclaimed analysis. It is sufficient to say that *Africa and the Victorians* has remained by far the most influential study of partition since its appearance in 1961. In historiographical terms the book

[14] E.A. Oroge, 'The Institution of Slavery in Yorubaland with Particular Reference to the Nineteenth Century', University of Birmingham Ph.D. Thesis, 1971. See also Claude Meillassoux ed., *L'esclavage en Afrique précoloniale* (1975).

[15] D.C. Dorward and A.I. Payne, 'Deforestation, the Decline of the Horse, and the Spread of the Tsetse Fly and Trypanosomiasis (*nagana*) in Nineteenth-Century Sierra Leone', *Journal of African History*, XVI, 2, (1975), pp. 239-56.

[16] A.G. Hopkins, 'Economic Imperialism in West Africa: Lagos, 1882-92', *Economic History Review*, 21, (1968), pp. 580-606.

drew on two main sources of inspiration, one in Europe and the other in Africa. First, the authors extended the revisionist interpretation of British overseas expansion in the nineteenth century which they had advanced in a celebrated article published in 1953.[17] They rejected Hobson's and Lenin's economic interpretations of imperialism and denied the novelty of the so-called 'new' imperialism at the end of the century. Robinson and Gallagher argued instead that expansion was continuous, and that the problem needing explanation was the shift from informal to formal means of control. In particular Robinson and Gallagher focussed on what they termed the 'official mind', arguing that the causes of partition had to be sought in the decisions made by the prominent politicians and officials who held office at the time. Second, Robinson and Gallagher were quick to take up (and contribute to) the main theme of liberal nationalist historiography, the policies and decisions of indigenous rulers and the process of nation-building in Africa, as this ran parallel to their own approach to European history. Following this method of dual analysis, Robinson and Gallagher came to see the scramble for Africa as arising out of local crises prompted by proto-nationalist and nationalist movements in Africa itself, beginning in Egypt in 1882 and reverberating around the continent thereafter. *Africa and the Victorians* was undoubtedly based on an amalgamation of the most promising lines of enquiry available at the time. It placed the interpretation of partition firmly in the context of politics and diplomacy, and it established the framework of discussion down to the present day.

Robinson and Gallagher's work has inspired so much research, much of it critical but all of it constructive, that it has now become necessary to issue periodic guides to the state of the debate![18] Further consideration has been given to the 'official mind', as for example in Uzoigwe's reassessment of Lord Salisbury's foreign policy;[19] sub-imperialisms have been identified as in Kanya-Forstner's examination of the role of the military in the Sudan;[20] proto-nationalists and resisters have been sought and found, as in Obaro Ikime's biography of Nana Olumu, the Itsekiri leader;[21] case

[17] R.E. Robinson and J. Gallagher, 'The Imperialism of Free Trade', *Economic History Review,* VI, 1 (1953), pp. 1-15.

[18] William Roger Louis, ed., *Imperialism: the Robinson and Gallagher Controversy* (1976).

[19] G.N. Uzoigwe, *Britain and the Conquest of Africa: the Age of Salisbury* (1974). See also the excellent review by Roy Bridges in *Journal of African History,* XVI, 4 (1975), pp. 631-4.

[20] A.S. Kanya-Forstner, *The Conquest of the Western Sudan* (1969).

[21] *Merchant Prince of the Niger Delta* (1968).

studies of local Afro-European relations have been undertaken, as exemplified in the detailed and quite indispensable work of Hargreaves;[22] and discussion has taken place on the question of which local crisis antedated or was more important than another, as witness Kanya-Forstner and Newbury's article dating partition from 1879 and locating its origins in Senegal rather than in 1882 and in Egypt.[23]

Africa and the Victorians has been shot at and shot through, but it sails on. The reason is simple: no one has succeeded in advancing an alternative explanation of greater power. Indeed, very few scholars have even attempted this formidable task, though there are many summaries of existing explanations. Sanderson's recent essay is perhaps the only study which clearly aims at establishing a new 'covering hypothesis' for the partition of Africa as a whole.[24] Sanderson must be given credit for his praiseworthy endeavour, but his argument, though erudite, is weakened by its apparent circularity. Briefly, Sanderson's case amounts to the claim that partition was a result of the destabilised political situation arising out of the decline of the military and political power which supported the Pax Britannica. The difficulty is not that this argument is untrue, but that it is a truism. It redefines the problem, but does not carry the discussion much further forward.

The beginnings of an alternative approach to partition began to appear with the rise of economic and social history from the mid-1960s onwards. Work undertaken by Newbury,[25] Klein,[26] and Hopkins,[27] among others, has indicated that there are grounds for supposing that an economic explanation of the scramble for West Africa can be advanced without running into the criticisms which

[22] J.D. Hargreaves, *Prelude to the Partition of West Africa* (1963), and *West Africa Partitioned:* Vol. I, *The Loaded Pause, 1885-89* (1974).

[23] C.W. Newbury and A.S. Kanya-Forstner, 'French Policy and the Origins of the Scramble for West Africa', *Journal of African History,* X, 2 (1969), pp. 253-76.

[24] G.N. Sanderson, 'The European Partition of Africa: Coincidence or Conjuncture?', *Journal of Imperial and Commonwealth History,* 3 (1974), pp. 1-54.

[25] C.W. Newbury, 'Trade and Authority in West Africa from 1850 to 1880', in L.H. Gann and Peter Duignan, eds., *Colonialism in Africa.* Vol. I *The History and Politics of Colonialism, 1870-1914* (1969), pp. 66-99; 'The Tariff Factor in Anglo-French West African Partition', in Prosser Gifford and William Roger Louis, eds., *France and Britain in Africa: Imperial Rivalry and Colonial Rule* (1971), pp. 221-59.

[26] Martin A. Klein, 'Social and Economic Factors in the Muslim Revolution in Senegambia', *Journal of African History,* XIII, 3 (1972), pp. 419-41.

[27] A.G. Hopkins, *An Economic History of West Africa* (1973), Ch. 4.

have been made of Hobson-Leninist theories.[28] Hopkins, for instance, has tried to show that the industrial revolution gave propulsion to mercantile capitalism rather than to finance capitalism in West Africa; that mercantile demands for new raw materials led to significant changes in the economic structure of export-producing regions, while at the same time tying them into the trade cycles transmitted by the industrial world; and that partition is to be explained in terms of a crisis of adaptation to the new economy made manifest in the long commercial depression which began in the 1870s, and in the conflicts which followed the intensified search for profits and revenue. Resistance and collaboration are seen in terms of the economic opportunities open to, and the demands made upon, African societies and the degree of response and stress they evoked. The history of Africa can still be joined with the history of European domestic problems and foreign policy, and the era of 'legitimate' commerce can be reinterpreted as containing the causes of partition. Methodologically, the main aim of this analysis is to enlarge the framework constructed by Robinson and Gallagher by shifting the discussion from individuals to processes; from elites in Africa and Europe to the interests they represented. However, it has to be said that the case has been presented in a rather schematic way, and has itself been criticised.[29]

The partition of Africa is obviously a fruitful subject for New Left writers, though at present little detailed historical research has been carried out from this perspective. At the level of generality the main emphasis has been on partition as increasing the dependence of Africa on Europe and furthering the integration and the exploitation of the continent. However, it can be expected that further attention will be paid to economic aspects of partition in the future, though it may well be that orthodox Marxist responses to New Left theories will dominate the literature. It would certainly be helpful to have a thorough analysis of changing modes of production in Africa in the nineteenth century. African history could then be related to more detailed work on types of capitalist presence

[28] At the same time it should be pointed out that many criticisms of Hobson and Lenin are attacks on stereotypes and are not based on a reading of the original texts. See also note 30 below.

[29] For example, J.F.A. Ajayi and R.A. Austen, 'Hopkins on Economic Imperialism in West Africa', *Economic History Review,* XXV, 2 (1972), pp. 303-6.

on the periphery, and to the re-thinking of the classic Marxist texts which is currently under way.[30]

The fourth bulge in the literature covers the era of formal rule (c. 1900-c. 1960). The colonial period is as much a study in imperial control and, ultimately, decline, as in imperial expansion, and it is only recently that it has begun to attract serious historical attention. However, the main historiographical trends are certainly worth noting, not least because they fit into the pattern of the other segments of history surveyed here.

Priorities during the era of liberal optimism were firmly fixed on recreating the history of Africans in their own continent. Studies of colonial rule were regarded as old-fashioned and were rarely undertaken. With the advantage of hindsight, it can be seen that the result of this bias was the neglect of some undeniably important subjects. For instance, very little work was done on any aspect of colonial policy, or on the modern transport systems which were one of the principal legacies of European rule.[31] The main exception to this generalisation lay in studies of resistance movements during partition and after, when the new rulers were faced with the task of turning formal possession into effective occupation.[32] These studies looked back to earlier state-forming movements identified by scholars such as Akinjogbin, and forward to the nation-building preoccupations at the end of colonial rule, as exemplified by Ranger's early work.[33] Robinson and Gallagher had argued that Africans who chose to resist were gallant anachronisms, unfitted for a place in the new colonial order. Against this view Hargreaves has made it clear that resisters as

[30] See, for example, the discussion and useful bibliography in Roger Owen and Bob Sutcliffe, eds. *Studies in the Theory of Imperialism* (1972); Kenneth J. Tarbuck, eds., Rosa Luxemburg, *The Accumulation of Capital – An Anti-Critique* and Nikolai I. Bukharin, *Imperialism and the Accumulation of Capital* (1972); George Lee, 'Rosa Luxemburg and the Impact of Imperialism', *Economic Journal* LXXX (1971), pp. 847-62; Walter Rodney, 'The Imperialist Partition of Africa', *Monthly Review,* 21, 11, 1970, pp. 103-14; and an article on Hobson by P.J. Cain forthcoming in the *Economic History Review,* 1978.

[31] It would be misleading to imply that the colonial theme was eliminated. For some valuable studies see Prosser Gifford and William Roger Louis (eds.), *Britain and Germany in Africa* (1967) and *France and Britain in Africa* (1971); and L.H. Gann and Peter Duignan, eds., *Colonialism in Africa, 1870-1960,* 5 vols (1969-75).

[32] For example, M. Crowder, ed., *West African Resistance: the Military Response to Colonial Occupation* (1971) and Robert Rotberg and Ali Mazrui, eds., *Protest and Power in Black Africa* (1970).

[33] T.O. Ranger, 'Connexions between "Primary Resistance" Movements and Modern Mass Nationalism in East and Central Africa', *Journal of African History,* IX, 3 and 4 (1968), pp. 537-53 and 631-41.

well as collaborators could gain from the colonial settlement,[34] while Pallinder-Law has shown that the distinction between resistance and collaboration, and indeed between gains and losses, is by no means easy to draw.[35] The debate on this subject is still very much alive.[36]

During the last few years there have been clear signs of a renewed interest in the colonial era. The revival has been inspired partly by scholars on the New Left, who have re-emphasised the role of the colonial state in retarding the development of Africa. Several detailed studies have appeared, though most are concerned with Central and East Africa.[37] Classic Marxist concerns have made themselves felt in studies of class formation among 'peasants' and wage-earners.[38] But interest in the history of the colonial period has encompassed all shades of opinion, and reflects a widespread feeling that the reaction against imperial history had reached the point where more was known about the ruled than about the rulers. Topics of current interest are varied and include the formation and direction of colonial policy,[39] the ideological justification for empire and the ways it influenced rulers' perceptions of the world,[40] the history of expatriate business in Africa,[41] and the great crises of colonial

[34] J.D. Hargreaves, 'West African States and the European Conquest', in L.H. Gann and Peter Duignan, eds., *Colonialism in Africa, 1870-1960.* Vol. I, *The History and Politics of Colonialism, 1870-1914* (1969), pp. 199-219.

[35] Agneta Pallinder-Law, 'Aborted Modernization in West Africa? The Case of Abeokuta', *Journal of African History,* XV, 1 (1974), pp. 65-82.

[36] See, for example, Ian Henderson, 'The Origins of Nationalism in East and Central Africa: the Zambian Case', *Journal of African History,* XI, 4 (1970), pp. 591-603; and Julian Cobbing, 'The Absent Priesthood: Another Look at the Rhodesian Risings of 1896-1897', *ibid,* XVIII, 1 (1977), pp. 61-84.

[37] For example, E.A. Brett, *Colonialism and Underdevelopment in East Africa: the Politics of Economic Change, 1919-39* (1973). On West Africa see G. Kay, ed., *The Political Economy of Colonialism in Ghana* (1972).

[38] On these subjects see the *Review of African Political Economy,* especially No. 3 (1975), and Richard Sandbrook and Robin Cohen, eds., *The Development of an African Working Class* (1975).

[39] For example, David Meredith, 'The British Government and Colonial Economic Policy, 1919-39', *Economic History Review,* XXVIII, 3 (1975), pp. 484-99, and the same author's Ph.D. thesis (Exeter 1976) which deals specifically with West Africa.

[40] T.O. Ranger, 'From Humanism to the Science of Man: Colonialism in Africa and the Understanding of Alien Societies', *Transactions of the Royal Historical Society,* 26 (1976), pp. 115-41.

[41] The *Journal of African History* has published a number of articles on this subject recently. See especially the contributions by Coquery-Vidrovitch, XVI, 4 (1975), pp. 595-621; Hopkins, XVII, 1 and 2 (1976), pp. 29-48 and 267-90; Vail, XVII, 3 (1976), pp. 389-416; Neil-Tomlinson, XVIII, 1 (1977), pp. 109-28; and the discussion between Vail and Neil-Tomlinson in XVIII, 2 (1977), pp. 283-6.

control – the two world wars and the economic slump.[42] The revival of imperial history is not to be seen as a turning away from African history, but as an extension of it. Historians of Africa should now feel free to argue for the importance of studying Europeans in Africa, whatever conclusions they may reach about the effects of their presence.

This survey has not been able to do more than hint at the rich and varied pioneering research of the past twenty years. The construction of historiographical categories inevitably produces an oversimplified account of work carried out by diverse minds in diverse continents. Yet it can be claimed that the main trends outlined here do provide signposts for non-specialists who do not know this particular wood very well, and perhaps even for specialists who look at the trees too closely. The schools of thought which have been discussed can fairly be regarded as setting the pace for new research. At the same time, it is as well to remember that they do not eclipse competing programmes, but continue to interact with them. Predicting future trends is difficult, and perhaps unwise, but it seems likely that Marxist and neo-Marxist influences will become prominent in all phases of the study of European expansion into Africa, and that the study of the colonial period in particular is likely to attract increasing attention. Defining historiographical trends is useful not only for those who wish to join them, but for those who do not, for gaps abound in the study of all periods of European expansion into Africa, and in all the historical specialisms – social, intellectual, political and economic. The advocates of each school of thought have all supposed that their viewpoint represents a higher and unsurmountable truth. Higher it may have been, but the record shows that its ascendancy has also been temporary. The undoubted advantages of following fashion should not be allowed to disguise the merits of being unfashionable too. The motto which Karl Marx placed at the end of the Preface to *Capital* should serve researchers of all persuasions: 'follow your own bent and let people say what they will'.

[42] The effects of World War I on Africa were discussed at a recent conference in London, and the papers appeared in a special issue of the *Journal of African History*, XIX/I, (1978). Professor Coquery-Vidrovitch organised a similar conference on the world slump and Africa in Paris in 1976, published as 'numero spécial" of the *Revue française d'histoire d'outre-mer*, LXIII (1976), pp. 375-776. World War II is beginning to attract attention now that the records are available for inspection. For example, Jane Bowden of the University of Birmingham is working on changes in the concept of 'development' during the late 1930s and early 1940s.

4. HISTORIOGRAPHY OF THE MAGHRIB

by

J.L. MIÈGE

I. THE EVOLUTION OF THE HISTORIOGRAPHY

The historiography of the Maghrib has been through three strongly contrasted periods between 1945 and today, in so far as concerns the themes treated, the character of works published, and their number. It is necessary to emphasize (as Henri Brunschwig has done in the case of Black Africa) the relatively low level of interest given to North African history, as also its poor quality, up to the eve of the Second World War. This is in spite of the fact that the 1930s marked a moment of abundant productivity – for Algeria especially – which even included works of quality, despite the colonialist view that characterized the epoque. These were books which for the most part would later be forgotten or would even become discredited, like the *Collection du Centenaire.*

1. 1945-1956/60

Between 1945 and 1956/60, there was a notable increase in the production of historical studies, but these did not differ in any essentials from those of the entire preceding period. Priority was given to relatively distant historical epoques, to archaeology and to art. In Morocco, political history – *histoire événementielle,* so to speak – lay at the centre of preoccupations, formulated according to a colonialist point of view. This was due especially to the stimulus and influence of Henri Terrasse, whose *Histoire du Maroc* has remained an inspired and indispensable tool, although composed in the most traditional idiom (108). In addition, a certain number of worthy and useful works were devoted to urban history (Caille, 21; Deverdun, 36; le Tourneau, 80).

In the three francophone countries of North Africa, during this period, a particularly important place was accorded to the publication of source materials, including *Sources inédites de l'histoire du Maroc.* which commenced publication as early as in 1906 under the direction of Robert de Cenival; the *Collection des documents inédits sur l'histoire de l'Algérie,* from 1930; and the *Documents inédits d'histoire tunisienne* (Granchamp).

Two works were particularly striking – due both to their novelty and to their place in a literature that was otherwise as dull as it was honest: J. Berque's thesis on the Seksawa of Morocco (12), and that of Hildebert Isnard on *La Vigne en Algérie* (65). The first introduced sociology into historical writing on the Maghreb and questioned the 'classical' interpretation of Moroccan history furnished by Robert Montagne in 1930 in his thesis *Les Berbères et le Makhzen dans le sud marocain.* The second – the work of a geographer – showed how after 1880 colonization had turned the Algerian economy towards a type of production, alien to the country's requirements. Arguing the baneful consequences of this development, he clearly separated himself from a self-congratulatory literature created in the climate of the centenary celebrations of the conquest of Algiers.

Equally, we should underline the labours of M. Emerit at the University of Algiers. His innovating, and excellently documented articles broke with established conventions, and have been strongly influential in the field. One can only regret that they did not lead to the much-awaited work of grand synthesis.

2. 1956/60-1970

These works opened a new era. Under the impulsion of Ch.-A. Julien (68) and of Renouvin, a series of 'professorial theses' (*grosses thèses*) have in three or four years raised North African history to a new level. By their new preoccupations, in which the influences of the *Annales,* founded by Lucien Febvre and Marc Bloch, has clearly been prominent (thus of social and economic history, and even 'global' history), by the range of their documentation, and also by their rupture with the self-satisfaction of the 'colonialist historiography', these books by Ganiage (43) and Poncet (97) in the case of Tunisia; Yacono (121), Nouschi (92), and later Ageron (4) for Algeria; and Miège (88) for Morocco, have marked an important step in historical research, and have been the spring board for numerous later works which widened these newly-opened directions.

This second period, from 1956/60 to about 1970, is thus one of decisive change. The completion of these 'professorial theses' – which ripened during the preceding decade – coincided with the rapid growth of a historical literature nourished by political passion. This literature was created in the context of the great crisis of a French conscience confronted with the decolonization of populous territories with which the metropolis had for a long time possessed numerous, narrow, and well-established relationships. Conflicting principles and irreconcilable passions came face to face in the great debate between "la justice et les liens du sang" (to use Albert Camus's celebrated phrase).

Recourse to history in polemical argument, as also to the history lessons that could be derived from it, resulted, during this period, in a multiplication in the number of works produced, but they were of very diverse quality, while the worst were often more abundant than the best. On the other hand, the current intensification of interest in this field has also meant that the Maghrib attracts an increasing number of researchers from overseas, notably scholars from English speaking countries (15 and 18) and from Italy (30). This enlargening of the ranks of researchers is one of the most positive developments of these years.

3. The 1970s

The third period, that running from 1968/70 to the present, is that in which the decolonization of history has occurred, a time apparently marked by a new serenity. In addition, the widening of the range of our interests has coincided with an enrichening of our methodological equipment. Above all, the period is characterized by the advent of a new generation of Maghribian historians who have formulated their history in quite novel terms. Coeval with these developments is the multiplication in the number of publications by non-French researchers, who frequently possess points of view very different from those characterizing French historiography. The tide of publication has risen, their number more than trippling between 1946/62 and 1963/76. Among the hundreds of titles that have thus appeared – we have collected almost two thousand of them – we shall have to make a somewhat arbitrary choice. We should add that these new departures in historical research on the Maghrib have already been the object of numerous reviews: Brett (15), Johnson (67), Wansbrough (118), Yacono (120).

In the rapid overview which follows, we chose to lay emphasis on the structure of research, the principal themes of modern and contemporary history, and finally on the directions taken by the most actively pursued branches of history.

II. THE INSTITUTIONAL CONTEXT

University organization is at once the signal and the source of the periodization worked out above. Before 1956, research was essentially

French and it was concentrated at two places: firstly, at Paris, under the direction of Augustin Bernard at the *Sorbonne,* and of Robert Montagne at the *Collège de France*; secondly, at the Faculty of Letters of Algiers, at which were concentrated, notably, Gàutier, Gsell, and Marcais. At Rabat and Tunis there were only the *Instituts des Hautes Etudes,* concerned for the most part with archaeology, art history and with medieval and early modern periods. Political sensibilities caused research in contemporary history to be put aside.

Between 1956 and 1960, there arose powerful structural changes in the conduct of historical writing and study, very clearly connected with the crisis of decolonization, on the one hand, and with the fundamental changes affecting historical studies in metropolitan France, on the other. The institutes at Rabat and Tunis were transformed into universities, in which contemporary history – right from the start – had a significant role to play. New specialists' chairs were created in France, notably at Toulouse, and at Aix-en-Provence, and in the ten years that followed, a singular emergence of new institutions marked the progress of this development: the installation of the *Archives d'Outre-Mer* at Aix-en-Provence; the foundation, again at Aix, of the *Centre de Recherches sur l'Afrique Méditerranéenne* (CRAM, soon to become the *Centre de Recherche sur les Sociétés Méditerranéennes,* or CRESM), with the publication of its *Annuaire*; and, besides, the beginning of the *Institut d'Histoire des Pays d'Outre-Mer*; the creation of the Maghrib Section of the *Centre d'Etudes des Relations Internationales,* inside the *Fondation Nationale des Sciences Politiques.* But more than anything, there also appeared a number of centres overseas directed towards the study of the Magrib, especially in the United Kingdom, the United States, and Italy. The latter were founded notably within the Institutes for the Study of History and Institutions of the Afro-Asiatic Countries which had been established at such centres as Pavia, Milan and Cagliari.

In France, similarly, the number of chairs occupied by historians specializing in North Africa, grew considerably. To those of Paris and Aix-en-Provence were added those of Tours (Ageron) and Lyon (Merad). Finally, in North Africa itself, a particularly spectacular development in research occured in Tunisia, marked by the appearance of a number of substantial journals: *Cahiers de Tunisie; Revue d'Histoire du Maghreb; Cahiers du CERES.* But Tunis was not alone; such change also affected Algiers, and, to a lesser extent, Rabat.

III. CURRENT RESEARCH PREOCCUPATIONS

Among areas of interest currently pursued, the most important concern the following four principal sectors.

1. The Pre-Colonial Economy

Research into the pre-colonial economy has multiplied in three essential directions:

i) In the first place we may note Mrs. Valensi's excellent little book on the Maghrib before 1930, and Gallisot's debate on the nature of the mode of production characterising the pre-colonial Maghrib. Do we define this mode of production as Asiatic or feudal, or is it a unique system peculiar to itself? The controversies on these issues have been lively, and the positions of the antagonists continuously evolving. These have resulted in a number of articles and to a special volume published by CRESM, and, secondly, in two round table discussions – one at Aix, in October 1975, and the other at Paris, in December 1976.

ii) On the other hand, research of a less theoretical character, but having for its focus the need to improve our knowledge of the actual facts, factual background of the pre-colonial economy, has also been proceeding apace. It is in terms of this empirical background, of which we know so little, that the specific character of the pre-colonial economy may be properly understood. This work has been particularly fruitful in the case of Morocco and Tunisia.

iii) Finally, interest has also focussed on the study of the economic crises affecting the economy of the Maghrib. We have been principally concerned with defining the nature of the relationships which they had with crises of an international character, as well as with working out their distinct characteristics. These were especially the objects of works by Nouschi (92) and Miège (88). Economic change, social crises, financial problems, appear to have developed in concert with the economic penetration of the Maghrib by Europe (10).

The analysis of pre-colonial crisis, also of French intervention, and the motives she had for it, have brought back into question the theory of imperialism itself. In respect of this requestioning of old ideas, it is sometimes the play of international diplomacy that has come to be emphasized as possessing the greater significance (for example, Guillen in respect of Germany); or, sometimes it is the special character of Italian colonialism (Malgeri, 85; Segre, 100; Miège, *L'Impérialisme colonial italien de 1870 à nos jours*); or else it is the spectre of the role of the politicians that is sometimes raised. The great thesis of Allain on Caillaux, is not so much a question, therefore, of the role of biography in general history; rather it is a question of inserting general history into biography (6).

A further example is Parson's synthesis – conducted in the most traditional vein of diplomatic history – concerning the implications of these international rivalries in the case of Morocco (95).

2. Nationalist reaction and the new history of the Maghrib

Connected with the economic problems discussed above, and assuming special importance in the last few years, has been the relationship between the development of 'nationalism' in the societies of the Maghrib and the desire of young historians for a body of historical writing concerning it.

History has played as key a role in the movements of opposition and resistance to colonization, as it has in the construction of the newly independent states of the Maghrib. It has been necessary to forge a historical vision in which their actual situation and their future both have a place. This intellectual movement was marked from the first by a reassessment of the lives of their national heroes. The Moroccans, in the 1930s, had founded their nationalist claims on the basis of criteria, simultaneously dominated by orientations both to the city and to the state, and leaving unnoted in the shadow, the question of peasant and popular resistance. But, since the movement which accompanied independence, they have recognised the essential role played by the different forms of mass action. In particular, we cite the new interpretations that have arisen concerning the role of Abd el Krim (*Colloque Abd el Krim et la République du Rif,* January 1973).

The most dynamic of these new centers of history located in the Maghrib, is that of Tunis. Already it is characterized by lively rivalries and fierce disputes between the proponents of different tendencies. If these young historians do not recoil before the most lively polemics, their stances are nevertheless fortified by a real care for historical precision and by scrupulous methodology. In fact, Amed Abdelsalem has demonstrated the extent to which the historian's discourse lies behind the whole cultural inventary of a nation at a given epoque (1).

Thus, to take two examples, Cherif has worked strictly within the grain of the *Annales* (24 and 25), whilst Temini has attempted to interpret anew the long-neglected sources of Ottoman power (107). Besides, the *Centre d'Etudes Economiques et Sociales* (CERES), founded in 1962, has played a vital role in the advancement of the social sciences in Tunisia, and during the last few years – since 1973, exactly – has included history among its various activities. In addition, two new sections have been created: that of the *Section d'études historiques du Maghreb,* and that of the *Section d'histoire du mouvement national.* The work so far produced under its auspices has been concerned almost exclusively with the 19th century, a period so rich in change. (Kraiem, 70; Tlili, 109). Tunisia constitutes an exception however, and Algeria and Morocco have not yet furnished a harvest of such comparable richness.

3. The new European contribution

To these movements towards substantial change, outlined above, and connected with the crises of colonization and decolonization, European historians have not been strangers, neither in the sense of the selection of new themes (notably that of the resistance), nor in that of the attempt to elaborate a more satisfactory level of interpretation.

One of the most important questions, raised in this respect, is that of the pertinence of the concepts utilized for explaining Maghribian history. The question is justified because of the inadequacy and indefinition of the terminology, and the bias it must contain through its derivation from European history. Such derivation must create a problem for the interpretation of a history based on different criteria, and it is thus arguable that it will be necessary to revise such notions as those of 'frontier', 'state', 'tribe', 'historical epoque', and 'social class'. The historiography of the formation of a national state has led to a number of particularly erudite studies. The collaborative work by Gellner and Micaud (49) – devoted almost entirely to Morocco – brings into question the rigidity of the notions lying behind the interpretations of events surrounding *Mont Markhzen* and *Bled Siba,* at the same time as demonstrating the importance of this myth as a political factor. For Sahli (99) the arbitrary imposition of European historical categories has masked the originality of the processes of national formation occuring in the Magrib. Patriotism, more than anti-colonialism, was the motor of Algerian resistance.

Thus, in the case of Morocco, an interpretation revolving around the role of the statist type of nationalism – that argued by Lahbabi (72), and, above all, by Laroui (73) in a recent and remarkable *thèse de doctorat d'Etat* – is opposed to one articulated around a tribal form of nationalism and patriotism (of which Magali Morsy has been a particularly eloquent advocate). Behind these differences are two conceptions diametrically opposed to one another, the one putting an emphasis on the specificity of a Maghribian evolution, the other exploiting universal historical categories, without however denying the significance of the former. In the Maghrib, more than elsewhere, therefore, history has seemed to be essentially an ideology, – "as murderous as any ideology".

So far as the study of the colonial period is concerned, one of the most intensely studied themes is that concerning the relationship between the growth of nationalism, on the one hand, and the development of the trade union movement on the other. The studies produced by Zghal (125) – starting from the basis of agrarian history – have been oriented towards the analysis of the birth of a Tunisian national consciousness. The thesis of Kraiem, on the other hand is concerned both with nationalism and trade unionism in Tunisia, between 1918 and 1929. In so far as concerns Moroccan agrarian problems, Pascons important articles prepared the way for an important *thèse de doctorat d'Etat,* completed in 1975, but still unpublished.

4. Culture and Elites

Interest has recently been directed towards problems of acculturation and cultural identity. They have been treated according to different foci, Gellner and Soumille, for example, examining them in relation to religious developments (48 and 102, respectively), Sourieau analysing them in respect of the press, while Turin and Colona dealt with them in relation to the influence of the school (112 and 26, respectively). A colloquium held at Stuttgart in March 1974 – the proceedings of which were published in the *Zeitschrift für Kulturaustausch* (no 4, 1975) – was devoted to the influence of France and Germany on the Maghrib, and of the Maghrib upon these two metropolitan countries. At the same time another colloquium was held at Tunis (18th-19th March 1974) on the theme of *Colonial Identity and National Consciousness,* the papers were also subsequently published by CERES.

The second theme, articulated around the notions of rupture and continuity (81) has focussed especially on the role of the elites: traditional elites, new elites, the relationship between the one and the other (Debbash, 33) and finally the world of the Jews. The role of the latter has been treated for pre-colonial times by Corcos (28); for the colonial period by Flamand (40) and for the phase of decolonization by Bemsimon (14b). Robert Attal's rich bibliography shows the new vigour of research in this field, as equally does the exploitation of Hebrew sources by Zafrani (123 and 124).

In contrast, certain areas have been neglected. This is notably the case with the publication of source materials and working aids. Only Tunisia has made an effort in this direction: for the modern and contemporary periods, especially, one can cite among others, the memoirs of Ibn Ali Dinar of Kairuani (*Al Muris fi Akhbar Ifrikian via Tunis*), Ibn Ali Dhiaf (*Ithaf Ahl Ezzaman*), Mohammed Bayram el Khamir (*Safovat et Ittilar*), General Khreddine, and of El Ouazir Essarej, etc. . . . For Morocco, one can only cite a few such excercises, for example those of Miège (90), and La Veronne (75). In Italy, the series *Italia in Africa,* published from 1955 onwards, is rich in documentary material, while Carlo Giglio has also published rich inventaries of Italian sources on the history of North Africa (50). A similar enterprise is taking place at Aix. In England bibliographies have been published on Libya (61) and Algeria (76).

Memoirs, statements and collections of speeches have been particularly important, although diverse in quality and concerned with the role and abilities of individual participants. Amongst them, we cite the memoirs of Mohamed Salah Myoli, of D. Cohen Hadria, of Sadok Zmerli for Tunisia; and those of Ferhat Abbas, Ait Ahmed Hocine, Bennali Malek, and Ouzegane Amar for Algeria.

IV. CONCLUSION

Numerous new directions are being opened each day; take for example the history of diet studied by Gast, or Lefebure's examination of the role of the brotherhoods (46 and 77, respectively). Or Goutalier's sortie into a period coeval with *l'histoire immédiate* (52).

Secondly, the publication of works of history written in Arabic becomes increasingly important, deserving its own quite separate treatment. Here we can only note a handful of items concerning Morocco, selected from an abundant literature: i) the works of Dawud, on Tetouan and on the reforms of 1904-08; ii) the valuable bibliographical guide of Ibn Sudah; iii) the biography of Shaykh Kattani.

The forthcoming publication of the *Guide de l'Histoire de l'Afrique au Nord du Sahara,* produced under the auspices of UNESCO, will be further evidence of the new dimensions taken by studies of the history of the Maghrib during the last decennium.

LITERATURE

1. Abdesselem, A., *Les historiens tunisiens des XVIIe, XVIIIe et XIXe siècles. Essais d'histoire culturelle* (Paris 1973).
2. Abun-Aasr, J.M., *History of the Maghreb* (Cambridge 1971).
3. Adam, A., *Casablanca* (Paris 1970), 2 vol.
4. Ageron, R., *Les Algériens musulmans et la France 1870-1919* (Paris 1968), 2 vol.
5. Ageron, C.R., *Politiques coloniales au Maghreb* (Paris 1975).
6. Allain, J.C., *Joseph Caillaux et la seconde crise marocaine* (Paris 1975), 3 vol.
7. Ashford, D.C., *Second and Third Generation Elites in the Maghreb* (Washington, DC, 1964).
8. Attal, R., *Les Juifs d'Afrique du Nord. Bibliographie* (Leiden 1973).
9. Ayache, G., "Société rifaine et pouvoir central marocain 1850-1920", in *Revue Historique,* 516 (1975) pp. 345-370.
10. Bellal, A., *L'investissement au Maroc 1912-1956* (Paris 1968).
11. Berque, J., *Structures sociales du Haut Atlas* (Paris 1955).
12. Berque, J., *Maghreb, Histoire et Sociétés* (Gembloux 1974).
13. Berque, J., *Le Maghreb entre deux guerres* (Paris).

14a. Bovill, E.W., *The Golden Trade of the Moors* (London 1951).

14b. Bensimon-Donati, D., *Immigrants d'Afrique du Nord en Israël* (Paris 1970).

15. Brett, M., "Problems in the Interpretation of the History of the Maghrib in the Light of Some Recent Publications", in *Journal of African History.* XIII (1972) no. 3, 489-506.
16. Brown, K., *People of Sale. Tradition and Change in Moroccan City 1830-1930* (Manchester, 1976).
17. Brown, L.C., *The Tunisia of Ahmed Bey 1837-1855* (Princeton 1974). 404 p.
18. Burke, E., *Precolonial Protest and Resistance 1860-1912* (Chicago 1976), 300 p.
19. Burke, E., III, "Pan-Islam and Moroccan Resistance to French Colonial Penetration 1900-1912", in *Journ. Afr. History,* XIII, 1 (1972).
20. Cahiers du Centre d'Etudes et de Recherches Marxistes (C.E.R.M.).
21. Caille, J., *La Ville de Rabat jusqu'au protectorat français* (Paris 1949), 3 vol.

22. C.E.R.E.S., *Identité culturelle et conscience nationale en Tunisie.* Actes du Colloque tenu à Tunis, 18-19 mars 1974. – Tunis: C.E.R.E.S., 1975 – 206-85 p.; 24 cm (*Cahiers du C.E.R.E.S.*, série sociologique. 2) Bilingue français-arabe.

23. Charnay, J.P., *La Vie musulmane en Afrique d'après la jurisprudence de la première moitié du XXe siècle* (Paris 1965).

24. Cherif, M.H., *Le Mouvement national tunisien, 1881-1956.*

25. Cherif, M.H., "Expansion européenne et difficultés tunisiennes de 1815 à 1830", in *Annales E.S.C.*, n° 3 (1970).

26. Colona, F., *Instituteurs Algériens 1883-1939* (Paris 1975).

27. Confer, V., *France and Algeria: the problem of civil and political reform 1870-1920.*

28. Corcos, D., *Studies in the History of the jews of Morocco* (Jérusalem 1976).

29. Cremadeilles, J., *Le P.C.F. et le Maroc 1920-1938* (Toulouse 1975), 2 vol. (T.3).

30. Cuisenier, J., *Economie et parenté. Leurs affinités de structure dans le domaine turc et dans le domaine arabe* (Paris La Haye, Mouton, 1975).

31. Curato, F., *La questione marochina e gli accordi italo-espagnoli del 1887 e del 1891* (Milan 1964), 2 vol.

32. Dabbab, M., *Index des revues et journaux tunisiens de langue française, 1907-1956 (Tunis 1973).*

33. Debbasch et al., *Mutations culturelles et coopération au Maghreb* (Paris 1969).

34. Ibid., *Pouvoir et administration au Maghreb. Etudes sur les élites* (Paris 1970).

35. Demeersmann, P., Articles de *Ibla.*

36. Deverdun, G., *Marrakech des origines à 1912* (Rabat 1959).

37. Drague, G., *Esquisse d'Histoire religieuse du Maroc* (Paris, s.d., 1952).

38. Emerit, M. ed., *L'Algérie à l'époque d'Abd el Kader* (Paris 1951).

39. Emerit, M., Articles in *Cahiers de Tunisie.*

40. Flamand, P., *Les Communautés israélites du Sud marocain* (Casablanca 1960).

41. Field, J.P., *L'Algérie, de Gaulle et l'armée (1954-1962)* (Grenoble 1975).

42. Galissot, B., *Le Patronat européen au Maroc* (Paris 1964).

43. Ganiage, J., *Les Origines du protectorat français en Tunisie, 1861-1881* (Paris 1959).

44. Garcia Figueras, T., Articles in *Africa,* Madrid.

45. Garcia Figueras, T., *La accion africana de Espana en torno al 98 (1860-1912)* (Madrid 1966), 2 vol.

46. Gast, M., *l'alimentation au Sahara* (Paris 1973).

47. Gellner, E., "The Struggle for Morocco's past", in *Middle East Journal* (1961) 17-90.

48. Gellner, E., *Saints of the Atlas* (London 1969).

49. Gellner, E. et Micaud, C. (eds.), *Arabs and Berbers. From Tribe to Nation in North Africa* (London 1973).

50. Giglio, C., *Inventory of the manuscript sources in Italy for the History of North Africa* (Leiden 1971 sq.), 3 vol.

51. Gordon, D.C., *North Africa's French Legacy 1954-1962* (Cambridge (M.) 1962).

52. Goutalier, R., *L'O.A.S. en Oranie* (Aix 1974).

53. Guillen, P., *L'Allemagne et le Maroc (1870-1905)* (Paris 1967).

54. Gulick, J., *Tripoli. A Modern Arab city (Cambridge 1967).*

55. Hajjaji, S.A., *The new Libya* (Tripoli 1972).

56. Hall, L.J., *The United States and Morocco 1776-1956* (Metuchen 1971).

57. Halstead, J.P., *Rebirth of a Nation: The Origins and Rise of Moroccan Nationalism* (Cambridge 1967).

58. Harbi, N., *Aux Origines du F.L.N., La mission du P.F.A.-M.T.L.D.* (Paris 1975).

59. Hart, D., *The Aït Waryaghar of the Moroccan Rif. An Ethnography and History* (New York 1976).

60. Hermassi, E., *Etat et Société au Maghreb. Etudes comparatives* (Paris 1975).

61. Hill, L.W., *Bibliography of Libya* (Durham 1959).

62. Hurewitz, J.C., *The Middle East and North Africa in World Politics.* (New Haven 1975).

63. *Introduction à l'Afrique du Nord contemporaine,* C.R.E.S.M. (Paris 1975).

64. *Italia in Africa* (Rome 1950 sq.).

65. Isnard, H., *La Vigne en Algérie* (Gap 1951).

66. Jemnitz, J., *The Danger of War and the Second International (1911)* (Budapest 1972).

67. Johnson, D., "Algeria: some problems of modern history", in *Journ. of Afr. History,* V. 2 (1974).

68. Julien, C.A., *Histoire de l'Algérie contemporaine* (Paris 1964).

69. Jurquet, J., *La Révolution nationale algérienne et le P.C.F.*, (Paris 1973), 2 vol.

70. Kraiem, M., *La Tunisie précoloniale* (Tunis 1973), 2 vol.

71. Lacheraf, M., *L'Algérie, Nation et Société* (Paris 1965).

72. Lahbabi, M., *Le Governement marocain à l'aube du XXe siècle* (Rabat 1958).

73. Laroui, A., *Origines sociales et culturelles du nationalisme marocain entre 1830 et 1912* (Paris 1976).

74. Laroui, A., *L'Histoire du Maghreb, un essai de synthèse* (Paris 1970).

75. La Veronne, C. de, *Documents inédits sur l'histoire du Maroc, France 1726-1728* (Paris 1975).

76. Lawless, R.I., *Algerian Bibliography, English Language Publications, 1830-1970* (London 1976).

77. Lefebure, *Colloque sur l'Elevage* (Aix 1976).

78. Lejri, M.S., *Evolution du mouvement national des origines à la querre mondiale* (Tunis 1974, sq.), 2 vol.

79. Leone, E. de, *La Colonizzazione dell'Africa del Nord* (Padoue 1960), 2. vol.

80. Le Tourneau, R., *Fès avant le Protectorat* (Casablanca 1949).

81. *Libye Nouvelle, rupture et continuité,* C.R.E.S.M. (Aix 1975).

82. Louis, P., *Tunisie du Sud, Ksars et villages de crètes* (Paris 1975).

83. Louis, P., Les Îles Kerkenah (Paris 1970).

84. Lyautey, *L'Africain. Textes et Lettres* (Paris 1953-1957), 4 vol.

85. Malgeri, F., *La guerra libica, 1911-1912* (Rome 1970).

86. Martel, A., *Les Confins Saharo-Tripolitains de la Tunisie 1881-1911* (Paris 1965), 2 vol.

87. Merad, A., *Le Réformisme musulman en Algérie de 1925 à 1940* (Paris 1967).

88. Miège, J.L., *Le Maroc et l'Europe* (Paris 1961-1963), 4 vol.

89. Miège, J.L., *Les Européens à Casablanca au XIXe siècle* (Paris 1955).

90. Miège, J.L., *Documents d'Histoire économique et sociale du Maroc* (Paris 1965).

91. Miège, J.L., "Le commerce transaharien de la Libye", in *R.O.M.* (Aix 1975).

92. Nouschi, A., *Enquête sur le niveau de vie des populations rurales constantinoises* (Paris 1961).

93. Nouschi, A., *Le Nationalisme algérien* (Paris 1962).

94. Palazzoli, C., ed., *Le Maroc politique. De l'indépendance à 1973* (Paris 1974).

95. Parson, F.V., *The Origins of the Morocco Question, 1880-1900* (Liverpool 1976).

96. Pascon, P., "L'histoire sociale et les structures agraires de la région de Haouz de Marrakech" (Paris 1975), Thèse inédite.

97. Poncet, J., *L'agriculture tunisienne depuis 1881* (Paris 1960).

98. *Race – L'Idéologie de Race au XIXe et XXe siècles.* Colloque d'Aix, 1975 (Marseille 1977).

99. Sahli, *Décoloniser l'histoire* (Paris 1965).

100. Segre, C.G., *Fourth Shore. The Italian colonization of Libya* (Chicago 1974).

101. Slama, B., *L'Insurrection de 1864 en Tunisie* (Tunis 1967).

102. Soumille, P., *Européens de Tunisie et questions religieuses, 1892-1901* (Aix 1975).

103. Souriau, Ch., *La Presse maghrébine* (Paris 1969).

104. Spillmann, G., *Napoléon III et le Royaume arabe d'Algérie* (Paris 1975).

105. Sraieb, N., *Colonisation, décolonisation et enseignement: l'exemple tunisien* (Tunis 1974).

106. Suliman, U.S., *Les Fondements idéologiques du pouvoir politique au Maghreb* (Aix 1976), 2 vol.

107. Temimi, A., *Recherches et documents d'Histoire Maghrebine* (Tunis 1971).

108. Terrasse, H., *Histoire du Maroc* (Casablanca 1952), 2 vol.

109. Tlili, B., *Etudes d'histoire sociale tunisienne du XIXe siècle* (Tunis 1974).

110. Troin, J.F., *Les Souks marocains* (Aix 1975), 2 vol.

111. Trout, F.E., *Morocco's Saharan frontiers* (Genève 1969).

112. Turin, Y., *Affrontements culturels dans l'Algérie coloniale* (Paris 1970).

113. Valesni, L., *Fellahs tunisiens. L'économie rurale et la vie des campagnes au XVIII et XIXe siècles* (Paris 1975, T.E.).

114. Valensi, L., *Le Maghreb avant la prise d'Alger* (Paris 1969).

115. Van Krieken, G.S., *Khayr al-Din et la Tunisie 1850-1881* (Leiden 1976).

116. Vatin, J.C., *L'Algérie politique, histoire et société* (Paris 1974).

117. Vilar Ramirex, J.B., *La Juderia de Tetuan* (Murcie 1969).

118. Wansbrough, J., "The decolonization of North African History", *Journal of African History,* IX, 4 (1968) pp. 643-650.

119. Waterbury, J., *Le Commandeur des croyants* (Paris 1975).

120. Yacono, X., in *Bulletin des Séances de l'Académie des Sciences d'Outre Mer,* 1 (1972).

121. Yacono, X., *La Colonisation des plaines du Cheliff* (Alger 1956), 2 vol.

122. Yacono, X., *Un Siècle de franc-maçonnerie algérienne* (Paris 1969).

123. Zafrani, H., *Etudes et recherches sur la vie intellectuelle juive au Maroc* (Paris 1972).

124. Zafrani, H., *Pédagogie juive en terre d'Islam* (Paris 1969).

125. Zghal, A., *Modernisation de l'agriculture et population semi-nomades* (La Haye 1967) 186 p.

126. Ziadeh, N., *Origins of Nationalism in Tunisia* (Beirut 1962).

Revues d'Histoire consacrées au Maghreb en cours de publication:

I.B.L.A., Revue de l'Institut des Belles Lettres Arabes, Tunis, depuis 1937.
Cahier de Tunis, Revue de la Faculté des Lettres de Tunis, depuis 1950.
Revue d'Histoire Magrébine, Tunis, depuis 1974.
Revue Tunisienne des Sciences Sociales, Revue du C.E.R.E.S., depuis 1962.
Revue de l'Occident Musulman et de la Méditerranée, Aix-en-Provence, depuis 1966.
Revue d'Histoire et de civilisation du Maghreb, Alger, depuis 1966.
Hesperis-Tamuda, Rabat, depuis 1922.

Ouvrages en langue arabe

Dawud, M., *Mukhtasar Tàrikh Titawàn* (Tétouan 1955), 2 vol.
Dawud, M., *Tàrikh Titawàn* (Tétouan 1955-1966), 15 vol.
Dawud, M., *Hafriyàt'an al-haraka al-dustùriya fi al-maghrib qabla al-himàya* (Rabat 1970).
Ghallab, A., *Difàan an al-dimuqràtiya* (Tanger 1966).
Ibn Sudah, A., *Dalil mu'arrikh al-maghrib al aqsà* (Casablanca 1965), 2 vol.
Kattani, M., *Tarjamah al-Shaykh Muhammad al-Kattàni al-shahid* (n.p. 1962).

5. FRENCH HISTORIOGRAPHY SINCE 1945 CONCERNING BLACK AFRICA

by

HENRI BRUNSCHWIG

By historiography we understand not the fact of writing history but the mode of writing it. We will present a history of historical writing by considering chronologically the volume of publications, the quality of their authors, and the currents of thought to which, whether consciously or not, they have been subject.

When, first of all, we consider the rhythm of production, it seems necessary to distinguish three periods in the development of historical studies on French black Africa: that prior to 1945, the period between 1945 and 1960, and, finally, that from 1960 until our own day.

I. BEFORE 1945

The first feature that strikes us, when we examine the bibliography, is its paucity prior to 1945. All African studies, not only history, suffered from this. A very rapid and superficial examination of the *Bibliographie de France* reveals that the chronological distribution of those boldly lettered items in which appears the word Africa – 'black' or 'white' – and which include all kinds of subject matters, not only hunting, soils, and meteorology, but also history – may be arranged as follows:

1939 : 19
1945 : 19
1961 : 57
1970 : 77
1975 : 92

In spite of its augmentation since 1945, this mediocre output corresponds with the persistent and general apathy of French public opinion vis-a-vis the colonies. Three brief quotations seem to be sufficient to illustrate this fact.

The whole world knows that colonial politics, narrowly defined, has for a long time been unpopular in France, but it is claimed that there has occurred a swing in public opinion favourable to these politics. I believe, Gentlemen, that it is necessary not to exaggerate this argument, and above all not to take what is simply a well-meaning indifference for a positive concern. (Commotion in the House). If such a swing in public opinion has indeed occurred, the cause, I am convinced, lies largely in the fact that the country believes that we are finished with those expeditions and distant conquests which have given rise to apprehension. (Repeated applause from the extreme left).
Gaston Doumergue[1]

We have an empire. Where do we find any awareness of this empire? We can perhaps imagine ourselves to be 100 millions, so as to cheer ourselves up. We prefer to remain 40 millions rather than to dispute among ourselves.

The empire was neglected by the France of 1918, which was intoxicated by the liberation of her metropolitan soil. Faithful to his life long destiny, and to the aspirations of the day, Clemenceau had lived the Európean peace passionately, without getting closely involved in the exigencies of our imperial life. And yet it is from there that our safety must derive in the event of a threat to it, whether that will be in the months of 1935, when we shall see the extent to which our national strength was wilted from the wounds of war, or whether it results from a possible international isolation. An imperial consciousness must be born . . . .
André Tardieu[2]

When shall we have in France a public opinion favourable to colonialism?
Georges Hardy[3]

Such indifference to black Africa is particularly evident in the case of the historian, in contrast to specialists of other kinds who deal with Africa. Perhaps the cause of this is to be found in the cultural tradition from which has derived that oft-repeated formulation – inherited from Herder and Hegel – in which black Africans are classed among the "peoples without history". Or can this lack of interest be located in the fact that the *métier* of the historian is characteristically bound up with the analysis of written sources, or else with the excavation of archaeological remains, whilst black Africa apparently lacks such documentary records, and possesses few historic sites. However, even if such views are shown to have

[1] Gaston Doumergue, in: *Journal Officiel, Chambre des Députés* (22nd Nov. 1894) p. 1955: against the granting of supplies for the Madagascar expedition.

[2] André Tardieu, *L'Epreuve du pouvoir* (Paris 1931) p. XVIII.

[3] Georges Hardy in *Marchés coloniaux du Monde* (6 June 1958) pp. 1541-1544.

been influential, the fact is that archival sources have been both abundant and accessible, and offer many possibilities for comparison with the numerous writings of explorers. Yet they have been hardly used.

When we consider the period in question – that prior to 1945 – the number of professional historians then concerned with the history of Africa, can be counted on one hand. Paul Cultru, and, three quarters of a century later, André Villard, both wrote general works on the history of Senegal (Cultru 1910; Villard 1942), while Gaffarel was concerned to depict the whole process of French conquest in Africa, then as much a matter of current events as of history (Gaffarel 1892). On the other hand, two other scholars – notably Georges Hardy in two important theses – were concerned with a more specialist approach to the origins of the French colonial presence in Africa; Schefer's massive work went back to a period well before the French Revolution. Typically, however, the concern is with the *French* in Africa, not with the peoples already there and fated to put up with their presence.

Besides this handful of books, the only places in which a scholarly interest in Africa was evinced, were the relevant chapters of text books of history dealing with French colonialism. Thus Gaffarel, again, dealt with the brief but significant period of colonialism that occurred during the years prior to 1905. Once again, it is worth noting the date: the treatment of this subject, undertaken in the first decade of the 20th century, could hardly be more than a balancing of accounts, or, more likely, a hymn of praise – not a history of colonial expansion in the strictest sense of the term. (Gaffarel 1906).

Georges Hardy, on the other hand, writing a generation later, could leave aside the limiting constraints of dates and write in the grand sense of *La Politique coloniale et le partage de la terre,* or simply on the 'History of French Colonialism' (Hardy 1928 and 1937).

In addition to books by specialist historians numerous authors of a different stamp had published works that purported to be history, but of a type that requires to be approached as if it were itself a source, and thus in the critical light that one would apply to more standard forms of documentation. These are the tales, reports, and accounts, produced by participants – soldiers, administrators, and explorers – and they are often very revealing. They are much more abundant than works by historians, properly speaking, and a list of them would be very long. I have thus selected just two rather prestigious names, those of Delafosse, whose principal work, published in 1912, resulted in an enquiry for the purpose of drafting an indigenous code of civil law, and of Marty, a specialist who has studied the role of Islam in the colonies of the AOF (*Afrique Occidentale Française*), notably in Senegal and Mauretania (Delafosse 1912; Marty 1915-1916).

We shall conclude this first section with two remarks. Firstly, it is striking to note that although France recruited African soldiers – drafting some 134,200 of them from French West Africa and French Equatorial Africa into Europe – interest in Africa did not awaken during the course of the First World War. These recruits undoubtedly contributed towards the greater orientation of African masses towards the West. The sudden development of education in French West Africa after 1920, a fact established by Denise Bouche, confirms it (Bouche 1975). But, no such influence occurred in the metropolitan country.

Nor is it true to say that the colonial exhibition at Vincennes in 1931 – or, for that matter, the efforts made by Albert Sarraut for what he called *La Mise en valeur des colonies françaises* (Paris, 1923 – were sufficient to stimulate historians to explore the archives to see what they might have to say about Africa. Similarly, movements for innovation in the field of history such as that of the *Revue de synthèse historique,* founded by Henri Berr in 1900, or that of the *Annales d'histoire économique et sociale,* founded by Marc Bloch and Lucien Febvre in 1929, have remained indifferent to black Africa. The only article to appear in *Annales* in which Africa was dealt with, before the late 50's, was one by Lemoine on the Belgian Congo. In 1957, however, there appeared my "Le Monde à l'heure de la décolonisation", in which I discussed the evolution of the Gold Coast; this was followed in 1962 by "Histoire, passé et frustration en Afrique noire". (Brunschwig 1957 and 1962).

Finally, and this is my second point at last, it is necessary to note that this tendency to reject Africa among historians was without doubt peculiar to France. The British lead was at that time considerable, despite our British colleagues' claims that this has since changed.

II. 1945-1960

The situation changed after 1945. This time – during the Second World War – it was not a question of blacks having come to France, but of large numbers of whites, having discovered black Africa. Africa had been one of the centres of organization for Free France. The ideology of the *Union Française* developed after the Brazzaville

Conference of 1944, and Tardieu's slogan of "100 million Frenchmen" became popular.

This change was expressed in the humanities by a three-pronged attack:

a) The *Institut français d'Afrique noire,* later to become the *Institut fondamental d'Afrique noire* was founded in Dakar in 1937. It took over the *Bulletin du Comité d'Etudes historiques et scientifiques de l'Afrique Occidentale Française,* which appeared from 1918-1928, and later, from 1939 onwards, published it in the new guise of the *Bulletin de l'IFAN.* In 1954 it was subdivided into a section for natural sciences and one for the humanities. From 1939, it published a series of *Memoirs,* some of which were important. In addition we must note the collections of *Ètudes* published by the regional IFAN Centres in Cameroun, Mauretania, Senegal, Niger, Haute Volta, Sudan and Dahomey (created between 1948 and 1953). Similarly, there was the *Office de la Recherche Scientifique des Territoires d'Outre-Mer,* created in 1943 by the Ministry for Overseas Territories, and sited at Brazzaville and Yaounde in 1947 and 1953, respectively.

When considering the activities of these institutions, we must note that they were oriented above all towards the natural sciences, rather than towards the humanities. Of the 60 reports published between 1939 and 1960, half concerned the natural sciences and only seven titles dealt with history. Only two of the latter were produced by professional historians, and both mark a retreat from the wider view of French colonialism which, for all its distortions, showed a willingness to see things in the round (Berbain 1942; Delcourt 1952).

b) The series *Colonies et Empires,* organized by Ch.-A. Julien, launched in 1948, and directed towards the general public, never succeeded in matching its own aspirations and ceased to appear after 1961. These publications were not confined to history. Indeed, the sole publishing successes were an anthology of new black African poetry, Senghor's *L'Orphée noir,* introduced by Sartre, and Gourou's *Les pays tropicaux.*

Some good history books were also published, but there were more along the well worn paths trodden by historians of European expansion, for example Ch.-A. Julien's thesis, on the voyages of discovery and the first commercial contacts made by Europeans overseas, and that of Gaston Martin on the history of slavery; black African history remained virtually non-existent. Besides, the character of the collection tended more towards popularization than to an interest in research (Julien 1948; Martin 1948).

c) Finally, it is necessary to comment on the African thrust into

France. The review *Présence Africaine* was launched in 1947 by a group of black and white intellectuals, and was dedicated to the victory of a 'new humanism', which would be adapted to the modern world.[4] Little preoccupied with history at the start, these black intellectuals would eventually arrive at it by way of their predominantly political concerns.

III. FROM AROUND 1960 TO THE PRESENT

History had thus gained little from a renewed interest in black Africa. The innovators in this domain were, instead, the Belgians, who were exploring new sources in the Vatican, perfecting methods for the utilization of oral sources, and revitalizing the study of the history of the Leopoldian Congo. In France, however, the most striking characteristic of this whole period was the powerful influence of ethnology on history.

The sociologist works on the living present, proceeding by oral enquiry, collecting traditions and analysing customs. In a period during which 'functional anthropology' had become dominant – isolating societies in time and space – this methodology tended to treat such custom as immutable. The historian, on the other hand, works more slowly and on a much more varied documentation, and seeks comparisons which illuminate his understanding of the particular people whom he is studying, caught in the specificity of a particular time and place.

To the extent that written and archaeological evidence is lacking, the historian must also have recourse to oral tradition. It is simply common sense. But when that 'historian' is not in fact a historian but a colonial administrator, and when the traditions which are gathered are not the traditions as told by a professional bard (griot), but stories translated by interpreters acting for officers and officials – like Le Herissé or Douglas – the result can only be dubious. This result is called 'ethno-history', a term coined, so I believe, by Hubert Deschamps.

The epidemic of ethno-history has been confined to France and its colonies. The terrain was prepared for it by the enquiries of administrators and officers uninitiated in historical method, by the existence of a class of educated blacks (*évolués*) deeply attached to their roots and eager to publish, and by the absence in French

[4] *Présence Africaine,* directed by Alioune Diop, was the subject of a *thèse de 3e cycle,* which Mohamadou Aliou will submit for examination in 1979 at Paris.

universities of specialists competent to judge the works submitted to them. From then onwards these Africanists have been attacked by a kind of fever, expressed in such slogans as "An old man that dies is a library lost", or else "Blacks have a memory infinitely superior to that of whites," – which appears to be no more evident than the power of their sexual instincts, so eloquently described by anthropologists of about the middle of the last century. And they insist on the urgency of recording traditions apparently threatened with loss. Yet on the one hand, real traditions transmitted from father to son within bardic families were not so fragile. On the other, there were abundant local archives which were no less menaced. Finally, the destruction of sources, whatever they are, is one of the constants of universal history, and very familiar to the historian.

This is not to argue that oral sources should be left aside by the historian, but rather that they should not be treated as if they existed in isolation. On the one hand they are more difficult to gather and to interpret than written documents, and yet, on the other, there are always opportunities for cross checking. Since 1954 a methodology has been worked out by Jan Vansina for this very purpose. He has rejected the term 'ethno-history' and insisted on the fact that oral sources must be treated like any other source, and together with others (Vansina 1960). I do not wish to trespass on an area about which Jean Stengers may wish to speak. However I must conclude that the French champions of ethno-history have not yet published works founded on oral traditions which I would regard as correctly researched and interpreted.

Besides Vansina, there are the British, for example Kathleen Stahl, and more recently John Lamphear, both of whom attempt to 'reconstruct' the history of black peoples through their oral traditions (Stahl 1964; Lamphear 1976). Such grand works of synthesis, in which all the humanities are brought together, and in which oral tradition is used judiciously, could also be applied to such francophone territories as Senegambia. The models for such attempts would be the works of Vansina and Wilks (Vansina 1973; Wilks 1975). But the French have not been attracted by the medium, except of course Yves Person in his monumental biography of Samori (Person 1968-76).

The first two volumes of Person's work encompass an admirable *tableau* of 19th century political geography of West Africa, – notably of Nigeria and Guinea. These books show the rise of the Dyula, Samori, and describe the institutions of the first of the empires he founded, an empire that did not founder even when buffetted by uprisings of animist peoples hostile to the advance of Islam (1888-1890). The threat of France, on the other hand, encouraged Samori to centre his second empire further to the east, and, without losing control over the main arteries of long-distance commerce, to accentuate the military character of the state, rendering it increasingly authoritarian. The third volume traces the details of the conflict with France between 1890 and 1898.

The change of tone is clear, moreover. All these works, Person's, those of Vansina, Stahl, Lamphear and Wilks, mark an involvement with African history in the full sense: 'a Dyula revolution'; the'Tio kingdom'; 'a history of the Chagga people'; 'the traditional history of the Jie'; 'Asante in the 19th century'; – these titles indicate an impressive and significant change in direction in which scholars of all nationalities working on black Africa are involved.

The final period is, in fact, one in which all serious historical writings on black Africa have appeared, and which is distinguished by the constant and powerful increase of the rate of publication; yet it also confirms what we have been claiming all along: the backwardness of France. Let us confine ourselves to a few examples:

a) The *Journal of African History* was founded in 1960; in France, however, only 20-25% of the pages of the *Cahiers d'Etudes Africaines* is concerned with history. Further, the only specialist review, the old *Revue d'Histoire des Colonies* (1913), to be transformed in 1958 into the *Revue Française d'Histoire d'Outre-Mer,* has no special African focus.

b) There are few chairs of African history in French universities. The first was created in 1960 at the *Ecole des Hautes Etudes* (H. Brunschwig); two more were introduced at the *Sorbonne* in 1961 (R. Mauny and H. Deschamps); other posts, generally categorized as 'contemporary history' lack specialization in black Africa.

I do not wish to lay too much emphasis on the small number of works published in France that happen to be useful, small at least in comparison with the large number of good English and American works (the latter, in fact, have generally appeared since 1960). Among them, nevertheless, it is worth mentioning the works of Mauny (1961); Schnapper (1961); Dampierre (1968); Verger (1968); Mazenot (1970); Michel (1972); Coquery-Vidrovitch (1972); Bouche (1975) and myself (1963), besides that of Person, referred to above. Coquery-Vidrovitch and I have also contributed to the series *Documents pour servir à l'Histoire de l'Afrique Equatoriale Française,* published by the *Ecole Pratique des Hautes Etudes,* under my own direction (Brunschwig 1966; 1969; Coquery-Vidrovitch 1969).

We should further remember that in the course of this period German historians have made an advance similar to that made by the Belgians after 1945. It seems to me that we may distinguish three directions in it: Marxist; the colonial question considered as one of the roots of National Socialism; the history of ideas and doctrines.

The general growth in output of what we may call truly historical works is partly explained by the emancipation of history from the domination of anthropology. This has given a new value to the former. Until about 1960, social anthropology (and sociology and ethnology) could be described as 'functionalist'. Considering human societies as natural systems, it had no need of history in order to explain their functioning, – no more than a physiologist has need of knowing the history of an organism in order to understand its activity.

Then Evans-Pritchard, in a contribution to a famous conference held at Oxford in 1950 (the papers remain, however, unpublished), and later at length in his *Essays in Social Anthropology,* argued that social anthropologists have a choice of two alternatives before them: to be historical or not to be. He suggested that the essential dynamism of social institutions made history an indispensable auxiliary science for an adequate anthropology, just as the latter is likewise a product of that same history.

These ideas were popularized after 1960 by Balandier, Mercier and others, and they engendered – in history, as in sociology – richer syntheses than had previously appeared. While the real successes have been foreign up till now (Vansina and Wilks, for example), French works are at hand.

Growth in output has clearly been dominated by the stimulus provided by decolonization between 1959 and 1960. New states concerned to integrate themselves into the international community, have felt the need for a history comparable to that of other nations. Their elites feel particularly strongly about this, for from such a history they expect to build that much-desired national consciousness which up till now these states have basically lacked. But these aspirations are not necessarily encountered in the work of young African historians. Many of them, encouraged by European ethnologists, have been animated more by traditional ethnical solidarities than by this new national sentiment. Here we may locate the ambiguity of the term 'history'. It may indeed define a succession of dated events, as in Europe, but each such event must be explained not merely by those preceding it, but by the totality of the conditions of life characteristic of a given epoque and providing its context. It can also define the way in which "men have tended to represent themselves in the past". Then it is, in fact, intimately connected with, and limited by, the study of specific tribes; chronology matters little, – the past with which one is concerned is isolated, more close to the gods than to other men.

An international congress on the history of Africa was held at Dakar in 1961, and its debates were summarized by a committee of three, R. Mauny, J. Vansina, and L.V. Thomas, all three oriented towards the study of oral traditions (Vansina, Mauny and Thomas 1964). It is significant that the member who represented contemporary history was the sociologist, L.V. Thomas. Warm controversy at this congress led to a rejection of the term 'ethno-history', as the participants did not want to appear on the international scene with a kind of history at odds with that of the rest of the world. But the ambiguity persists, and it is this problem without doubt that explains the backwardness of French-speaking African historians in contrast to those who write in English. These last – educated in London, but returning to continue their work in Ghana, Nigeria, Dar es Salaam, etc. – have published works of history of a universal and contemporary stature. But French-speaking African historians capable of emulating Dike, Boahen, Ajayi, Obichere, etc., are slow to show themselves; this may be due to the fact that sociology has turned out to be more attractive to Africans, or because they have abandoned erudition for popularization (like Abdoulaye Ly, the author of a thesis on *La Compagnie du Sénégal,* or like Ki-Zerbo who, nevertheless, was the author of the monumental *Histoire de l'Afrique noire*).

But black French-speaking historians have progressed more rapidly than the specialists of the old metropolis; this is because the young Frenchman, when considering his career, knows that specialization in black Africa will not bode him well in French universities where this domain continues to be considered marginal. Even if their works remain to be published, and even if, in some cases, they are not yet completed, I shall nevertheless remark on the best among them, that is of those currently known to me. André Salifou, a historical specialist of the Niger Delta, has published several studies on this topic and in 1968 he defended in Toulouse his *doctorat d'Etat*: *Colonisation et Sociétés indigènes au Niger de la fin du 19e siècle au début de la 2e guerre mondiale.* In addition, Barry Cissoko, Diallo, Ly-Tall and Niang published good historical monographs during the period between 1972 and 1975.

M'Bokolo, of Zaire, ex-student of the *Ecole Normale Supérieure* and a graduate in both history and sociology, has brilliantly presented a *thèse de 3e cycle* on *Le Comptoir français du Gabon.* Its interest lies in the fact that he, an African, has analysed the secondary materials and the western archives better than a European would have known how to do, in order to explain the opinions, reactions and beliefs of pre-colonial peoples. He is now *maître-assistant* at the *Ecole des Hautes Etudes* and is putting together a team for the purpose of collaborating on his *doctorat d'Etat* on *Sécheresses, épidémies et famines en Afrique Occidentale Française au 19e siècle.* Mutambe Makombo from Zaire has written an excellent *doctorat d'Etat* (Paris, 1978) on *Le Congo belge, 1940-1960. De l'émergence des "évolués" à l'indépendance.* Adalbert Owona is about to complete a doctorate on Camerounian national consciousness, and Luc Garcia one on the French conquest of Dahomey. Excellent *thèses de 3e cycle* have been written on the press. In particular that of Clement Koudessa Lokossou, on the relationship between the press of Dahomey and the colonial administration between 1894 and 1960, and of Mrs. Rabearimanana on that of Madagascar from 1947 to 1956.

There are many others and some of them can be found in the remarkable *Bibliographie générale de Mali* by Paule Brasseur (vol. II (1961-1970), Dakar, 1976). What I wish to emphasize is the tendency among the African students of history – history in the western sense of the term – to take the baton from the French, who had first dealt with it.

Let me conclude with a comment on what seems at first sight to be a rather derisory aspect of these African histories, and of the polemical accusation of 'ethno-centrism' in which their authors tend to dress up each others works. On the one hand, Africans have had much greater difficulty than Europeans, in avoiding the snares of anachronism, because they are not endowed with that abundantly documented history, nor by those numerous vestiges of the past, that enable us, with comparative ease, to abstract ourselves from the present.

On the other hand, the historian who claims to 'reconstruct' pre-colonial history, in reality constructs nothing at all. In plucking a history of a western sort out of diverse oral traditions, he is attempting to build a national history – which may indeed be needed, but which, with its chronology and its vocabulary, corresponds little to the vision that Africans once had of their past.

LITERATURE

Boubacar Barry, *Le Royaume de Waalo. Le Sénégal avant la conquête* (Paris 1972).

Suzanne Berbain, *Le Comptoir français de Juda au 18e siècle* (Paris 1942).

Henri Blet *Histoire de la colonisation française,* 3 volumes, (Paris 1946-50).

Denise Bouche, *L'Enseignement dans les territoires français de l'Afrique occidentale de 1817 à 1920,* 2 volumes (Lille and Paris 1975).

Paule Brasseur, *Bibliographie générale de Mali,* Vol. I (until 1960), Vol. II (1961-1970) (Dakar 1964-1976).

Henri Brunschwig, "Le monde à l'heure de la décolonisation", *Annales E.S.C.* (1957).

Henri Brunschwig, "Histoire, passé et frustration en Afrique noire", *Annales E.S.C.* (1962).

Henri Brunschwig, *L'Avènement de l'Afrique noire du 19e siècle à nos jours* (Paris 1963).

Henri Brunschwig, *Brazza Explorateur. L'Ogoué* (Paris 1966).

Henri Brunschwig, *Les Traités Makoko 1880-1882* (Paris 1969).

Henri Brunschwig, *Le Partage de l'Afrique noire* (Paris 1971).

Catherine Coquery-Vidrovitch, *Brazza et la prise de possession du Congo 1883-1885* (Paris 1969).

Catherine Coquery-Vidrovitch, *Le Congo au temps des grandes compagnies concessionnaires* (Paris 1972).

Paul Cultru, *Histoire de Sénégal du 15e siècle à 1870* (Paris 1910).

Eric de Dampierre, *Un Ancien royaume banda du Haut-Oubangui* (Paris 1968).

Maurice Delafosse, *Haut-Sénégal et Niger,* 3 volumes (Paris 1912).

André Delcourt, *Les Français et les établissements français du Sénégal de 1713 à 1763* (Dakar 1952).

Hubert Deschamps, *Traditions orales et archives au Gabon* (Paris 1962).

Thierno Diallo, *Les Institutions politiques du Fouta-Djallon au XIXe siècle* (Dakar 1972).

E.E. Evans-Pritchard, *Essays in Social Anthropology* (London 1962).

Paul Gaffarel, *La Conquête de l'Afrique* (1st edition Paris 1892, 4th edition, 1903).

Paul Gaffarel, *Histoire de l'expansion coloniale de la France depuis 1870 jusqu'en 1905* (Marseille 1906).

Luc Garcia, *La Genèse de l'administration française au Dahomey 1894-1920* (thèse de 3e cycle) (Paris 1969 ms).

Pierre Gourou, *Les Pays tropicaux* (Paris 1948).

Gabriel Hanotaux et Alfred Martineau, *Histoire de la Colonisation française et de l'expansion de la France dans le monde,* 6 volumes (Paris 1929-1933).

Georges Hardy, *L'Enseignement au Sénégal de 1817 à 1854* (Paris 1920).

Georges Hardy, *La Mise en valeur du Sénégal de 1817 à 1854* (Paris 1921).

Georges Hardy, *Histoire de la colonisation française* (Paris 1928).

Georges Hardy, *La Politique coloniale et le partage de la terre* (Paris 1937).

Charles-André Julien, *Les Voyages de la découverte et les premiers éstablissements (XVe-XVI siècles)* (Paris 1948).

J. Ki-Zerbo, *L'Histoire de l'Afrique noire* (Paris 1972).

John Lamphear, *The Traditional History of the Jie of Uganda* (Oxford 1976).

R.-J. Lemoine, "Finance et colonisation. Le Congo belge", *Annales E.S.C.* (1934).

Clement Koudessa, *La Presse au Dahomey de 1894 à 1960. Evolution et réaction face à l'administration coloniale* (thèse de 3e cycle) (Paris 1978, m.s.).

Abdoulaye Ly, *La Compagnie du Sénégal* (Paris 1958).

Madina Ly-Tall, *Contribution à l'histoire de l'Empire du Mali (XIIIe-XVIe siècles). Limites, principales provinces, institutions politiques* (Dakar 1977).

Gaston Martin, *L'Histoire de l'esclavage dans les colonies françaises* (Paris 1948).

Paul Marty, *L'Islam en Maurétanie et au Sénégal* (Paris 1915-1916).

Raymond Mauny, *Tableau géographique de l'Ouest Africa* (Dakar 1961).

Georges Mazenot, *La Likouala Mossaka: Histoire de la pénétration du Haut-Congo: 1878-1920* (Paris 1970).

M'Bokolo, *La France et les Français en Afrique équatoriale. Le Comptoir du Gabon 1839-1974,* (thèse de 3e cycle) (Paris 1974, m.s.).

Marc Michel, *La Mission Marchand, 1895-1899* (Paris/La Haye 1972).

Djihil Tamsir Niang, *Soundiata ou l'époque mandingue* (Paris 1960).

Yves Person, *Samori: Une Révolution dyula,* 3 volumes (IFAN Dakar, Volume I 1968; Volume II 1970, Volume III 1976).

Lucile Rabearimanana, *La Presse d'opinion à Madagascar de 1947 à 1956. Contribution à l'Histoire du Nationalisme malgache du lendemain de l'insurrection à la Loi-Cadre* (Paris-Antananarivo 1978).

André Salifou, *Le Damagaran ou Sultanat de Zinder au 19e siècle* (Niamey 1971).

André Salifou, *Kaoussan ou la révolte senoussiste* (Niamey 1973).

Albert Sarraut, *La Mise en valeur des colonies françaises* (Paris 1923).

Christian Schefer, *Instructions générales données de 1763 à 1870 aux gouverneurs et ordonnateurs des établissements français en Afrique occidentale*, 2 volumes (Paris 1921).

Bernard Schnapper, *La Politique et le commerce français dans le Golfe de Guinée* (Paris 1961).

Léopold Sédar Senghor, *L'Orphée noir* (Paris 1948) (introduction by J.-P. Sartre).

Sékéné Mody Sissoko, *Tombouctou et l'Empire songhay: épanouissement du Soudan nigérien aux XV-XVIe siècles* (Dakar/Abidjan 1975).

Kathleen Stahl, *The History of the Chagga People of Kilimanjaro* (Boston 1964).

Jan Vansina, "Recording the oral history of the Bakuba, I. Method". *Journal of African History* (1960) Volume I, 43-51.

Jan Vansina, *The Tio Kingdom of the Middle Congo* (Oxford 1973).

Jan Vansina, Raymond Mauny, L.V. Thomas (editors), *The Historian in Tropical Africa. Studies presented and discussed at the 4th International African seminar at Dakar, Senegal, 1961* (London 1964).

Pierre Verger, *Flux et reflux de la traite des nègres entre le Golfe de Bénin et le Bahia de Todos os Santos* (Paris 1969).

André Villard, *Histoire du Sénégal* (Dakar 1942).

Ivor Wilks, *Asante in the 19th century* (Cambridge 1975).

PART III

THE SMALL COLONIAL POWERS

6. IBERIAN HISTORIOGRAPHY ON EUROPEAN EXPANSION SINCE WORLD WAR II

by

G.D. WINIUS

The aim of this essay is to comment upon the historiography of the European expansion as published by Iberian presses during the 20th century and more particularly since 1945. My observations are necessarily for new-comers to the Hispanic field or, more likely, for those primarily concerned with contiguous expansion, i.e. with the Dutch, English or French empires. I have not attempted a bibliography, though I do mention some book titles. And, nota bene: I have not attempted to encompass what the presses of Latin and North America or Europe have produced on the Iberian expansion. I was indeed tempted to do so, but consider what I encountered: in the Spanish or Portuguese-speaking countries of the Americas, nearly every book about any event or place prior to the era of independence is technically expansion history. One would have to be a super bibliographer of 24 countries to discern the trends, the backgrounds of the writers and the political conditions which either inspired or inhibited the works in each country. As a mere historian whose bibliography cards sometimes get mixed up with old Christmas cards, I decided to stick to the Iberian peninsula – which I know, or think I do.

I must say at the outset that the work done by Iberians on their own expansion is of very high quality; it is a pity that most expansionists in contiguous fields know what they do of the Spanish and Portuguese empires exclusively through the works of foreigners: English-speaking historians like Charles Boxer, Bailey Diffie and John Parry and Frenchmen like Pierre Chaunu and Frédéric Mauro. It is also true, however, that of the major writers on expansion history among the Iberians themselves, only two, Armando Cortesão and Vitorino Magalhães Godinho, both Portuguese, have published anything of importance in either French or English. It boils down to this: too many writers on the Dutch East India Company or English East India Company, or on the non-Hispanic Caribbean, neglect Spanish and Portuguese works which involve their periods merely because they are unaware of them. Their books and articles would be stronger and wiser if they consulted what Iberian writers have produced, even if this means acquiring a reading knowledge of one or both of the languages to do so.

As a beginning, it might be most useful if I were to give you an idea of what kind of history is written – or not written – by Spanish and Portuguese authors on the expansion, and by the not inconsiderable number of Latin Americans who are published by presses of the Peninsula. You will look in vain for some topics and find others treated in abundance. It is well to know the what and the why; then you can search in the right places, or, conversely, not bother to look at all.

First, it is well to keep in mind that the world in which both Spanish and Portuguese historians have worked is an isolated one. Some of this is no doubt due to the existence until recent years of the Franco and Salazar dictatorships, but I think these regimes have had more influence on what got published than upon the academic and cultural environment per se. Northern European historians, or I should say historians of the Common Market countries in order to include the Italians, have formed something of a common intellectual community since the war; they create associations and attend international conferences – and so, of course, do the U.S. and Canadian historians. This naturally gives them an international outlook. It is not unusual at all to find a Dutchman, for example, specializing in German or French or U.S. history. The Spanish, and to a lesser extent, the Portuguese, however, are not international in outlook and seldom partake in foreign historical congresses (I hasten to except José Gentil da Silva and Magalhaes Godinho, who worked abroad for extended periods, and the extremely internationally-minded Captain Avelino Teixeira da Mota). They are by and large uninterested in any history but their own; they seldom study it beyond the rather elementary level – with the sole exception of ancient history, which in a way is their own, too. About so far as a Spaniard or Portuguese is likely to go is to write a relation of his country's past as it is linked with another's, as in the relations of Portugal with the Hanseatic League, for example. Even this is rare.

Hence it is that I am talking about Spanish colonial history as written by Spaniards and Portuguese colonial history as written by Portuguese. If I broaden this occasionally to include Spanish overseas history as written by Latin Americans and published by Spanish presses or Portuguese colonial history written by Brazilians and published in Coimbra or Lisbon, do not assume from this that I am touching upon any sort of internationalism or trans-Atlantic cooperation. There is no counterpart in the Hispanic world of Pan-

Slavism, or even Pan-Americanism.[1] It is simply a reflection of the fact that to undertake research topics involving their own colonial period, Latin Americans must reside in Spain or Portugal for more or less extended periods. While there they make contacts. And I suppose there is a certain amount of prestige involved in being published by an Iberian press, and, as in the case of the Escuela de Estudios Hispano Americanos, superior distribution.

Iberians may get along very well with one another – I do not hesitate to state that there is no more cordial or outgoing society than theirs. But anyone who knows them at all knows that they like to pick their own associates. Their own voluntary professional organizations have not been successful in the past, perhaps, as one Spanish scholar and humorist, Fernando Dias Plaja, suggests, because everyone perceives them as being dominated by enemies and rivals – while lacking motivation to effect the organizing and dominating to one's own advantage. Iberians prefer to live their intellectual lives in less formal groups of basically like-minded friends with whom in any case they do not directly compete. Whether numbers of Spaniards and Portuguese will appear at European historical congresses once these two countries have applied for membership in the European Economic Community is anybody's guess. My guess is that the Iberians are basically unwilling to commit themselves to the institutionalized and the ongoing. There is the Spanish word "duende" – which is untranslatable, but if one is said to have "duende" it is meant that the spirit is moving him and that he embodies the essence of something. Obviously the very idea of a 7th annual meeting of an organization – or a 37th or 38th does not have "duende".

But Iberians know that when the spirit does strike, everyone can have a profitable time, and fun besides. It is in this light I think, that two Portuguese historians, Avelino Teixeira da Mota and the late Armando Cortesão, organized two thematic conferences in the early 70's, one on the Tordesillas agreement and another on the voyage of Magellan. These included both Spanish and Portuguese participants and in fact were held in Spain. They were a great success. A Dutchman, an Englishman or an American would immediately have founded a new international society with annual or

[1] If the Luso-Brazilian Colloquium comes to mind as an exception, please note that it was created by North Americans, most notably Lewis Hanke and first met at Duke University in 1947. To judge from the two I have attended, the Portuguese merely group together and complain that the Brazilians have monopolized the whole conference. The organisation at this writing appears moribund.

semi-annual meetings. It is at this point that Iberians would have broken into separate little groups and all returned to their favorite cafés.

The isolation is therefore more voluntary and temperamental that it is geographic or political, and it follows that we are dealing with highly individualistic peoples, ones who are loath to follow others' styles or fashions. One of the most popular current topics in America and Europe today is the history of slavery and the slave trade; among Spanish and Portuguese writers, one will find hardly any historiography at all on the subject. It simply does not seem to interest them; and to speculate why this is would make me sound too much like Américo Castro, who explains everything on the basis of the Reconquista. But fundamentally I suspect: 1) Iberians never blame themselves for the sins of their ancestors; and 2) an African slave was an outsider to their culture; once he assimilated it, he was likely no longer a slave, but part of their civilization, hence not worth writing about separately. I will welcome all additional explanations, but perhaps it is best to say that Iberians do not march to the beat of distant historical drums.

There is, in fact, almost a total absence of familiar contemporary themes in Iberian writings on the Iberian expansion, and I think this is largely to be explained in terms of the era in which Spain and Portugal lost their American colonies: not very recently. The Netherlands, England and France all surrendered their major colonies 30 years ago, or less; Brazil and Spanish America have been gone for 150. Hence, the kind of debate that has recently taken place, between French or British pro-colonialists and anti-colonialists, or between Indonesian and Dutch historians is all but inapplicable to the Iberian case. For example, writers in the newly formed nations, or in other cases, those critics residing in the former metropolitan nations, accuse the mother country of having industrialized itself at the expense of the former dependency. If researchers are looking for a similar strain in Hispanic expansion historiography, they can forget it. Spain and Portugal were separated from their American colonies a good half century before the modern industrial era, besides which, everybody knows that until the past decade Spain could not by the wildest flights of imagination have been considered an industrialized nation at all. It is too early to know what a newly-independent Mozambique or Angola will say about Portugal's role in Africa in more modern times, if indeed they do not say it in sterile Marxist terms. But it is well to bear in mind that in the 1950's the nearest thing to automation in Portugal was the bottling plant for Sagres Beer; in the 1960's a few assembly plants were built by European auto manufacturers to avoid duties and taxes. Probably the nastiest thing that historians of the future can write about Portugal in Africa is what Latin Americans have long assumed about their former Spanish overlords – that they were *gachupines* (Mexican argot for "the men with the spurs") – and a rapacious lot of parasites who deserved to be kicked out, or worse. This hardly makes for novel historical interpretation, and those former colonials nurtured in the Iberian cultures are too realistic about human nature to pretend that, had the positions been reversed, they would have behaved themselves any differently than the Spaniards did.

No essay on any aspect of Iberian historiography during the Franco and Salazar eras could be complete without a reference of some sort to censorship. Yet the problem is more subtle than it might appear to those who would automatically assume that Iberian censorship was anything like the censorship of communist states – which it scarcely resembled, at least so far as historians and books were concerned. In fact, just what its influence might have been on writing about the expansion of Europe is impossible to estimate. But I think it was at best indirect.

In the first place, there was never any censorship of books on the Peninsula – only that of newspapers and broadcasting.[2] And in the second, the Iberian dictatorships, unlike the communist ones, never demanded that historians or other scholars actually infuse propaganda into their books to make them conform to a grand design. Just as the Inquisition did, they merely required that the works under consideration not contain anything objectionable. If it seems contradictory of me to say in one breath that there was no censorship of books and in the next that, in effect, there was, please consider that monographs of the sort expansionists produce would seldom ring enough cash registers in Spain or Portugal to warrant publication by a commercial publisher; practically all of them had to find subsidy, and in the relatively poor Iberian lands, this all but automatically meant government subsidy. Of course nobody of sound mind would ask his patrons for money to publish a book criticising their integrity, honesty and judgement. So it can not be entirely coincidental that the books which were submitted to governmental agencies and later published via their largesse, concerned a century long gone and safely far away and then stuck unusually close to the facts. In effect, writings were self-censored; the real casualties were invisible – books which never got written at all.

[2] Although in some instances, books once published were banned from sale or confiscated.

It would be misleading to assume, however, that the authors necessarily yearned to choose their subjects differently or write otherwise about them. I have long suspected that even if strictly left alone, nineteen out of twenty historians of the Iberian Peninsula temperamentally prefer the era of Cervantes or Camões, Philip II or Henry the Navigator – nothing more recent.

There are proportionally fewer professional historians working in Spain and Portugal than in northern Europe and North America, if only because there are fewer universities per inhabitant. To supplement those, there are far more clerics around than in northern countries, mostly members of religious orders, and many seem to have the leisure and subsidy to compose and publish books, some of which are no more than bouquets of documents concerning the history of their particular fraternity, but a few of which have high merit. Then thirdly, in a peninsula where it seems every tenth man considers himself an intellectual, those who do not write poetry write history – some of it good. The works of the Spaniard, Gregório Marañon, a physician, and those of the Portuguese admirals Gago Coutinho and Botelho de Sousa, attest this. But the point is that neither the clerics nor the amateur feel at all obligated to write about the expansion movement in any context other than that which appeals to them personally. The clerics turn out missionary history and the amateurs write of battles or who-discovered-what-first, in other words, hobby stuff. I do not wish to disparage it; it can be highly useful. But this helps explain why there are so many minutely topical studies in existence, so many annotated volumes of specialized documents and so relatively few interpretations or broad perspectives. I do not know enough about the book market in Spain to hazard a guess whether a synthesis like John H. Parry's *Spanish Seaborne Empire* would sell many copies, but there are surveys of narrower scope in Portuguese expansion history, such as Damião Peres' *Descobrimentos Portuguezes* and Duarte Leite's *História dos Descobrimentos Portuguezes,* which apparently show that there is a market for Spanish or Portuguese expansion written by an Iberian.[3] One can only speculate as to why the lacuna has not been filled. Probably it is because those qualified to fill it have not felt the challenge – nor felt a particular desire for royalties.

[3] Since composing this article I learn from C.R. Boxer that his *Portuguese Seaborne Empire,* among other works, has just appeared in Portuguese. In general, Portuguese readership is more attuned to the expansion than is the Spanish.

Let me now turn to a brief examination of the salient features of the historiography in each land as it touches the expansion. I might confess that it was at this point where I came perilously close on several occasions to becoming lost among book titles; one failure of an author's resolve and a would-be historiographical essay becomes no more than a critical bibliography. I finally avoided the dilemma by simply choosing what features I considered the most typical or interesting and grouping my titles around them.

Spain is a much bigger country than Portugal and its engagement in European wars and politics has been enormously greater, especially in the 16th and 17th centuries. It is therefore much easier for Spanish historians to ignore their overseas expansion if they wish to, concerning themselves exclusively with the *Reconquista,* with the Catholic Kings, or Charles V, or Philip II. On the other hand, the whole kernel of Portuguese history lies in the expansion, and historians there have never lost sight of it, if only because every trail seems to lead into the water. Reinforcing this natural tendency toward overseas history has been the fact that the government's whole policy in recent times has been imperialistic. Right up until the fall of Marcelo Caetano in the *revolução* of April, 1974, it has worked directly and indirectly to inspire and stimulate study of the *ultramar.*

Spain's Contribution

To have judged from the vantage point of 1892 in Spain, it would have seemed that interest in overseas history there was assured. Both before and around this 400th anniversary of Columbus' great voyage, Spaniards created a wealth of exhibits, documentary reprints, histories, catalogues, commemorations and colloquia to celebrate not only the discovery of America, but also the exploration era in general. The afterglow, however, did not last long. In 1898, it was interrupted by imperial events, much closer at hand: Theodore Roosevelt's Rough Riders on San Juan Hill and Admiral Dewey at Manila Bay: to wit, the inglorious end of Spain's overseas history. It would then seem as if Spanish scholars turned their backs on empire for 40 years and became, as it were, Continentals. Much less did other European historians pay homage to Spain in America during this period; Spanish expansion became the exclusive property of the Americans, both North and South. As the great Spanish bibliographer, Benito Sánchez Alonso lamented: "One can thumb through whole volumes on end of the great historical journals without finding any such studies at all. . . ."

This is not to say that some works were not produced during

this fallow period; Sánchez Alonso's *Fuentes de la historia española y hispanoamericana* provided at least a few dozen titles of books and articles published between 1900 and 1940, but, of these, hardly any seemed familiar to me. To judge from their absence in citations of recent synthetic works on the Spanish empire by historians like Clarence Haring, Bailey Diffie, J.H. Parry or Pierre Chaunu, hardly any *were* significant either. On one Hispanicist's recommendation, I used Gervasio Artiñano y de Galdácano's 1917 history of commerce with the Indies during the Habsburg period, (*Historia del comercio de las Índias durante el domínio de las Aústrias,* Barcelona, 1917), and I know that Padre Pablo Hernández 's 2-volume work on the Jesuit missions in Paraguay is a classic. It was published in 1913. (*Organizaciones sociales de las misiones del Paraguay,* 2 vols., Barcelona, 1913). But hardly any other works are in frequent use, except one on the Indian tribute system of New Spain, by a former director of the Archive of the Indies, (José de la Peña Cámara's *El "Tributo": sus orignes y su implantación en Nueva España,* Sevilla, 1934). A good bit of the output of Spanish publishers on expansion topics in the period prior to the outbreak of the civil war and immediately afterwards was by Spanish American authors, most notably Sílvio Zavala, J.M. Ots Capedequí and Guillermo Cespedes de Castillo. But these writers never published there exclusively; much of their work remains part of the expansion literature of the New World. In at least one instance, however, the contribution was not eastbound, but westward: one of Spain's best expansionists was the late Daniel Cosío Villegas, who fled Spain during the conflict and settled in Mexico.

The modern era of expansion history in Spain dates from 1940, just after the end of the Civil War, and it is tempting to speculate that if an external catastrophe turned Spaniard's attention inwards, an internal one focused it outward again. In that year, a University of Madrid professor, Antonio Ballesteros y Beretta, known most widely abroad as author and editor of a compendious and sprawling (but somewhat disorganized) *Historia de España* (1918-1935), founded an institute attached to the national university and named for Gonzalo Fernández de Oviedo, 16th century *conquistador,* chronicler and biographer of Columbus. Its chief organ, the *Revista de Indias,* was published by the then-new government agency, the *Consejo Superior de Investigaciones Científicas,* or C.S.I.C., designed to stimulate scholarship in the social sciences. Over the past 36 years, the *Revista* has carried both literary and historical articles, but the preponderance historical, and in recent times, articles of modern subject matter and treatment, from those on social classes in colonial Perú to ones on political institutions in the Rio de la

Plata region. It also is beginning to carry a smattering of articles on subjects which reflect a growing interest in the social sciences, such as ones on historical demography. No serious writer on Spanish overseas history can afford to ignore it.

Although the founding of the *Instituto Fernández de Oviedo* was the signal event in the revival of expansion studies in Spain, only four years later, *the Faculdad de Filosofía y Letras* of the University of Seville brought into existence what proved to be an even more important catalyst for expansion scholarship, the *Escuela de Estudios Hispano-Americanos.* Seville was the city associated with Spanish expansion from the earliest days, and it possessed the records of the famous *Casa de Contratación,* the body which regulated Spanish trade with the Indies. Since the building which once housed it has now become the *Archivo General de Indias,* or Archive of the Indies, Seville is naturally the focus of scholars throughout the world interested in the Spanish expansion. And it is perhaps inevitable that the Escuela's publications should have the pick of the best literature produced by them, and that it should attract the cream of the Spanish university teachers and students interested in the *ultramar.* For any combination of reasons, the *Escuela's* publications are fatter, richer and more varied – and most of us feel of higher quality – than the *Revista de Indias.* A typical issue of the *Anuário de Estudios Americanos,* as the review is called, is about twice as thick as a double number of the *Revista,* in recent years often published only once per annum. In addition, the Escuela also puts out a very important monographic series, which at last count totalled 187 volumes, not counting the issues of the *Anuário* itself. Many Latin-American scholars choose the *Anuário* and the monograph series as vehicles because these publications may be second only to the *Hispanic-American Historical Review* (or perhaps it is vice versa) in their ability to reach expansion scholars in every country. Even the German, Ernst Schäfer, published his classic study of the Council of the Indies, the steering body of the Spanish empire, in the monograph series. (*El Consejo Real y Supremo de las Indias en la administración colonial,* 1947). Although most of its writers prefer the century of discoveries, the series is extremely wide in scope, covering subjects from colonial architecture in the Antilles to viceregal administrations in the time of Carlos IV, commerce between the Canary Islands and the Americas, military sieges and biographies.[4] It is also underwritten by the C.S.I.C.

[4] The following are a few titles suggestive of the way in which researchers working on the Spanish empire in the 16th century can utilize the Escuela's output, though one would have to read the whole listing to see if one's own research interest was represented. Antonio Muro Orejón, Florentino Perez-

Before leaving the Spanish side, I might call attention to two important series, which, though not specifically labelled expansion history, contain large helpings of it, often on topics not sufficiently covered elsewhere.

The first of these is the 5-volume *Historia Social y Económica de España y América,* first published in Barcelona between 1956 and 1958, under the editorship of the late Jaime Vicens Vives. Vicens Vives was a Catalan, and those familiar with Spain will know immediately that *Cataluña* is the province whose indigenous language most resembles medieval Provençal and which has historically been closest to France in culture and outreach. Vicens Vives was an admirer of Lucien Febvre and Fernand Braudel and a follower of the *Annales* school; his premature death in 1960 robbed Spain of its best historian. His *Historia Social y Económica* was written by his followers under his close personal direction, and it certainly provides the best overview of the Spanish empire as yet written in any language, even though, as the original title suggests, the history of the Americas takes second place to that of Spain and the subject matter is principally social and economic. It is full of fresh insights, new data and new approaches. It is only a pity that the Catalans have never shown any great affinity for the expansion and that the disciples of Vicens Vives did not continue to write about it along the same lines. (Please note that the subsequent editions have dropped the words "Social y Económica", from the title and merely call it *Historia de España y América*).

Embid, and Francisco Morales Padrón have written with some scope of the "expansion century" or furnished materials useful to the scholar who specializes in that period.

Gimenez Fernandez, Manuel, *Hernán Cortés y su revolución comunera en la Nueva Espana*, Seville: Escuela de Estudios Hispanoamericanos (hereafter EEH, 1950).

Perez-Embid, Florentino, *Los descubrimientos en el Atlántico hasta el tratado de Tordesillas* (Seville: EEH, 1948).

León Pinelo, Antonio, *El Grán Canciller de las Índias* (Seville: EEH, 1954).

Morales Padrón, Francisco, *Fisonomia de la Conquista Indiana* (Seville: EEH, 1955).

Muro Orejón, Antonio, *Cristóbal Colón: el original de la capitulación 1492* (Seville: EEH, 1951).

Muro Orejón Antonio, *Ordenanzas Reales del Consejo de las Indias* (Seville: EEH, 1957).

Muro Orejón, Antonio, *Las Leyes Nuevas* (Seville: EEH, 1961).

Sanchez Bella, Ismael, *La organización financiera de las Indias.* (Seville: EEH, 1968).

Ramos Perez, Demetrio, *Ximénez de Quesada y el Epitome de la conquista del Nuevo Reino de Granada.* (Seville: EEH, 1972).

The second series is not a continuous history, as is the *Historia de España y América,* but a group of 18 separately-assigned volumes, whose topics were conceived by the late Antonio Ballesteros y Beretta, whom I have already mentioned in connection with the founding of the *Instituto Gonzalez de Oviedo* and the *Revista de Indias.* Its inception dates from 1935, although if I am not mistaken, several of its volumes have still not reached the printer! This is the *Historia de América y de los Pueblos Americanos.* As in all such sweepingly conceived projects, some of its titles are superior, others reputedly rather pedestrian. I have used and found vols. VI and XI excellent (A. Melón and R. de Gordejuela, *Los primeros tiempos de la colonización* and F. Esteve Barba, *El Descubrimiento de Chile,* both dating from shortly after the war), but I have never worked regularly in a library which possessed the whole set, or at least those volumes published to date. Incidentally, I have never seen the volumes shelved as a series; they always seem to be scattered throughout a library, catalogued solely according to author and region – a natural consequence of the infrequency with which contributions have been published.

Portuguese Historiography

Although Portugal is a much smaller country and its output of historical material is much less profuse, it has not – at least up until April 1974, – suffered anything like the loss of interest in its overseas history that Spain did in the years 1898-1940. As I indicated earlier, practically all of Portugal's significance to the rest of the world has been derived from its maritime expansion, and only one or two of the significant Portuguese historians have tried to avoid it – like António Oliveira Marques (though as I will show later, he has written the one worthwhile summary of the modern Portuguese empire to appear during the Salazar-Caetano era). Moreover, partly out of national pride, but mostly out of national policy, the Salazar government was only too happy to inspire, sponsor or promote anything which called attention to Portugal's long presence in Asia or Africa, as if this would soften hearts already hardened against colonialism. But note that neither the government nor individuals have shown a comparable interest in Brazil.

So far as I can determine, there have been around one hundred Portuguese historians since the war who have produced writing more significant than a *licentiatura* thesis, and, of these, perhaps thirty or forty have written at least an article or two about the expansion. Some, like Teixeira da Mota, Botelho de Sousa and Humberto Leitão were military men with good scholarly instincts, but on the fringes of the academic community. Two important ones were academic historians based in France, namely Vitorino Magalhães Godinho and José Gentil da Silva. More were *catedráticos* and *adsistentes* in Portuguese universities, like Luís de Albuquerque, or even *profesores de liceu,* like Joel Serrão. And several listed themselves merely as *historiador,* which meant they actually worked at a business and were ashamed of it, or else they did nothing.

By a wide margin, they have contented themselves with historiography of the classical sort – political, diplomatic, military, some economic and with a little administrative thrown in. This is because Portugal itself is old-fashioned, and because the recent government was highly unsympathetic to history that was not Europe-centered. Whatever smacked of anthropology or ethnic African or ethnic Asian left it cold. Moreover, unless they were able to study abroad, most of the younger historians were not exposed in their course work or teacher-relationships to modern social scientific approaches which would enrich their viewpoints. It has only been in the last few years that one could see signs of change – most, as it were, by osmosis. Now that António Oliveira Marques and Vitorino Magalhães Godinho are both teaching again in Portugal, this might alter somewhat; Marques has studied in Germany and taught in the U.S. Godinho, who recently has been Minister of Education, spent long years in France and both are apostles of the *Annales* approach.

The Infante Dom Henriques, alias Henry the Navigator, was the most important individual ever produced by Portugal, and happily for those who study him, his enigmatic nature lends itself to considerable interpretation. It is only concerning his person and the exploration era which he inaugurated – about a century's span in all – that the Portuguese have produced any significant controversies. And these have tended to revolve around only two real issues: Henry's nature and the policy of secrecy during the reign of King João II. I will address my remarks to these.

Regarding the first issue, that of Henry himself, the signal Portuguese achievement since the war has been his re-humanization. Long apotheosized as an intellectual, as a quasi-mystical seer and as sponsor of a nautical and astronomical school on Cape Sagres, Henry's name was so surrounded by an aureole in the 1920's that the late Jaime Cortesão created a furor when he suggested that Henry was not a virgin! But in the 1940's and 1950's things changed. Two respected historical veterans, Captain Avelino Teixeira da Mota and Tomas Marcondes de Sousa, a Brazilian who published many of his articles in Portugal, denied quietly but effectively that Henry was any of these things. To cite, among others, only his

"Ainda a suposta escola de Sagres" (1953).[5] Marcondes de Sousa showed convincingly that the nautical school notion had never existed before the 18th century, and that the so-called "astronomers" in Henry's service were probably only astrologers, in any case not connected by a shred of evidence to Sagres. He and Teixeira da Mota suggested that there was not even any evidence that Henry was especially learned or preoccupied by exploration, but rather an extraordinarily busy man with a finger in every affair in Portugal. He even wanted to make money.

It is amusing that this debunking did not prevent the Salazar government from erecting a gigantic and rather silly limestone monument at the water's very edge in Belem, showing Henry standing on what looks like the stone prow of a boat, staring heroically out to sea, while throngs jostle up from behind him. Lisbon taxi drivers, incidentally, seemed rather more prepared to accept the scholar's findings. The joke they told had Henry saying to those behind him: "Don't push, boys, I can't swim".

Rather understandably, I think, the rehumanization of Henry has not yet crept into textbooks, either Portuguese or foreign. I reason it this way: people like Henry better the way they thought he was. The altarpiece attributed to Nuno Gonçalves in Lisbon's Museu de Arte Antiga, the greatest national treasure of Portugal outside the Jerónimos monastery, contains the only accurate depiction of the prince, robed in black and contrasting sharply with the more sumptuous raiment of his family and its courtiers. Everyone carries this in mind. If one projects this dark figure upon the desolate Cape of Sagres, where Henry once lived in his Vila do Infante, high above the pounding surf, one truly wishes to believe in all the legends. Accordingly, they will die slowly, and might not die at all.

Misconceptions about Henry are shared the world over and have at least romanticised Portugal, but there is one other in Portuguese historiography which has not been so widely known outside the community of scholars specializing in the field, but whose effect can only be described as disastrous. As the U.S. historian Bailey Diffie has written, the confusion it has created in the minds of foreign historians has tended to deprive Portugal of due credit for its real and matchless achievements. This is the so-called "policy of silence", or "sigillum silentio" theory, which unlike the nautical school notions of Henry the Navigator, does not even possess the respectability of a tradition which dates

[5] To be found in the *Revista de Historia* I (1953) (São Paulo).

back to the 18th century. Instead, it originated with the late Jaime Cortesão in 1924. The belief holds that in the reign of King João II, discoveries made by Portuguese navigators were kept from the rest of Europe, especially Castile, whom the Portuguese feared as a more powerful rival; it is based on a few decrees of that monarch which forbid the transmission of charts, maps and other data to foreigners. According to the theory as fully developed, the Portuguese almost certainly discovered America before Columbus. The late Samuel Eliot Morison, Columbus' biographer, was scathing in his denunciation of it as "... perhaps the most preposterous (theory) in modern history because it uses the absence of evidence as positive evidence that the Portuguese discovered everything. Yet it has converted almost every Portuguese historian and is taught in Portuguese schools".[6]

It was the late Duarte Leite, a Brazilian who was long professor of astronomy and geodesy at the University of Coimbra, who fired the first salvo at it as early as 1931, although the fullest and best summary of his thinking is found in his posthumous *História dos Descobrimentos Portuguezes* (1959).[7] Among the writers in the Portuguese language who have defended the "silence" theory are Costa Brochado, Admiral Gago Coutinho and Jaime Cortesão's younger brother, Armando. Marcondes de Sousa, just mentioned as a debunker of the nautical school, joined Leite in his attack. Damião Peres, already mentioned as having written a scholarly history of the Portuguese discoveries, performed the difficult manoeuvre of rejecting most of the secrecy arguments, but retaining of them something akin to a fig leaf. The most convincing attack on the "sigillum silentio", however, comes not from a Portuguese or a Brazilian, but from an American, Bailey W. Diffie. His article in *Terrae Incognitae* I (1969), "Foreigners in Portugal and the 'Policy of Silence'", shows that the quantity of foreigners in residence during the period, together with the number of them employed by the crown, would have made any pretensions to secrecy extremely improbable.

Beyond these two controversies, plus a few minor ones involving who-discovered-what-first, Portuguese historians have contributed a number of solid, non-political monographs to various phases of expansion history since World War II.

[6] Samuel Eliot Morison, *The European Discovery of America; The Northern Voyages. A.D. 500-1600* (New York 1971), p. 110.

[7] See also his *Descobridores de Brasil* (1931) and *Os Falses Precursores de Cabral* (1946).

To mention them here would not be as lengthy a task as citing the monograph titles of the Spanish *Escuela de Estudios Hispano-Americanos,* but certainly beyond my allotted space. I tend to favor works I know and have found valuable. But I can cite a few as typical, all published in Lisbon. Alexandre Lobato's *Os Portuguezes em Moçambique de 1489 à 1530* (3 vols, 1948-1951) is scholarly and authoritative. Francisco Paulo Mendes da Luz's *O Conselho da Índia* (1952) offers many insights into the nature of the Spanish bureaucracy and its colonial aims during Portugal's "captivity", and Humberto Leitão's *Os Portuguezes em Sólor e Timor, 1515-1702* (1948) meticulously fills a gap in expansion historiography. These excellent studies, however, contain no startingly original interpretations which would attract the attention of historians outside their special field. But then again, very few works of this era did.

Despite all the verbal assaults on Portugal's recent empire made in the United Nations and all the counterattacks mounted by the Portuguese, and in spite of the generous amounts of argumentation and political propaganda turned off Portuguese government presses – much of it using historical argumentation – there are practically no works in Portuguese of a scholarly nature which reflect either a defiantly pro- or anti-colonial bias. A very few authors, most notably Father António da Silva Rego, who is featured below, tried their hands at writing some pieces which resemble, but do not quite qualify as pro-colonial expansion history (viz. his *História da Colonização Moderna,* no more than a text piece to be used in the training of colonial officials). Most scholars left propaganda writing strictly to the propagandists.

In fact, so far as I know, there was only a single book, written under unusual circumstances and at the very end of the Salazar-Caetano era, which surveyed the phenomenon of dictatorship in Portugal and attempted to "tell things as they really were". This was António H. de Oliveira Marques' *History of Portugal* in two volumes, both published by the Columbia University Press in 1972. Forced to leave Portugal in 1965, Marques taught at Auburn University for one year and then at the University of Florida for three. Upon Salazar's incapacitation in 1968, he learned that Marcelo Caetano (a historian and a former professor of his) would tacitly permit him back in the country. Meanwhile he had been commissioned by Columbia to write the above work. It appeared in English after Marques had returned to Lisbon. Caetano, however, was no Salazar, firm and decisive; he made no attempt to ban the book, perhaps because it was in English and therefore seemed relatively harmless. I saw it for sale in several Lisbon bookstores in 1973. Although it is not primarily concerned with the expansion, there are four chapters exclusively devoted to overseas history, which is also mentioned frequently in other passages throughout the work. The final chapter, entitled "The Overseas Empire in the Twentieth Century" unerringly brushes aside all the camouflage of the colonial propagandists, and in brief compass it reveals the protective twistings and turnings of governmental colonial policy at various junctures. The account is balanced and fair, however, and Marques faithfully mirrors the régime's attempts to bring prosperity to Angola and Mozambique while taking a strong hand against the rebels and striving to discourage manifestation of ethnic African culture at the expense of Lusitanization. Caetano was so upset that he reportedly sought to refute Marques in a long book review – which was of course far more civilized than having him sent to Peniche or Caxias prisons.

What might ultimately have happened will never be known. In 1973 there appeared Vol. I of Marques' history in a new, all Portuguese edition, greatly expanded and augmented. Vol. I, however, extended only through the 18th century, and the régime was not overly sensitive about that era. A historian who tended more to the official viewpoint told me that the real question involved what would occur when Vol. II was distributed. Before that occured, the *revoluçao* of April, 1974, did. Marques, nonetheless, still deserves to be saluted for his conviction – or temerity.

In my opinion, Portugal has produced only one historiographer in the postwar years, who approaches in colonial history the status that Oliveira Marques has achieved in general Portuguese history: Vitorino Magalhães Godinho. His main fault is that he never uses one word when nine will do, which is somewhat usual these days for a French-trained scholar, but he is without peer as an economic historian of Portugal's empire; only Frédéric Mauro rivals him in any respect. One can simply discard the older writers as sketchy and amateurish, like João Lúcio de Azevedo, who was good in his day. Godinho's bulky *thèse complémentaire* at the Sorbonne was printed in 1969 by S.E.V.P.E.N. as *L'Économie de l'Empire Portugais aux XVe et XVIe Siècles,* and he later expanded it into an even thicker two-volume set in his native language. His earlier volume on the Henrician discoveries and his two volumes of *Ensaios,* or essays, on other aspects of Portuguese economic history, including the sugar fleets of Brazil, are indispensable. My only grudge against him is that he never constructs any chapter or sub-chapter for easy accessibility. He makes you read every last word.

One other expansionist, Father António da Silva Rego, rivals and even surpasses him in importance, but his contribution is of an entirely different sort. If this essay has a hero – I realize scholarly works are not supposed to have them – it is he. His contributions to expansion history are extraordinary, and none the less so because they were made (in Richard Hammond's words) "out of Portugal's persistent belief in herself as an imperial power" rather than in and for themselves. A priest and a former colonial resident, author of several books, including an excellent history of Portuguese missionary activity in India before the arrival of Francis Xavier,[8] he fervently believed that Portugal's overseas presence and *Civilização Cristã* were synonomous and contiguous – and that to become convinced of this, one only had to read the documents. These he was determined to make available to scholars throughout the world, as a kind of secular evangelism on behalf of Portugal's rightful and historical claims. He had already done much along these lines by compiling 12 volumes of documentation on Portuguese missions in India (not to be confused with his own study in one volume on the same subject) and by inspiring his friends, Artúr Basílio de Sá and António Brásio, to carry out similar projects for Indonesia and Angola. All three series were published by the Agência Geral do Ultramar, the publications agency attached to the Ministerio do Ultramar, or Overseas Ministry.[9] But Silva Rego had even bigger things in mind.

In 1951, with a preliminary grant from the Overseas Ministry, he began collecting microfilms from the Goan archives. In 1952, the Overseas Minister, Sarmento Rodrigues, broadened this microfilming activity to other archives outside Portugal which contained important information on Portuguese expansion, and he arranged for filing of the negatives in a repository in Lisbon, to be called the Filmoteca Ultramarina Portuguesa. Finally, in 1955, Silva Rego prevailed on him to create a special studies center, called the Centro de Estudos Históricos Ultramarinos, to house the Filmoteca, prepare and publish its catalogues, and to welcome scholars. And

[8] *História das Missões do Padroado Português no Oriente* (Lisbon: Agência Geral das Colónias, 1949). Only one volume has been written.

[9] This agency, founded by the *Ministério do Ultramar,* was the most important publisher of studies on the expansion until the creation of the C.E.H.U. Before 1952 it was called the *Agência Geral das Colónias,* but changed its name from "Colonias" to "Ultramar" at the same time as its parent organization. Since the C.E.H.U. did not publish monographs, the *Agência* continued to perform this important function. All its functions have now been incorporated into a new entity, the *Junta de Investigacoes Científicas do Ultramar,* successor to the C.E.H.U. and all other organs, including the *Junta de Investigacõos do Ultramar.*

meanwhile, the redoutable scholar-priest sought and obtained Gulbenkian Foundation help to subsidize new publications. Thus came into being a dream, complete with a fine library, richly-appointed rooms, copious staff, many offices and plenty of money, all presided over by an oil portrait of Pope John XXIII, whom Silva Rego particularly admired. There was thus absolutely nothing anachronistic about the operation, except for the reason which called it into being.

Henceforth, for nearly twenty years, the Centro de Estudos Históricos Ultramarinos poured forth documental calendars, annotated documents, a model journal, called *Stúdia,* and either reprints of long-unavailable books on the Portuguese expansion or first printings of informative works which had lain for centuries in manuscript, such as Frei Paulo da Trindade's *Conquista Espiritual do Oriente (ca. 1635).* To mention all of these is impossible in a short essay such as this, but I intend to do so in a forthcoming issue of our Centre's Bulletin, *Itinerario.* I will give some "for instances". There were, besides the calendared documents of the archives in Goa, Madrid, Macau and other places, the contents of the *Gavetas,* or drawers, of all but previously unknown manuscripts, largely on the *ultramar,* from the Arquivo Nacional da Torre do Tombo, another five volumes of overseas documentation from other sources, called the *Documentação Ultramarina,* and reprints of extremely rare historical sources like António de Oliveira de Cadornega's history of the Angolan wars, originally published in 1680. Then there were the ambitious *Documents on the Portuguese in Mozambique and Central Africa, 1497-1840,* with side-by-side English translations of the Portuguese, a project partly sponsored by the National Archives of Rhodesia and Nyasaland. (Only 8 volumes, I think, were ever published, bringing the story to 1588, and it is a fairly safe bet that no more ever will be).

In my opinion, the importance of these publications, together with the earlier documentation inspired by Silva Rego, surpasses all else achieved in either Spanish or Portuguese circles since the war. When one puts with them the documental volumes published in Goa under the editorship of the late Panduronga S.S. Pissurlencar, plus the output of the *Monumenta Henricina,* the 14-volume documental series inspired by Henry the Navigator's 500th anniversary, everything else done on the expansion in the Peninsula seems trivial by comparison. (Silva Rego, incidentally, had a hand in most of those, too, and was responsible for the recent publication of volume VI to VIII of the *Documentos Remetidos da India*).

If Silva Rego failed in his main objective, it was not that the historians had deserted him; it was merely that he overestimated our influence. But he left a lasting historical legacy as a by-product, one which will endure at least as long as film and paper do. It is now within the power of any university library whose purse-strings are not triple-knotted shut (as many are these days) to become a respectable source of information about Portuguese overseas history, where scholars thousands of leagues from Goa and Lisbon can carry on a good deal of preliminary research on a variety of topics. For the life work of any historian, the achievement is a magnificent one.

The role of the foreign Iberianists

At the beginning of this essay, I performed an artificial task, one akin to entering a pond with a net and sorting out all the different kinds of fish into little pens or compounds. To wit, I proposed only to consider Iberian works on the Iberian expansion and to exclude all the others. On this, or any other subject, one does not restrict one's choice only to paperbacks, or exclusively to the works of certain authors, but reads anything which can provide information and insights. Now it is time to let the fish escape, having measured, weighed and described them.

If the total Iberian contribution, including source material as well as monographs and articles, is taken together, then I would judge that it easily forms the most significant part of the literature on its own expansion tradition. I do not think I could do much research on any topic if I did not have access to this body of work, but was offered only the works of foreign historians, as excellent as some of these are. For in effect what the British, American and Latin American historians have largely done, is to view the Iberian expansion from their own vantagepoints and sift out of it what they value or wish to know. The Latin Americans are interested in their own countries' history (and so, I might add, are the Asians and Africans from nations like Ceylon, The Philippines and Japan, once penetrated by the Iberians), the other former colonial nations like Britain and France are largely interested in Iberia as comparative manifestations of empire, and the North Americans are interested because they share a hemisphere with the former Iberian colonies, besides which they are so big and so rich that they dabble in everything. Then, the Americans, the British, the Dutch and to some extent the Caribbean nations, are concerned with the history of slavery, which involves them to a greater or lesser extent in the history of Angola, or perhaps of the *asiento.* All these interests have produced a significant amount of expansion historiography dealing with the Iberians.

Above all, British and American authors have provided the synthetic works on the two Iberian empires which Spanish and Portuguese authors themselves have never supplied. Edward Gaylord Bourne's *Spain in America* (1904) was in some respects the pioneering work of this genre, but Roger B. Merriman's *Rise of the Spanish Empire in the Old World and the New* (4 vols., New York, 1918-1934) provided a more up to date narrative, while Clarence H. Haring's *The Spanish Empire in America* (New York, 1947) gave readers the first truly modern and satisfactory institutional and thematic treatment of the subject. It has been translated into Spanish, and no expansionist should ever be allowed to sally forth into the professional world without having studied it. In 1966, John H. Parry's *Spanish Seaborne Empire* was published, a perceptive and stylish work which rivals Haring's (if any book ever really rivals another) and is far more readable. Finally, another synthesis by Lyle N. McAlister is nearing publication in the "Europe and the World in the Age of Expansion" series; in my opinion, it promises to be a masterpiece. One can safely gather from this recitation that the English-speaking writers excel in creating the overview.

The Portuguese empire as a whole is not quite so lavishly served, but it attracted fewer scholars until recently. Leaving F.C. Danver's derivative and defective *The Portuguese in India* aside, the first satisfactory book on any aspect of the empire was that of Richard C. Whiteway, a former British civil servant, published in 1899. This was his *Rise of the Portuguese Power in India.* For what it is – purely military and political history, it holds up quite as well today as it did when it was written. It gave readers no coverage, though, of the Henrician discovery era. For this they had to make do with an old biography of the prince written five years before the turn of the century by C. Raymond Beazley. Edgar Prestage's *Portuguese Pioneers* (1933) partly filled this gap: it was a conscientious survey of the empire from its earliest days through the discovery of India and Brazil, and it was forced to do duty for another third of a century. The trouble was that it took all the claims of Henry's nautical school and the policy of silence seriously because Prestage based his views too literally on the prevailing views of Portuguese writers of his day. Neither Whiteway nor Prestage were superseded or supplemented until Charles R. Boxer wrote his *Four Centuries of Portuguese Expansion, 1415-1825: a Succinct Survey,* Johannesburg, 1965, and his *Portuguese Seaborne Empire,* New York 1969. In a way, these studies left readers somewhat dependent on the earlier works because they were either (in the case of the *Four Centuries*) too brief to enter into the same breadth of detail or (in the *Portuguese*

Seaborne Empire) they covered different territory. It is only this year that Bailey Diffie and myself have attempted, in our *Foundations of the Portuguese Empire,* to update both Prestage and Whiteway with comparable syntheses which take advantage of the most modern research. Before taking leave of survey material, I might also mention Donald F. Lach's *Asia in the Making of Europe,* Vol. I (really two volumes, called "Books 1 & 2") which amounts to a near encyclopaedic treatment of the Portuguese in Asia – from p. 87 to about p. 750.

In a very real sense, those of us who have synthesized have done so not because there has been any failure of the Iberian historiography apparatus, but because, as I pointed out above, our concern is to see our own history in relation to theirs – and we need the summaries for our own purposes. They perhaps need them less; it is the foreigners, not knowing how to drive from Sevilla to Madrid, who buy the road maps. In writing my own synthesis I also became aware that – as I am sure my fellow synthesizers are happy to admit – the contributions of the modern Spanish and Portuguese historiographers are usually first-rate, and that my survey could hardly have been adequate without them.

In closing, I would like to observe that every Portuguese and Spanish historian I have met or associated with has been unfailingly kind, helpful and genuinely interested in my work. As a genre, the Iberians may show little interest in Jean Baptiste Colbert, Kitchener, or Coen, in other words, subjects outside their own horizons, but they exhibit a keen interest and appreciation for the work we foreigners have done in their own sphere. This was even so when Charles Boxer crossed swords with Portuguese officialdom on the issue of racial tolerance (with his *Race Relations in the Portuguese Colonial Empire, 1415-1825,* Oxford, 1963). Although Father Silva Rego devoutly believed in the opposite point of view, his regard for Boxer – and their friendship – never faltered and the one respected Portuguese historian who attacked him in immoderate terms later bitterly regretted having done so. This, however, was an extreme case.[10] Historians like Lewis Hanke, Arthur P. Whitaker, William Lytle Schurz and others have been unfailingly honored and treated with esteem – and, more importantly, their books are read and even translated. It would perhaps not be going too far to say that we and they, the Iberianists and the Iberians, are all members of the same fraternity.

[10] The Portuguese never doubted that Boxer liked them. Another writer, James Duffy, gave them the impression that he was not only anti-imperial, but anti-Portuguese.

7. DUTCH HISTORIOGRAPHY ON EUROPEAN EXPANSION SINCE 1945

by

H.L. WESSELING

I. INTRODUCTION

If one sets out to describe and analyse historiographical developments in a certain country, it is not enough to enumerate a series of important publications, institutions, or scholars. In order to understand the historical discipline of a country, attention must be paid not only to the contributions of individuals, but also to the impact of national traditions and international developments. Both in time and space, three levels of analysis can be distinguished: person, country, and international community on the one hand, and on the other, long, middling and short term. Every historian has his place within a definite historical culture which usually bears national and international characteristics. Every historical production can be seen within the context of a certain historiographical trend or "conjuncture," as well as forming part of a general historiographical structure.

But this is only one, viz., the "endogenous," approach to the problem. It is concerned with the changes stemming from the scientific ideas themselves. There is also the "exogenous" approach, which stresses developments in the society in which historical research is done and historical studies are written. Thus, the growing interest in overseas history, and the changing approach to it, are closely connected with the socio-political context within which historiography is taking place.

The great importance of this aspect for the historical discipline has long been known. Every generation interrogates the past anew and in its own manner, which is why Geyl has called history "an argument without an end". In so far as the study of overseas history is concerned, the extent to which it has been quantitatively and qualitatively influenced by the course, and, even, the outcome of that history itself, is all too clear. Therefore, if we want to understand the development of post-1945 Dutch historiography on

European expansion, we should not only pay attention to new insights and individual accomplishments, but also to the influence of national traditions, socio-political changes, and international scientific trends and innovations.

In this essay I shall first deal with the traditions of Dutch overseas history and their impact on contemporary historical work; then turn to socio-political and scholarly changes after 1945; and finally, I shall attempt to assess the value of Dutch historiography of the last thirty years, within an international and comparative context.

II. TRADITIONS

At first sight, with respect to overseas history, it seems awkward to use such terms as "tradition" and "long term." Indeed, history itself, as an independent academic discipline, is still rather young, hardly more than a century old. In the beginning, its character was mainly nationalist and in any case had a European orientation. For non-European history, therefore, we must turn (even today) not only – and not even in the first place – to the historical discipline in the narrow sense, as it is practised within the history departments, but to what are known as Oriental studies: sinology, indology, islamology etc. Only from this perspective may one speak of a long-standing tradition. The training of colonial civil servants, which was only academised at a fairly late date, was based upon linguistic and ethnological studies. Sinology in Leiden saw the light with the institution of a chair in the year 1875, whilst the study of Islam rose to great heights under the direction of Snouck Hurgronje,[1] although of course, Arabics, albeit with a different orientation, had existed for a long time before that. Obviously, the ascendance of these studies is closely connected with developments in Indonesia itself, where the forever increasing intensity of the Dutch presence stimulated the need for scientific study of indigenous traditions (adat-law),[2] Arabic influences, the role of the Chinese and so on.[3] This development coincided with the international renaissance of the university in the second half of the nineteenth century.

[1] Snouck Hurgronje, C. *Mekka*; mit Bilder-Atlas (3 vols. 's-Gravenhage 1888-1889).

[2] The most important scholar in this field was C. van Vollenhoven, author of a.o. *Het Adatrecht van Nederlandsch-Indië* (3 vols. Leiden 1906-1933). See also the 45-volume series of Adatrechtbundels, edited by the Commissie voor het Adatrecht ('s-Gravenhage 1910-1955).

[3] For Oriental studies see Woltjer J.J., *De Leidse universiteit in verleden en heden* (Leiden 1965).

Thus, we are dealing with the 19th century, as one can hardly speak of genuine overseas history before that date. Of course, in the wider sense of interest in the world outside Europe, such as in the form of travel accounts, we could go back much further. Here we meet with the age-old tradition of the Netherlands as a seafaring and mercantile nation. Holland has always been a country with world-wide economic interests, turned away from the continent and strongly orientated towards the seas, a country with a great commercial and maritime empire, and, later, a colonial empire. The effects of this are very apparent today, not only in a certain mental outlook and interest, but especially in the form of its remains, rich collections of manuscripts, maps, documents and travel accounts.

Consequently, one of the most important activities in the field of the history of European expansion lies in rendering accessible this wealth of material. It is well known that these collections, for the earlier period, cover a much wider geographical area than that which would later develop into the Dutch colonial empire. In fact, very important data can be found concerning the early history of Japan, China, Taiwan, Sri Lanka and parts of Africa and America. The collections are housed mainly in three locations, namely the General State Archives (A.R.A.) in The Hague, the Royal Institute of Linguistics and Anthropology (K.I.T.L.V.)[4] in Leiden and the Royal Tropical Institute in Amsterdam.[5] The A.R.A., of course, is by far the most important: from the earlier period, it contains both the archives of the East and West India Companies (V.O.C. and W.I.C.) as well as many other collections.

For the 19th and 20th centuries, the archives of the Ministry of the Colonies are of primary importance; those dealing with the period 1850-1900, it may be mentioned, are located in a safe, but somewhat sinister bunker in Schaarsbergen, and for the period thereafter in a building of the Ministry of the Interior in The Hague. The collections of the K.I.T.L.V. in Leiden are mainly concerned with Indonesian history of the 19th and 20th centuries, as are those of the Tropical Institute; the first possess more of a cultural character, while the latter are more of interest to economic historians. Naturally there are many more private, municipal and national archives, and these are sometimes of the utmost importance.

[4] A survey of publications published by the K.I.T.L.V. in the first 125 years of its existence has been prepared by F.G.P. Jaquet in: *Overzicht van publikaties uitgegeven door het Koninklijk Instituut voor Taal-, Land- en Volkenkunde 1851-1976* (Leiden 1976).

[5] The library of the Tropical Institute is very important but it is rather poor in unpublished material.

Even though much work has yet to be done, various guides, publications, inventories, etc. have appeared in the last few years which make these collections accessible. As part of a large Unesco project, the A.R.A. is compiling lists of archival material pertaining to the history of overseas territories. The Latin-America guide has been published by M. Roessingh.[6] A guide pertaining to the sources in the Netherlands for the history of Africa is recently published.[7] A work that also deserves particular mention in this context is the series of publications that is being edited by F. Jaquet, under the title: *Gids van de in Nederland aanwezige bronnen betreffende de geschiedenis van Azië en Oceanië 1796-1949* (Guide to the Sources in the Netherlands Concerning the History of Asia and Oceania 1796-1949). M. Roessingh is preparing a guide for the sources up to 1796.[8]

Besides the issuing of guides and inventories there is, of course, the editing and publishing of the sources themselves. Without any attempt at completeness, four series should be mentioned. Firstly, the publications of the Linschoten-vereniging, the Dutch version of the Hakluyt Society, consisting of a series of travel accounts mainly from the 17th century, of which so far more than 75 issues have been published.

Secondly, the publications of the R.G.P. (State Historical Publications). This series has long been an Utrecht speciality, the Emeritus Professor Coolhaas editing and annotating mainly the older sources and his successor, Prof. Van der Wal, the recent and contemporary ones. Of his series *Generale Missiven van Gouverneurs-Generaal en Raden aan Heren XVII der Verenigde Oostindische Compagnie,* (General Missives of Governors-General and Councils to the Gentlemen XVII of the V.O.C.) Professor Coolhaas has so far produced five large volumes. These reports (the 'general missives')

[6] Roessingh, M.P.H. *Guide to the Sources in the Netherlands for the History of Latin America* (The Hague 1968) (Guide to the Sources of the History of the Nations, A. Latin America, III, 2).

[7] Roessingh, M.P.H. and Visser, W. *Guide to the Sources in the Netherlands for the History of Africa South of the Sahara* (Munich 1978). (Guide to the Sources of the History of the Nations II, 9). A copy of the typewritten text in Dutch can be used in the reading room of the Algemeen Rijksarchief in The Hague. See also Carson, P. *Materials for West African history in the Archives of Belgium and Holland* (London 1962) (Guide to Materials for West African History in European Archives, 1).

[8] Jaquet, F.G.P. *Gids van de in Nederland aanwezige bronnen betreffende de geschiedenis van Nederlands-Indië/Indonesië, 1816-1942* (Leiden 1968). To date 7 vols. have been published, the last one in 1973. Vol. 1 (a list of bibliographical works) has also been published in *Internationale Spectator,* 22 (1968).

from the administration in Batavia contain a wealth of information about all the Asian dealings of the VOC. The five volumes printed so far deal with the 17th century (1610-1697), while another five are planned for the 18th century.[9]

Professor Van der Wal started at the other end of colonial history with his source publications on Dutch-Indonesian relations during the period of decolonisation (1945-1950). Undertaken on the initiative of the Dutch Government six volumes of this latter work so far have been published.[10] A third important series consists of source publications pertaining to the history of the Netherlands-East-Indies, edited by a committee of the N.H.G. (the Dutch Historical Society). This is another series for which we must thank Prof. Van der Wal, who has worked on educational policy in the Netherlands-Indies (1900-1940) and on political developments in the years 1891-1942, particularly with regard to the *Volksraad.*[11] Still other volumes appeared in this series; for example, about the nationalist movement, edited by R.C. Kwantes,[12] and about economic policy by the hand of P. Creutzberg. Mr. Creutzberg[13] is also the creative stimulus behind the fourth and last, very recent important series of source publications, *Changing Economy in Indonesia: A Selection of Statistical Source Material from the Early 19th Century up to 1940.* This is a series of statistical surveys of various economic activities and variables such as production, trade,

[9] Coolhaas, W.Ph. *Generale Missiven van Gouverneurs-Generaal en Raden aan Heren XVII der Verenigde Oostindische Compagnie* ('s-Gravenhage 1960-). (Rijks Geschiedkundige Publicatiën, Grote Serie).
To date Vol. 1 (1610-1638) in 1960, Vol. 2 (1639-1655) in 1964. Vol. 3 (1655-1674) in 1968, Vol. 4 (1675-1685) in 1971, Vol. 5 (1686-1697) in 1975 and Vol. 6 (1698-1713) in 1976 have been published.

[10] Wal, S.L. van der. *Officiële bescheiden betreffende de Nederlands-Indonesische betrekkingen, 1945-1950* ('s-Gravenhage 1971-), (Rijks Geschiedkundige Publicatiën, Kleine Serie, 36, 37, 38, 39, 41, 44).

[11] Wal, S.L. van der. *Het onderwijsbeleid in Nederlands-Indië 1900-1940; een bronnenpublikatie* (Groningen 1963) (Uitgaven van de Commissie voor bronnenpublicatie betreffende de geschiedenis van Nederlands-Indië 1900-1942 van het Historisch Genootschap (henceforth cited as CBNI), 1). Wal. S.L. van der. *De Volksraad en de staatkundige ontwikkeling van Nederlands-Indië; een bronnenpublikatie* (Groningen 1964-1965. 2 vols), Vol. 1 (1891-1926) published in 1964. Vol. 2 (1927-1942) published in 1965. CBNI, 2-3.
Wal, S.L. van der. *De opkomst van de nationalistische beweging in Nederlands-Indië; een bronnenpublikatie* (Groningen 1967) CBNI, 4.

[12] Kwantes, R.C. *De ontwikkeling van de nationalistische beweging in Nederlandsch-Indië* (Groningen 1975-). To date vol. 1 (1917-medio 1923) in 1975, CBNI, 8, has appeared.

[13] Creutzberg, P. *Het ekonomisch beleid in Nederlands-Indië; capita selecta; een bronnenpublikatie* (Groningen 1972-1975). Vol. 1 appeared in 1972, Vol. 2 in 1974 and Vol. 3 (in two parts) in 1975. CBNI, 5, 6, 7.

transport and so on. The whole series is planned to comprise some fifteen volumes, of which seven are well under way, and two have appeared since last year. The subjects of these are, respectively: "Indonesian Export Crops" and "Public Finance."[14]

It appears from the above that these source publications, particularly for the 19th and 20th century, are mainly concerned with Asia, and more especially with Indonesia, although some work has been done for the Caribbean area (such as the *West-Indisch-Plakkaatboek*).[15] This concentration on Indonesia for the 19th and 20th centuries is rather natural. The 19th century, from a colonial point of view, was for the Netherlands a period of contraction as well as intensification. Contraction in a geographical sense, on Indonesia, and intensification in the administrative, social and economic sense. As I have said, administrative difficulties resulting from this have, in many cases, provided the primary impulse to a more scientific approach to the study of colonial problems, and thus to what is still sometimes referred to as "Oriental studies." This tradition dates roughly from the middle of the 19th century and is thus about a hundred years old.[16] Very important in this context is the academic organisation of the training of colonial officers, a training which received international praise.[17] The history of this remains yet to be written, but we may here limit ourselves to observing that, after some wandering, it became concentrated in Leiden and Utrecht. The fact is significant, as it explains why overseas history is still exercised mainly from these two universities. Another important factor in the growth of these studies

[14] Creutzberg, P. *Changing Economy in Indonesia; a Selection of Statistical Source Material from the Early 19th Century up to 1940;* initiated by W.M.F. Mansvelt (The Hague 1975-). To date Vol. 1 (Indonesia's Export Crops, 1816-1940) in 1975 and Vol. 2 (Public Finance, 1816-1939) in 1976, have appeared.

[15] *West-Indisch plakaatboek;* onder redactie van J.A. Schiltkamp en J.Th. de Smidt (Amsterdam, 1973-). To date Vol. 1 (*Plakaten, ordonnantiën en andere wetten, uitgevaardigd in Suriname 1667-1817*), edited by J.Th. de Smidt in co-operation with T. van der Lee, (Werken der Vereeniging tot uitgaaf der Bronnen van het Oud-Vaderlandsch Recht, 3e reeks, 24-1), has been published (2 parts, 1973).

[16] See on this the biographical essays collected in: *Honderd jaar studie van Indonesië, 1850-1950; levensbeschrijvingen van twaalf Nederlandse onderzoekers* (Den Haag 1976).

[17] Wesseling, H.L. "Le modèle colonial hollandais dans la théorie coloniale française", *Revue française d'histoire d'outre-mer* 64 (1976) Nr. 231, pp. 223-255. Also as "The Dutch Colonial Model in French Colonial Theory, 1890-1914," with a commentary by R.F. Betts in *Proceedings of the Second Annual Meeting of the French Colonial Historical Society* (Athens, Georgia 1977) pp. 107-130.

was, of course, the international trend which in this period led to the so-called geographical movement throughout Europe, a movement stimulating the study of geography and ethnology; the Dutch part of this chapter also remains, as yet, unwritten. As regards the ideological and scientific aspects of overseas history, it can be said without much exaggeration that both of them have for a long time, in fact up to 1945, borne a strongly 19th century character. Ideologically, of course, there were considerable differences in the valuation of Dutch rule, of the roles of Coen and Van den Bosch, the so-called ethical policy and so on, but in general the approach remained predominantly Eurocentric, and the perspective colonialist.[18] A remarkable exception to this is the history of Indonesia from a Marxist viewpoint by S.J. Rutgers.[19] Equally exceptional but much more important is J.C. van Leur's dissertation of 1934, to which I shall come back later.[20] Generally speaking, however, the approach remained oldfashioned and colonialistic, oriented toward military and political history, although, of course, Gonggrijp's *Economic History* must also be mentioned.[21]

III. NEW TRENDS AND DEVELOPMENTS SINCE 1945

Much was changed after the Second World War, on the one hand by decolonization, and on the other by the expansion of new world powers like the U.S. and the Soviet Union. Historical perspective was influenced by this in two different, and to a certain extent contradictory, ways. In the first place, the new power relations led to increased attention to the extra-European world, and to a more general discussion of the European point of view. This discussion was particularly stimulated by Professors Romein of Amsterdam and Locher of Leiden; and in fact, Amsterdam and Leiden were the two universities to have substantiated this new interest in the form of chairs and institutes. In Amsterdam, this led to the founding of the institutes for Eastern European Studies and for North American Studies, and later on, on an inter-

[18] See also the very useful historiographical introduction by J.S. Wigboldus to Burger, D.H. *Sociologisch-economische geschiedenis van Indonesia* (Wageningen 1975).

[19] Rutgers, S.J. en J.A. Huber. *Indonesië* (Amsterdam, 1937-1947. 2 vols). Vol. 1, 1947. Vol. 2 (*Het koloniale systeem in de periode tussen de eerste en tweede wereldoorlog*), 1947.

[20] See below pages 131-132.

[21] Gonggrijp, G. *Schets eener economische geschiedenis van Nederlandsch-Indië* (Haarlem 1928, 1938, 1949, 1957).

university level, for Latin American Studies, the C.E.D.L.A.[22] In Leiden, the teaching of non-European history received much attention and was stimulated by the presence of the K.I.T.L.V.[23] (Royal Institute of Linguistics and Anthropology) and the newly-founded African Study Centre[24] and the Centre for Chinese Studies.

Inversely, decolonization itself led to a great rupture in the traditional, namely colonial, practice of non-European history. The break between the pre-war and post-war periods indeed seems to have been sharper and more consequential in the Netherlands than anywhere else. Undoubtedly the trauma of decolonization has been relatively considerable, owing to the length and cruelty of the process and the painful and lingering aftermath of the New Guinea question.[25] Scholarly relations between the Netherlands and Indonesia came to an almost complete end, only to be revived in the past few years. Dutch scholars played a much smaller part in the new overseas universities than the French and English did in their former colonies, while, inversely, Indonesian researchers hardly visited the Netherlands. Of course, apart from educational traditions, language was an important obstacle here. But it seems that in the Netherlands the younger generation suffered more from a bad conscience about the long and greedy colonial past than it did elsewhere, and that consequently the aversion to colonial history was greater. Probably connected with this is the fact that Third World ideologies and development fever are particularly flourishing in the Netherlands. In the field of overseas studies, this in turn has led to an American-inspired approach strongly concentrated on the present, one possessing a sociological and economical orientation, and which the Institute of Social Studies in the Hague has become an important centre of. Not much room was thus left for historical reflection.[26]

[22] Centro de Estudios y Documentacion Latinoamericanos publishing in co-operation with the Caribbean Department of K.I.T.L.V. (established in 1972) the *Boletín de estudios latinoamericanos y del Caribe.*

[23] Its main journal is called *Bijdragen tot de taal-, land- en volkenkunde* (1853–), while its main series of separate publications is formed by the *Verhandelingen van het Koninklijk Instituut voor Taal-, Land- en Volkenkunde* (1938–).

[24] Publishes as a journal of research and communication *Kroniek van Afrika* (since 1976 called *African Perspectives*).

[25] Lijphart, A. *The Trauma of Decolonization; the Dutch and West New Guinea* (New Haven-London 1966). (Yale Studies in Political Science, 17).

[26] For a brief analysis of Dutch knowledge and expertise concerning Indonesia, and of the a-historical approach to Third World problems characteristic in the Netherlands, see Jong, J.J.P. de, "Indonesië-kennis in Nederland als factor in de samenwerking met Indonesië", *Internationale Spectator* 30 (1976) 6, pp. 325-331.

At the universities the consequence of this was that colonial history drew practically no interest at all, and, in so far as it did, did not want to call itself by that name any more. It was re-baptised with neutral but awkward names such as "overseas history" or "history of the East-West-encounter." In the 'seventies, attention to this field of history revived, owing, from the socio-political side, to a normalization of relations with Indonesia and the increased importance of the Third World and, from the scholarly side, to the growing historical-mindedness of the social sciences, and a certain scepticism with regard to the possibilities for social engineering.

The loss of the unifying colonial-historical orientation naturally led to great theoretical uncertainty both about the definition of overseas history as a field of research, and about the most relevant methods and approaches. The discussion about Asia-centric, or Indonesia-centric, or region-centric historiography was very lively, though it must be remarked that its theoretical aspects, both in articles and in the broad studies undertaken by Romein and Wertheim,[27] received more attention than their practical application, such as in regional historical studies. To cut a long story short, it would be now out of the question to study Asian history solely in terms of Dutch history, but it is equally clear that separate studies from the Dutch standpoint, which would yield valuable data and insights, are still missing in many fields.[28]

But, of course, developments in overseas history were not only influenced by the changing world around it, but also by the development of the historical discipline itself. In this respect, two major trends must be mentioned which are both, in the last issue, connected with the increasingly scientific character of historical work. The first of these movements stresses that history must make use of the models, methods, and above all the concepts of the social sciences, particularly those of economics and sociology. For overseas

[27] Romein, J.M. en J.E. Romein. *De eeuw van Azië; opkomst, ontwikkeling en overwinning van het modern-aziatisch nationalisme* (Leiden 1956). Translated as: *The Asian Century; a History of Modern Nationalism in Asia*; with a forew. by K.M. Panikkar (Berkeley-Los Angeles 1962).
Wertheim, W.F. *Indonesian Society in Transition; a Study of Social Change* (The Hague-Bandung 1956, 2nd rev. ed. 1959).
Wertheim, W.F. *East-West Parallels; Sociological Approaches to Modern Asia* (The Hague 1964).
Wertheim, W.F. *Evolutie en revolutie; de golfslag der emancipatie* (Amsterdam 1971). Translated as: *Evolution and Revolution; the Rising Waves of Emancipation* (Harmondsworth 1974) (Pelican books, A 1529).

[28] Fasseur, C. "Java in de negentiende eeuw: Europa-centrisch of Indonesiëcentrisch? *Kleio,* 17 (1976) 9, pp. 941-949.

history, one should turn also to cultural anthropology and non-western sociology. It is a noteworthy fact that, chronologically, this movement among historians coincides with the trend, mentioned earlier, among social scientists toward a more historical approach. The second movement attempts to put the scientific character of history into practice by the application of exact methods and techniques. Quantitative, or, as Chaunu, one of the masters of this discipline, has it, serial history, which has its origins particularly in France (Labrousse, Simiand, Meuvret), has developed into a historical method which, after victories gained in the field of economic history and later in that of social history, has now proceeded on to themes of cultural history, and particularly of the history of mentalities.[29] These developments have naturally not occurred without impact on Dutch historiography in general, nor on that of European expansion in particular. In the field of Indonesian history, and in particular with respect to the current orientation towards the social sicences, there has actually been a precursor whose name must not be left out of any survey of post-war historiography, even though he died prematurely during the war. I am referring, of course, to the work of J.C. van Leur.

Van Leur, who was born in 1908 and was killed in 1942 in the Battle of the Java Sea, was a man of feverish activity and remarkable originality. Just like many eminent scholars in Indonesian studies, he was trained in Leiden at the school for colonial civil servants. After this, at the age of 26, he wrote a dissertation on some aspects of the early Asian trade.[30] As an civil servant in the Dutch East Indies he made a rapid career, but also remained active as a scholar. His scholarly fervour is apparent from the fact that the bibliography of the writings of this author, who died at hardly 34 years of age, adds up to almost fifty titles. The variety and the often contemporary orientation of his articles, dealing with many aspects of the world crisis of his time, testify to his social engagement and broad interest.

The originality of the work of Van Leur lies in the fact that he sensed, and tried to materialise, two of the major trends in post-war

[29] See on this for example Chaunu, Pierre, "Un nouveau champ pour l'histoire sérielle: le quantitatif au troisième niveau". *Mélanges en l'honneur de Fernand Braudel,* 1 (1973) pp. 105-125.

[30] Leur, J.C. van. *Eenige beschouwingen betreffende den ouden Aziatischen handel* (Middelburg 1934). A translation of this book, as of his other works can be found in Leur, J.C. van, *Indonesian Trade and Society; Essays in Asian Social and Economic History* (The Hague-Bandung 1955) (Selected Studies on Indonesia by Dutch Scholars, 1). For his necrology see note 16.

historiographical developments: the abandonment of the Eurocentric viewpoint and the application of sociological categories. Van Leur reacted against the exclusively Dutch-oriented approach, by which perspective became distorted and much historical reality rendered invisible. "Most historians," he wrote, "see the Asiatic world through the eyes of the Dutch ruler: from the deck of the ship, the rampart of the fortress, the high gallery of the trading house."[31]

But Van Leur's criticism is at the same time more general and more fundamental. The periodisation of history, and the place in it allotted to Asia are questioned by him. For instance, in one extensive article he examined the questionable virtues of applying such concepts as "the 18th century" to Indonesian history, concluding that in this case the concept has no heuristic value. Nothing of the great changes which make for the typical character of this period in European history can be traced in the Indonesian past. Up to 1800, it simply remains part of Asia.[32]

This leads us to the second main characteristic of Van Leur's historical approach, namely the application of concepts from sociology, in particular those of Max Weber. Using Weber's concept of the ideal type – as for example those of "peasant culture," "patrimonial bureaucratic states," "peddling trade" – he attempts to describe Asian history as part of universal history, but with its own character. In this way it is possible to do justice to the peculiarities of various cultures without either wrapping them up entirely in too abstract and too general a set of categories, or discussing them as merely exotic and incomprehensible.

Van Leur's book is not based on any new primary research. It is, in fact, a volume of original, erudite and stimulating observations on comparative history. Its significance, as with many great theses, is to be sought above all in the discussion following it and the studies stimulated by it. Generally speaking, one might say that historians have reacted to Van Leur's theses perhaps no less enthusiastically, but still with more hesitation, than sociologists.

To begin with these last, the man who has contributed more than anyone else to the spreading of Van Leur's work among Dutch historians, and later in international scholarly circles, by means of English translations, has been Prof. Wertheim. Trained as a lawyer,

[31] Leur, J.C. van. *Indonesian Trade and Society*, p. 162.

[32] Leur, J.C. van. "Eenige aantekeningen betreffende de mogelijkheid der 18de eeuw als categorie in de Indische geschiedschrijving," *Tijdschrift voor Indische Taal-, Land- en Volkenkunde*, 80 (1940), pp. 544-567. Translated in *Indonesian Trade and Society*.

but known in the course of his scholarly career mainly as a sociologist, Wertheim has made major contributions to overseas history as well. His sociological approach, concentrated especially on Asia, bears the mark of a strong historical orientation. In his work, attention is paid not only to the problems of modern Indonesia in a broad Asian context but also to its historical background. His studies are concerned both with socio-economic structures and with ideologies, such as Marxism, nationalism, 19th century-anti-colonialism.[33] Moreover, during his Amsterdam professorate, Wertheim has not only been active by means of his own publications, but has also stimulated a large number of students, so that we may speak of an Amsterdam historical-sociological school.

The most important work to be stimulated by Van Leur is the dissertation by Mrs. Meilink-Roelofsz, fortunately published in English as: *Asian Trade and European Influence in the Indonesian Archipelago between 1500 and about 1630.*[34] In this very fine piece of historical scholarship, not written from any "deck, rampart or gallery," but from a well-entrenched position in the State Archives, a very detailed analysis, based mainly on the V.O.C.-archive, is made of the Asian trade network in the first, and of the parts played in it by Portuguese and Dutch merchants in the second place. In this priority given to Asian trade, the book clearly differs from the traditional approach, with its exclusive concentration on the role of the European merchants.

The history of trade, and economic history in general, is the terrain for which traditionally quantitative or serial methods have most readily lent themselves, and historically, it is not surprising that here serial history has had its earliest developments. This leads us to the second scientific movement in post-war historiography which has also influenced the history of expansion, namely, historical statistic research. The best-known example, of course, is the voluminous study by the Chaunus on *Séville et l'Atlantique.*[35] In spite of much important work done in the field of V.O.C.-history, such as the above-mentioned book by Mrs. Meilink-Roelofsz and

[33] See note 27.
[34] Meilink-Roelofsz, M.A.P. *Asian Trade and European Influence in the Indonesian Archipelago between 1500 and about 1630* ('s-Gravenhage 1962, 1969).
[35] Chaunu, Pierre et Huguette. *Séville et l'Atlantique, 1504-1650* (Paris 1955 f.f.).

the work of the Danish historians Glamann and, later, Steensgaard,[36] a historical statistical survey of all the material is still lacking. Therefore Prof. Schöffer and Dr. Bruijn have initiated a research project into the archives of the V.O.C. in Asia for the whole period of 1595-1802. This work, which has not yet been finished, but whose publication may be expected in 1979, will bring to light much important new data, among others that concerning monetary and demographic history. This is already apparent from a number of articles and contributions by the participating researchers.[37] The final results will comprise several volumes and will be published in English under the title *Dutch-Asiatic Shipping in the Seventeenth and Eighteenth Centuries.* The bulk of this publication will be taken up by a very detailed tabular survey, in which a great quantity of data (length of the journey, crew, tonnage, value of the freight, etc.) is given for every ship. In an extensive introduction the history and organisation of the V.O.C. will be described, as well as nautical and technical problems, such as the equipment and organisation of ship-building and navigation.

IV. BALANCE

It is unusual in a historiographical survey to deal with future publications, but inadvertently this is what has happened here. Let us therefore quickly return to the past and, after these general observations about historiographical trends and developments, now try to put Dutch historiography concerning European expansion into the balance. As a more complete survey can be found in various bibliographies (a new edition of Prof. Coolhaas' well-known *Critical*

[36] Glamann, K. *Dutch-Asiatic Trade 1620-1740* (Copenhagen-The Hague 1958). Steensgaard, N. *Carracks, Caravans and Companies: the Structural Crisis in the European-Asian Trade in the Early 17th Century* (Lund 1973) (Scandinavian Institute of Asian Studies monograph series, 17). Published also as: *The Asian Trade Revolution of the Seventeenth Century; the East India Companies and the Decline of the Caravan Trade* (Chicago 1974).

[37] Bruijn, J.R. "De personeelsbehoefte van de VOC overzee en aan boord, bezien in Aziatisch en Nederlands perspectief." *Bijdragen en mededelingen betreffende de geschiedenis der Nederlanden* 91 (1976) 2, pp. 218-248. Gaastra, F.S. "De Verenigde Oost-Indische Compagnie in de zeventiende en achttiende eeuw: de groei van een bedrijf; geld tegen goederen: een structurele verandering in het Nederlands-Aziatisch handelsverkeer." *Bijdragen en mededelingen betreffende de geschiedenis der Nederlanden* 91 (1976) 2, pp. 196-217.
Schöffer, I. "The Import of Bullion and Coin," to be published in: Aymard, M. et J. Revel (eds.), *Capitalisme hollandais et capitalisme mondial.*

Survey is being prepared by Schutte and Stevens)[38] I may confine myself to the mentioning of some accomplishments and flaws of Dutch historiography, seen in a comparative context.

The first striking feature, then, is a rapid growth in the number of researchers in this field. Although statistical data is lacking, it is nevertheless clear that this is a fairly recent phenomenon, dating roughly, we might suggest, from the beginning of the 'seventies and the causes of which I have already dealt with. A superficial glance at the lists of researchers published in our *Newsletters* shows that these are mainly young historians. From this it appears that a change of guard has taken place, and that a new generation, often with new interests and insights, is making itself heard. Thus the number of researchers is fairly large, probably about a hundred, more or less spread out all over the Netherlands, although tending towards concentration in Utrecht, Amsterdam and Leiden. There is, however, a great quantitative discrepancy between ongoing research on the one hand, and publications on the other. To put it in a different way, due to this change of generation, historical production is still rather limited when set against the number of researchers. Let us hope that, when the balance is drawn up next time, say in ten years, this discrepancy will have been overcome. For the time being, it is easier to discern what is missing than what exists. The gaps are more conspicuous than the accomplishments.

Still, to begin with these last, I have already mentioned several important works: source publications, monographs, larger research projects and smaller articles. Thematically, chronologically as well as geographically, it is possible to distinguish the main directions: thematically, economic and mercantile history; chronologically, the seventeenth and twentieth centuries; and geographically, Indonesia. It is, of course, natural that historiography in the Netherlands should be concentrated on Indonesia. The Dutch presence there has, after all, been longer and more influential than elsewhere, while the archival material is accordingly more plentiful. For the history of

[38] Coolhaas, W.Ph. *A Critical Survey of Studies on Dutch Colonial History* ('s-Gravenhage 1960) (Koninklijk Instituut voor Taal-, Land- en Volkenkunde, Bibliographical series, 4).
To cover current research in all parts of the world on the colonial history of Indonesia the best aid to research is a bi-annual documentation journal of the K.I.T.L.V., *Excerpta Indonesica* (1970–). The Leiden Centre for the History of European Expansion attempts to cover the whole field of Dutch expansion. See *Newsletter* Vol. 2 no. 1 and no. 3 (continuing under the name of *Itinerario*).

the Caribbean it is striking that the weightier studies on both Surinam and Curaçao have been written not by historians but by sociologists: Van Lier and Hoetink.[39] Research in economic history, and into the history of the West-Indies, is almost totally lacking, although plans are being made in this direction.[40] Important Dutch contributions, however, have been made in the last few years to the history of the Atlantic slave-trade, that unglorious link between American and West-African history.[41]

With regard to African history, the Dutch contribution is very limited. Some publications by individual researchers might be mentioned,[42] but there is no question of any systematic or continuous research. The almost total disappearance of interest in the history of Southern Africa, and the rather abrupt breaking off of the relations with South African historians are a conspicuous fact, but not one difficult to explain.

With respect to the study of Dutch expansion in Asia, the emphases lie, chronologically, mainly on its beginning and end, that is to say the 17th and 20th centuries. Thematically, in the first period, most interest centres on mercantile history, and in the second on

[39] Hoetink, H. *Het patroon van de oude Curaçaose samenleving; een sociologische studie* (Assen 1958. 2nd ed. Oranjestad-Tiel 1966).
Hoetink, H. *De gespleten samenleving in het Caribische gebied; bijdragen tot de sociologie der rasrelaties in gesegmenteerde maatschappijen* (Assen 1962). See the abridged translation: *The Two Variants in Caribbean Race Relations; a Contribution to the Sociology of Segmented Societies* (London 1967).
Lier, R.A.J. van. *Samenleving in een grensgebied; een sociaal-historische studie van de maatschappij in Suriname* ('s-Gravenhage 1949. 2nd ed. Deventer 1971). Transl. ed.: *Frontier Society; a Social Analysis of the History of Surinam* (The Hague 1971) (Koninklijk Instituut voor Taal-, Land- en Volkenkunde, Translation series, 14).

[40] Mention must be made of a very recent contribution by Soest, J. van, *Olie als water; de Curaçaose economie in de eerste helft van de twintigste eeuw* (Curaçao 1976). He applies a quantitative approach to the economy of Curaçao c. 1900- c. 1950.

[41] Emmer, P.C. *Engeland, Nederland en de slavenhandel in de negentiende eeuw* (Leiden 1974).
Dantzig, A. van. *Het Nederlandse aandeel in de slavenhandel* (Bussum 1968) (Fibulareeks, 27).

[42] For some rare, but valuable Dutch studies on Africa outside the well-defined boundaries of Dutch expansion see for example Schipper, J. *Koloniale opinies over Kongo; een onderzoek naar enkele opvattingen van de koloniale samenleving in Belgisch Kongo over Kongo, zijn ontwikkeling en zijn inwoners (1940-1960)* (Leiden 1970) and Laan, H.L. van der. *The Lebanese Traders in Sierra Leone* (The Hague 1975).

socio-economic and political history. Geographically, in the first period, most emphasis has been laid on East and South-east Asia, and in the second on Indonesia, particularly Java. Most striking from an international perspective is the scantiness of literature about the 19th century, and especially about what might be called "Dutch Imperialism".[43] Of course, in the general literature some attention is paid to it, but these books are either out of date, such as the studies by De Graaf and Vlekke[44] – however remarkable they may be – or they have an exclusive orientation towards economic history, for example the studies by Boeke and Burger.[45] Baudet and Brugmans have edited an impressive volume of articles on the twentieth century, but this is more important as a source than as a treatment of the issue.[46] Fairly recently, Mr. Fasseur and Mr. Van 't Veer have provided us with important books treating two of the highlights, or nightmares, of our 19th century colonial past, viz., the Cultivation System and the Atjeh War.[47] Still, the number of missing studies is far more conspicuous. This is true of Dutch-centered as well as of Indonesia-centered historical research, especially in so far as regional case studies are concerned. A comparison with international literature points to the lack of studies on the Colonial Office, colonial civil servants (training, motives

[43] See, however, a special issue of *Bijdragen en mededelingen betreffende de geschiedenis der Nederlanden,* 86 (1971) with nine contributions dealing with Dutch expansion in Indonesia in the age of modern imperialism.

[44] Vlekke, B.M.H. *Nusantara; a History of the East Indian Archipelago* (3rd pr. Cambridge, Mass. 1945. Orig. ed. 1943).
Vlekke, B.M.H. *Nusantara; a History of Indonesia* (wholly rev. ed. The Hague-Bandung 1959).
Graaf, H.J. de *Geschiedenis van Indonesië* ('s-Gravenhage-Bandung 1949).

[45] Boeke, J.H. *Indische economie;* boek 1-2 (Haarlem 1940).
Boeke, J.H. *Economics and Economic Policy of Dual Societies as Exemplified by Indonesia* (Haarlem 1953).
Indonesian Economics; the Concept of Dualism in Theory and Policy, by J.H. Boeke, G. Gonggrijp, J. van Gelderen a.o. (The Hague 1961) (Selected studies on Indonesia by Dutch scholars, 6).
Burger, D.H. *Sociologisch-economische geschiedenis van Indonesia;* met een historiografische introductie door J.S. Wigboldus (2 vols. Wageningen 1975).

[46] *Balans van beleid; terugblik op de laatste halve eeuw van Nederlandsch-Indië;* met medew. van A.P.A.A. Bernard, H.J. Friedericy e.a. Uitgeg. door H. Baudet en I.J. Brugmans (Assen 1961).

[47] Veer, P. van 't. *De Atjeh-oorlog* (Amsterdam 1969); Fasseur, C., *Kultuurstelsel en koloniale baten; de Nederlandse exploitatie van Java 1840-1860* (Leiden 1975).

etc.), the role of missionary activities,[48] the colonial army and the colonial wars, colonial lobbies, the imperialist ideology, public opinion, the history of geography and anthropology,[49] social Darwinism, education[50] and so on, although in the field of cultural history the important work of Mr. Nieuwenhuys should be mentioned.[51] In comparison with foreign research (for example about Africa) there is a striking absence of detailed regional historical studies aimed at demographical change, social and economic development, the influence of trading links, administration and education, social stratification and mobility, the role of Indonesians in Dutch administrative bodies, protest movements, the position of the Chinese, etcetera.

The problem is somewhat different with regard to the more specific question of Dutch imperialism. Years ago already, Dr. Tichelman, who has recently published a social-historical study about Indonesia with a broad orientation, in every sense,[52] rightly maintained that the book about Dutch imperialism had yet to be written.[53] This still holds true, in spite of a number of relevant articles published in the mean-time.[54] It might even be questioned whether a Dutch imperialism has existed at all. The position of the Netherlands is paradoxical, in so far as it has been both the most imperialistic nation, in the sense of economic exploitation and *mise*

[48] See, however, a number of studies on missiological aspects: Jongeling, M.C. *Het zendingsconsulaat in Nederlands-Indië 1906-1942* (Arnhem 1968).
Koetsier, C.H. *Zending als dienst aan de samenleving; over de houding van zending en kerk ten opzichte van sociaal-economische vraagstukken in Indonesië in het bijzonder op Midden-Java* (Delft 1975).
Kamma, F.C. "*Dit wonderlijke werk*"; *het probleem van de communicatie tussen oost en west gebaseerd op de ervaringen in het zendingswerk op Nieuw Guinea (Irian Jaya) 1855-1972; een socio-missiologische benadering.* (Oegstgeest 1976).

[49] Ellen, R.F. "The Development of Anthropology and Colonial Policy in the Netherlands: 1800-1960," *Journal of the History of the Behavioral Sciences,* 12 (1976) 4, pp. 303-324.

[50] See, however, Kroeskamp, H. *Early Schoolmasters in a Developing Country; a History of Experiments in School Education in 19th century Indonesia* (Assen 1974).

[51] Nieuwenhuys, R. *Oost-Indische spiegel; wat Nederlandse schrijvers en dichters over Indonesië hebben geschreven vanaf de eerste jaren der Compagnie tot op heden* (Amsterdam 1973).

[52] Tichelman, F. *Stagnatie en beweging; sociaal-historische beschouwingen over Java en Indonesië in Aziatisch verband* (Amsterdam 1975).

[53] Tichelman, F. "Het Nederlandse imperialisme." *NRC-Handelsblad,* 9-7-1975.

[54] See note 43.

en valeur, and the least imperialistic, because it did not follow a policy of formal expansion, and even abandoned its last possessions in Africa shortly before the final partition of that continent. Consequently, the history of Dutch imperialism would be difficult to incorporate into the general discussion about European imperialism, which is strongly dominated by the problems surrounding the partition of Africa and by international rivalries, or, to put it more generally, the problems of international relations. Rather, for an analysis of Dutch imperialism, we will have to make use of concepts such as "informal" or "peripheral" imperialism, or of Marxist concepts, although from what we have seen of this last approach, expectations should not be too high.

But let me finish in a more optimistic way. If interest in the history of European expansion does indeed continue to increase, which we can only hope for, and if Dutch historians remain true to their traditional pre-occupations, while at the same time receiving fresh inspiration through internationally discussed hypotheses, we can be confident about the future. Developments in the 'seventies and 'eighties may, in that case, lead to the result that the contribution of Dutch historians to the historiography of expansion will assume the important place one would have expected it to occupy, in view of the abundant material at their disposal.

8. THE HISTORY OF EUROPEAN EXPANSION: A REVIEW ON GERMAN-LANGUAGE WRITING SINCE WORLD WAR II

by

HELMUT BLEY

A report on German-language writing on a theme as general as the history of European expansion cannot produce a very unified picture. It is not simply a matter of a wide range of questions, but also of countries that differ in their political outlooks and in their organisation of research. Historiographies may represent the conservative-liberal traditions of Switzerland, the Marxist-Leninist approaches of the German Democratic Republic (GDR), or the very confusing situation in West Germany in which conflicting lines of thought have derived from mutually antagonistic bodies of assumption. Austria's contribution seems to be so marginal with respect to our theme that it can be kept in the background. In order to show the development of particular tendencies, it will be necessary to risk over-simplification and over-categorization. This report must therefore be selective and will not provide a completely annotated bibliography of the subject. In particular, the flood of individual monographs dealing with overseas history had necessarily to be omitted if they focussed on the overseas regions themselves, in spite of the fact that they discuss important aspects of European expansion. Our main concern will be to deal as adequately as possible with the "European side" of the expansion process.

My first duty is to explain why, after 1945, no wide-ranging specialized research on the European aspects of the European expansion developed in West Germany, and why GDR-historiography, after its fresh and successful start in the field of German colonial history in the 1950's, somehow became derailed by political developments. The first point devolves upon a story of self-imposed isolation. It developed out of a paradox. Since WW II the desire to reintegrate the future Federal Republic of Germany into Western Europe, after the barbarism of Nazism, became a powerful intellectual force, leading to the reassessment of the "European heritage," the "values" derived from Europe's particular character, and the reinvented mythology of the *Abendland.* So long as world history was in question – and this was indeed the very issue that emerged in the forefront of discussion after two World Wars – the contribution of Europe to *Universalgeschichte* was significant. By implication this approach produced a strong tendency toward generalization. It integrated philosophical and religious interests by focussing on the meaning of human existence. In the context of history it meant a broad debate on historical anthropology and cultural history. Tendencies and consequences of this approach will be discussed first. Although I am aware that this approach was not confined to regions in which the German language was spoken – names like Arnold Toynbee and Teilhard de Chardin indicate this – I shall concentrate on the German/Swiss context. My procedure will be to look at the *Saeculum*-group which concentrated itself around the periodical *Saeculum,* founded in 1950.

The second point to be discussed is that, in spite of the rather small number of persons involved, there developed an important and continuous tradition of writing on comparative colonial history. This tradition obtained its main stimulus from the powerful German historiographic tradition in analyzing the thoughts of politicians, political thinkers and administrators. The links between this research and our theme stem from the close relationship between the study of political thought and the history of the modern state and its foreign relations. An example of this tradition can be found in the 17 volumes, so far produced, of the *Beiträge zur Kolonial- und Überseegeschichte,* edited by Rudolf von Albertini (Zürich) and Heinz Gollwitzer (Münster), including the major books of these two scholars.

A third major field of attention which distinguished German work in both the GDR and West Germany from that of Western Europe, is connected with German history itself – which by dint of having made Europe its victim, became in turn Europe's own history: the history of European expansion is also that of an expansion within Europe. In this context it could be argued that it is rather artificial to distinguish a boundary between overseas and intra-continental expansion, one that merely reflects the special experience of Western Europe in contrast to that of Central and Eastern Europe. This aspect could be discussed in the formative context of early modern times – say, in that of the German, Polish and Scandinavian debates on Baltic rivalry, and its connections with the growing Atlantic system, or it could be looked at in the frame-work of Immanuel Wallerstein's concept of a modern world system, which tries to integrate the European and overseas aspects of expansion.

However, I intend to concentrate on the results of the controversial German-language debate on the role of Germany in the classic period of imperialism prior to 1914, in which both elements, expansion of Europe and expansion in Europe have become inseparable issues. German research in this field has looked with particular interest at connections between internal developments and the directions and cumulative effects of expansion; it has also been concerned with expansionist thinking. In so far as general interest in the theories of imperialism is concerned, this German debate did not take the route of the Gallagher-Robinson approach to the origins of overseas expansion in the 19th century, that is to say that of their influential concept of formal and informal empire. The German debate in East and West was far more concerned with what its practitioners called the structural crisis of the *Kaiserreich,* with the far-reaching influences of this crisis upon expansionist thinking, foreign and colonial policy, and with the increased readiness to regard a European war as inevitable (even if it were unnecessary).

A fourth major field – more theoretical than concerned with actual detailed research, and relating to the general history of European expansion – was developed by political scientists and political economists when reviving the debate on the laws regulating the creation and stages of the world market. This of course is closely connected with the neo-marxist and GDR interest in periodization, and in the stages of the various modes of production. Its timing was related to the beginnings of the debate on "neo-colonialism" and underdevelopment. I will try to interpret this discussion (which obviously has its forerunners and counterparts on the international scene) in terms of the GDR-debate in the *Jahrbuch für Wirtschaftsgeschichte,* and the West German and West Berlin debate sparked off by the so called "capital logic group". I am aware that, in most of the relevant publications, historical data are but scantily used, since what was at issue was a reinterpretation of history itself. Genuine historical research, in a conceptual frame, has not yet been attempted. Yet, it is a challenge to the discipline as a whole, that the main sources from which the impulse to generalize and interpret history are derived, are located outside the history departments. This is due both to the lack of initiative and to the reluctance to synthesize so characteristic of professional historians. It will not be possible here, even by means of a short appraisal, to discuss that growing production of works by social scientists in general, and historians in particular, consisting largely of regional studies of African, Latin American and Asian countries. In so far as these studies include historical aspects, they indirectly contribute to the history of expansion. Methodologically they are usually linked with the relevant internationally-oriented schools of area-studies. The setting up of collaborative teams and research centres has resulted from a practical interest in development aid and from their function as advisers to government agencies; only very exceptionally they have developed in conjunction with university institutes. Because of these practical connections, historians are seldom at the centre of activities with the exceptions of those involved in Latin American studies.

I. GERMAN *UNIVERSALGESCHICHTE*;[1] A ROAD TO ISOLATION

Traditions of descriptive historiography were revived immediately after WW II when Egmont Zechlin, in cooperation with Eberhard Vietsch, wrote the first volume of a *Maritime Weltgeschichte* (1947).[2] So far as the 15th and 16th centuries were concerned he based himself on his earlier paper published in the *Neue Propyläen Weltgeschichte* (1941),[3] and gave a colourful picture of international rivalry without an Eurocentric bias. If one looks at the fascinating chapter on economic and military rivalry in the Indian Ocean, it can be seen that he had synthesized all of the knowledge available, at that time, not only that concerning European political and commercial powers, but also those of Asia. But in a sense the book remained an isolated event; volume II was never completed, and it did not have the impact upon German research on early European expansion that one would have expected. The same happened to Percy Ernst Schramm's book on the foreign trade traditions of the German seaports (1950). Although *Deutschland und Übersee* is a very early example of research in "free-trade imperialism," it lacked an appropriate conceptual framework.[4]

During the early fifties, the period of reconstruction, German intellectual interest took a different route. It tried to bring an interest in philosophical anthropology into relationship with theories of world history, reflecting a desire to reestablish humanitarian ideas in post-fascist Germany. Within this framework the concept of *Universalgeschichte* became far more ambitious than had been the case in descriptive approaches to World History.

[1] A good introduction by Ernst Schulin in the reader: Ernst Schulin, *Universalgeschichte*, Neue Wissenschaftliche Bibliothek (Köln 1974). Einleitung, pp. 11-67.

[2] Egmont Zechlin, *Maritime Weltgeschichte* (Hamburg 1947).

[3] Egmont Zechlin, *Die grossen Entdeckungen und ihre Vorgeschichte*, Die Neue Propyläen-Weltgeschichte, Vol. 3 (Berlin 1941).

[4] Percy Ernst Schramm, *Deutschland und Übersee* (Hamburg 1950).

The newly founded periodical *Saeculum* (1950), which offered a platform to historians of ancient and medieval Europe and to those concerned with the ancient civilizations of Asia, typified this development. The key question concerned the development of world history, and, further, as aspects of the former, the relationship between the cultural and religious heritage of the old Asian and Latin American cultures on the one hand and the unifying force of European expansion on the other. The grounds for this type of very general interest in *Universalgeschichte* had been prepared by Karl Jaspers in his *Vom Ursprung und Ziel der Geschichte* (1949),[5] which divided history into periods based on criteria derived from changes in the basic structure of human thinking. A similar set of concerns produced Freyer's *Weltgeschichte Europas* (1948),[6] which connected traditions of sociology practices in the Weimar Republic with conservative theories current in West German post-war scholarship. The *Saeculum*-group[7] – with Stadtmüller, Köhler, Franke, Spuler and others – bringing together historians, sinologists and islamicists – was concerned mainly with the intellectual consequences and impact upon mankind of European expansion, but only, however, with that part of mankind represented by the ancient high cultures. The group demanded a regional focus that would avoid creating histories that were merely prehistories of European conquest. In fact, they had become so radical that the European impact was lost to sight. Thus, for example Oskar Köhler saw even 20th century world-history, not as a global, integrated development, but basically as a system of regional developments which were "only connected through modern technology." He stated that although intercultural change might be very important, the real impulses for the developments relevant for world history came out of the internal conditions of those "regional worlds."

The effect of this thinking was that the research tended to center on the intellectual developments in the different regional "worlds." In reconstructing the rich internal structures of the high civilizations European intellectual history was combined with traditions of orientalist studies. This type of thinking maintained its momentum throughout the sixties and was expressed in the main textbooks, such as in Valjavec's *Historia Mundi* (in 1960 renamed *Weltgeschichte*

[5] Karl Jaspers, *Vom Ursprung und Ziel der Geschichte* (1949).

[6] Hans Freyer, *Weltgeschichte Europas* (2 Vols.; 1948).

[7] *Saeculum, Jahrbuch für Universalgeschichte* (Freiburg/München, I, 1950) established by Georg Stadtmüller, editor (1976) Oskar Köhler.

der Gegenwart).[8] It also characterizes the *Saeculum Weltgeschichte* with its Volume VII published as late as 1975.[9] Traditionally, in the study of cultural history, each decade brought a number of new attacks on the ideological battlefield against what was vaguely called "left thinking" and "left approaches," – whatever might have been meant by such interpretations. These attacks served very strong and direct ideological purposes. For instance in the *Weltgeschichte der Gegenwart* (1962) one of the main spokesmen of the "Ordo-liberal" school (which favoured a free enterprise society), Wilhelm Röpke, argued that on the basis of its fundamentally moral intellectual force, Europe had been able to produce the One World Civilization.[10] Whether envied, hated, or admired, the spirit of Europe could not be transplanted; unfortunately the European success-story overseas to date had merely consisted of a transfer of material civilization. The final victory would be won by a future transplantation of its eternal values. Röpke ended with the classical sentence: "This is the new white mans burden, in a very humble way, but directed towards the most ambitious and difficult aim of all." The strengthening of this thinking in the seventies, bearing many marks of the German tradition of *Kulturkritik* can be strongly associated with the development of a counter-offensive to the onslaughts against traditional historiography formulated during the period of student rebellion, and to the lead developed by neo-marxist influenced thought occuring within the same context.

The *Saeculum*-group, for instance, between 1971 and 1976, reinforced their debate on cultural history with a sceptical revival of conservative thinking. Köhler drafted a *Historische Anthropologie* (1974) and was able to summarize the essence of European history in a sentence like: "There were two experiences, which perhaps could be called the basic elements forming the *abendländische – europäische Geschichte,* and which have either emerged into full

[8] Historia Mundi, Ein Handbuch der Weltgeschichte in 10 Vols. Vol. 8, *Die überseeische Welt und ihre Erschliessung* (Bern/München 1959). Established by Fritz Kern, ed. by Fritz Valjavec. German language authors: Hermann Trimborn, Rüdiger Schott, Richard Konetzke.

[9] *Saeculum Weltgeschichte* in 7 Vols. (Freiburg/Basel/Wien 1965-1975) ed. by Herbert Franke, Helmut Hoffmann, Hubert Jedin, Oskar Köhler, Peter Meinhold, Gerd Tellenbach, Hermann Trimborn and Joseph Vogt. Vol. 7, Werdende Einheit und wachsende Widersprüchlichkeit der politischen Welt – Die Weltrelingionen – Selbst – und Weltverständnis nach der Revolution – Geschichte in der Gegenwart, by Heinrich Dumoulin, Oskar Köhler, Peter Meinhold, Berthold Spuler and Rolf Trauzettel.

[10] Fritz Valjavec, *Weltgeschichte der Gegenwart* (1962).

consciousness or been retained at the level of the unconscious memory: the decline of the Roman Empire and the delayed readvent of Christ. Even though the content of these experiences might have been transformed into new forms, the basic impetus originally behind them maintained momentum." (*Saeculum Weltgeschichte* VII, S 502).[11] Köhler, in these obscure words, tried to reinforce the idea that behind modern expansionism was the old ideology of the one Empire, and further that chiliastic desires remained the moving forces behind, for instance, the Marxist theory of society. Köhler attempts to understand world history as the *Weg der Menschheit zu sich selbst.* As a consequence of his kind of thinking he minimized, to an extreme degree, the role of economic and political factors in historical development, in contrast to the role of the cultural and religious spheres. He was thus enabled to formulate: "The 'first' (Western) and the 'second' (Socialist states) worlds are essentially aggregations of economic-technical, military and political organisation. . . . Those worlds (despite all claims of being historical units *im Innersten*) are not, therefore, integrated except in terms of those technical elements." (*Saeculum Weltgeschichte* VII, 186). This type of approach has obvious consequences for researchers concerned to communicate with those involved in other branches of history, not to speak of colleagues working in the more systematic social sciences. A tendency towards "global" reflection had developed which failed to lead towards new fields of enquiry. It necessarily avoided an analysis of social, economic and political phenomena. It explained expansion as a mere technical process resulting from European rationality. It could not encourage an interest in comparative studies because it imputed that "cultures" had to be regarded as unique entities in their own right. Another consequence of this reduction of history to cultural and religious aspects is the apologetic tendency with regard to the impact of the European expansion on the rest of the world.[12]

[11] Oskar Köhler, Versuch einer "Historischen Anthropologie." *Saeculum,* 25 (1974) pp. 129-246.

[12] However, it has to be observed that a counter tendency away from isolation developed at the level of textbooks through the wide participation of international scholars. A good example is the "Fischer Weltgeschichte" a paperback series, published from 1965 on and edited by Jean Bollack (Paris). 34 volumes are planned. It mainly represents French and Italian social and economic historians. Vol. 22 is by Richard Konetzke: *Süd und Mittel-Amerika* I (1965).

II. *BEITRÄGE ZUR KOLONIAL- UND ÜBERSEEGESCHICHTE*[13]

However, despite the isolationist tendencies of the *Universalgeschichte*, which were supported by similar developments within oriental studies, certain other traditions of overseas history survived. In the early sixties Albertini and Gollwitzer started from a different position to that of the *Saeculum*-group. Both were closely concerned with the general history of the modern European state, and maintained a strong interest in the history of political ideas connected with the process of state-formation. Gollwitzer, especially, extended this traditional interest by integrating the methods of social history into his research, no longer restricting the history of political and social ideas to the small body of leading thinkers and politicians. In a sense it was a parallel development to Conze's group, whose work in social history bypassed the much narrower concepts of Meinecke and Ritter. Typical products of this approach were Albertini's and Gollwitzer's most important books. Albertini's book on *Dekolonisation* (1966) was a comparative analysis of European official colonial thinking since 1919.[14] This analysis was completed by his history of European colonial policy (1976) co-authored with Wirz.[15] Gollwitzer wrote a history on the concept of the "yellow peril";[16] in 1972 he published the first volume of *Geschichte des weltpolitischen Denken* and is now writing the second volume.[17] Both approaches offered opportunities for specialised research. So the *Beiträge zur Kolonial- und Überseegeschichte* are dominated by books about theories concerning the colonial policy held by politicians and administrators, as well as by books on broader intellectual ideas. The history of French colonialism in North-Africa and in South East Asia have been subjected to particular attention.[18] The same tendency can be

[13] Beiträge zur Kolonial- und Überseegeschichte, ed. by Rudolf von Albertini and Heinz Gollwitzer, publ. at Westdeutscher Verlag Köln, now at Atlantis, Zürich/Freiburg. For a complete list see in Rudolf von Albertini, *Europäische Kolonialherrschaft*, Vol. 14 (1976) – Vol. I was von Albertini's *Dekolonisation* (1966).

[14] Rudolf von Albertini, *Dekolonisation, Die Diskussion über Verwaltung und Zukunft der Kolonien 1919-1960* (Köln 1966).

[15] Rudolf von Albertini, in cooperation with Albert Wirz, *Europäische Kolonialherrschaft 1880-1940*, Beiträge zur Kolonial- und Überseegeschichte, 14 (1976).

[16] Heinz Gollwitzer, *Die Gelbe Gefahr, Geschichte eines Schlagwortes, Studien zum imperialistischen Denken* (Göttingen 1962).

[17] Heinz Gollwitzer, *Geschichte des weltpolitischen Denkens. 1, Vom Zeitalter der Entdeckungen bis zum Beginn des Imperialismus* (Göttingen 1972).

[18] See Beiträge, Vols. 2, 4, 7, 8.

observed in the work of scholars possessing no special connections with the group. A typical title in this context is E. Schulin, *Handelsstaat England.*[19] Schulin's introduction to a reader about *Universalgeschichte,* included a good summary of German traditions of this kind of history. G. Hamann's *The Discovery of the Southern Hemisphere* (1965) was the main Austrian contribution, dealing with the history of geographical knowledge since the 15th century.[20] Also influenced by Gollwitzer was a dissertation on the London World Exhibition of 1851 (U. Haltern 1971).[21]

A rather independent but strong special line of overseas historiography is provided by Latin American and Iberian studies, which grew out of studies on the Habsburg empire. In terms of methodology, the books and articles of Konetzke,[22] Kellenbenz,[23] Klaveren,[24] Wolff[25] are closely connected with concepts of social history developed by German medievalists. They are partly influenced by Otto Brunner, and deal with economic history. But in fact it is Konetzke who dominates German production of text books on world history, especially in so far as Latin American history is concerned.

III. HISTORY OF GERMAN IMPERIALISM

The main stimuli leading to research on expansion, both in West Germany and in the GDR, developed out of reinterpretations of the history of the *Kaiserreich,* out of investigations into the reasons for German expansionism, and out of the analysis of the origins of World War I. Because it related social and economic factors underlying the belated processes of industrialization and state-formation, to ideas and policies concerning expansion (overseas and in Europe) on the one hand, and to internal tensions within the *Kaiserreich* on

[19] Ernst Schulin, *Handelsstaat England* (Wiesbaden 1969).

[20] Günther Hamann, *Der Eintritt der südlichen Hemisphäre in die Europäische Geschichte* (Wien 1968).

[21] Uwe Haltern, *Die Londoner Weltausstellung 1851,* Diss. phil. (Münster 1971).

[22] Many publications, i.a. Richard Konetzke, *Süd- und Mittelamerika I, Die Indianerkulturen Altamerikas und die spanisch-portugiesische Kolonialherrschaft,* Fischer Weltgeschichte, 22 (1965).

[23] Hermann Kellenbenz, his early study: *Unternehmerkräfte im Hamburger Portugal-und Spanienhandel, 1590-1625* (Hamburg 1954).

[24] Jacob van Klaveren, *Europäische Wirtschaftsgeschichte Spaniens im 16. und 17. Jahrhundert* (1960).

[25] Inge Wolff, *Regierung und Verwaltung der kolonial-spanischen Städte in Hochperu 1538-1650* (Köln/Wien 1970).

the other, there developed – especially in West Germany – a broad variety of approaches, in so far as methodology and interpretation were concerned, and this had a profound influence on historical and political debate. The history of German imperialism of that period thus became the most important German contribution to the issue of expansion. The reasons for such a concentration of attention upon the phase of German imperialism that occured prior to 1918, were fourfold.

1. An initial analysis of the origins of Nazi-Germany suggested continuity with the *Kaiserreich.*

2. Scholars of GDR universities systematically applied Lenin's theory of imperialism to the German situation and rewrote the history of the *Kaiserreich,* combining it with a permanent and effective attack on West German historiographic traditions.

3. Connected with both of the above developments, two myths, current in West Germany, – characterizing the national-liberal historiography of the Weimar Republic – were destined for destruction. Firstly, that after World War I the allied powers had used their declaration of German war-guilt to justify reparations. Secondly, that they had justified the annexation of German colonies, by the mandate-system, by alleging cruel mismanagement. German historians had thus specialised in attacking what they called the *Kriegsschuldlüge* and the *koloniale Schuldlüge,* and apologetic tendencies of course prevailed.

4. The timing of new departures in historical writing was influenced by the fact that around 1956 the relevant files of German government departments were returned to Potsdam, Merseburg, Bonn and Koblenz from Moscow, London and Washington. New sources could thus be tapped.

Colonial history had its beginning in the research group of Walter Markov in Leipzig. From 1959 books were produced that concentrated on the first period of German colonial expansion (i.e. that preceding the beginning of the "monopoly" stage, which Lenin had dated around 1900); – on the movement of colonization (Nussbaum)[26] in East Africa (Müller[27] and Büttner[28]), in Kamerun

[26] Manfred Nussbaum, *Vom "Kolonialenthusiasmus" zur Kolonialpolitik der Monopole. Zur deutschen Kolonialpolitik unter Bismarck, Caprivi, Hohenlohe* (Berlin 1962). Studien zur Kolonialgeschichte und Geschichte der nationalen und kolonialen Befreiungsbewegung, ed. by Walter Markov, Vol. 8.

[27] Fritz Ferdinand Müller, *Deutschland-Zanzibar-Ostafrika, Geschichte einer deutschen Kolonialeroberung 1884-1890* (Berlin 1959).

[28] Kurt Büttner, *Die Anfänge der deutschen Kolonialpolitik in Ostafrika* (Berlin 1959) Markov Studien, 1.

and China (Stöcker)[29] in South-West-Africa (Drechsler),[30] on missions (Loth).[31] Their theoretical concern was mainly one of ordering the periodization of colonial history according to types of economic organization; at the same time they stressed the importance of African resistance. Attacks on the myth of "good German colonial goverment" – still much alive – frequently took the form of open agitation. Because almost all of the writers either had become involved in the academic side of the development of GDR politics towards the Third world, or were reoriented towards the more theoretical aspects of imperialism, this group disintegrated, putting aside the study of colonial history and of an African history possessing its own regional perspective. Thus, no important new historical tradition could be constructed. It can be justly stated that in terms of African studies the anthropologists took the place of the historians (e.g. Walter Rusch[32] and Thea Büttner[33]).

West German production started a few years later, but more along the line of individual enterprise. Parts of it were often delayed by difficulties in gaining access to GDR archives. The works of Bley[34] on South West Africa, Hausen,[35] Diehn [36] and Wirz[37] on

[29] Helmuth Stöcker, *Deutschland und China im 19. Jahrhundert, Das Eindringen des deutschen Kapitalismus* (Berlin 1958).
Helmut Stöcker (editor), *Kamerun unter deutscher Kolonialherrschaft* (2 vols. Berlin 1960 and 1968).

[30] Horst Drechsler, *Südwestafrika unter deutschen Kolonialherrschaft* (Berlin 1966).

[31] Heinrich Loth, *Die christliche Mission in Südwestafrika, Zur destruktiven Rolle der Rheinischen Missionsgesellschaft beim Prozess der Staatsbildung in Südwestafrika (1842-1893),* (Berlin 1963), Markov Studien, 9.

[32] Walter Rusch, *Klassen und Staat in Buganda vor der Kolonialzeit* (Berlin 1975).

[33] Thea Büttner, see her article "Das präkoloniale Afrika und die Diskussion zur asiatischen Produktionsweise," *Jahrbuch für Wirtschaftsgeschichte* (1967), which gives further examples of her work.

[34] Helmut Bley, *Kolonialherrschaft und Sozialstruktur in Deutsch-Südwestafrika 1894-1914* (Hamburg 1968); English edition: *South-West Africa under German Rule* (London 1971).

[35] Karin Hausen, *Deutsche Kolonialherrschaft in Afrika, Wirtschaftsinteressen und Kolonialverwaltung in Kamerun vor 1914* (1970), Beiträge zur Kolonial- und Überseegeschichte, 6.

[36] Otto Diehn, *Kaufmannschaft und deutsche Eingeborenenpolitik in Togo und Kamerun von der Jahrhundertwende bis zum Ausbruch des Weltkrieges,* Diss. phil. (Hamburg 1956), unpubl.

[37] Albert Wirz, *Vom Sklavenhandel zum kolonialen Handel, Wirtschaftsräume und Wirtschaftsformen in Kamerun vor 1914* (1974), Beiträge zur Kolonial- und Überseegeschichte, 10.

Cameroon, Tetzlaff[38] and Bald[39] on East Africa were products of the few West German islands of overseas studies: Bley in the Overseas Section of Zechlin, in the History Department at Hamburg; Hausen at Münster (Gollwitzer); Wirz at Zürich (Albertini); Tetzlaff in the *Arbeitstelle für Afrika* of Ansprenger at Berlin; Bald possessing contact with the *Afrika-Studienstelle* of the *Ifo-Institut für Wirtschaftforschungen* at Munich, then led by Wilhelm Marquardt and with the *Arnold Bergsträsser Institut* in Freiburg. In spite of the existence of these institutes of overseas studies, West German production was not influenced by them, reflecting in the main the more general streams of historiography. Bley's book on South West Africa tried to combine a social and intellectual history of the *Kaiserreich* (thus of the development of totalitarian politics) with those new concepts of African history which arose in the sixties.

Karin Hausen contributed to the debate on the theoretical interpretation of imperialism, Tetzlaff and Bald to that on economic pressure groups, Wirz to that on the conceptual contents of an economic history of West Africa. A regional bias inevitably crept in; colonial history became the history of Africa, a tendency also affecting the work of British and American scholars like Iliffe[40] and Austen,[41] who had worked in the German archives on similar themes and at the same time as German historians. In so far as its reception within German historiography was concerned, this colonial history was regarded as part and parcel of the ongoing debate on German imperialism, because, in the meantime, the debate on the long and short term origins of World War I had gained momentum. The fierce academic dispute over Fritz Fischer's *Griff nach der Weltmacht* (1961) overshadowed the discussion of expansionism.[42]

Although Fischer's book was essentially concerned with the question of German war-aims and expansionism during World War I (based on the newly available documentation spoken of above), throughout the introduction and the first chapter on the origins of

[38] Rainer Tetzlaff, *Koloniale Entwicklung und Ausbeutung. Wirtschafts- und Sozialgeschichte Deutsch-Ostafrikas 1885-1914* (Berlin 1970).

[39] Detlef Bald, *Deutsch-Ostafrika 1900-1914, eine Studie über Verwaltung, Interessengruppen und wirtschaftliche Erschlieszung* (München 1970). Afrika-Studien IFO-Institut für Wirtschaftsforschung, 54. Bald worked at the Arnold Bergsträsser Institut in Freiburg, which has a strong interest in development studies.

[40] John Iliffe, *Tanganyika under German rule 1905-1912* (Cambridge 1969).

[41] Ralph A. Austen, *Northwest Tanzania under German and British Rule, Colonial policy and tribal politics, 1889-1939* (New Haven 1968).

[42] Fritz Fischer, *Griff nach der Weltmacht. Die Kriegszielpolitik des kaiserlichen Deutschlands 1914/18* (Düsseldorf 1961). 3 revised editions (1963).

the war, he had dealt with the question of German expansionism before the War and that of the problems of continuity within German politics underlying the origins of the Second World War. This initial discussion was greeted simultaneously with both enthusiasm and hostility within the discipline.[43] Fischer was seen as influenced by radical democratic traditions characteristic of the Weimar Republic, and as being closely related to the lines of research established by Eckart Kehr,[44] George Hallgarten[45] and Hans Rosenberg.[46] Fischer's contribution (which was the result of a collaborative project producing a number of dissertations) led to intensified research on the whole *Kaiserreich* epoch, including the period of Bismarck, as well as a central thesis, or chain of argumentation, concerning the origins and directions of German expansionism since 1870.

In this thesis, links were formulated between the Great Depression of 1873-97 on the one hand, and the conservative reorganisation of the *Reich* that had resulted in an expansionist coalition between East Elbian landlords and organised industry on the other. In consequence, internal tensions had so increased that they had a cumulative effect on expansionist tendencies within Europe and abroad. Research concentrated either on the Bismarck period (Rosenberg, Böhme[47] and Wehler[48]) or on the internal and external structural crisis that developed after 1903 (Stegman,[49] Witt,[50] Saul,[51] Berghahn[52]). With regard to the primary aims of expansion,

[43] Several readers on the debate have been published. See bibliography Section III 8.1 in: Hans Ulrich Wehler, *Das Deutsche Kaiserreich 1871-1918* (Göttingen 1975, 2nd edition), p. 265.

[44] His most famous book is: Eckart Kehr, *Schlachtflottenbau und Parteipolitik 1894-1901* (Berlin 1930). A collection of his articles: Eckart Kehr, *Der Primat der Innenpolitik, Gesammelte Aufsätze zur preussisch-deutschen Sozialgeschichte im 19. und 20. Jahrhundert,* ed. by H.U. Wehler (Berlin 1965).

[45] George W.F. Hallgarten, *Imperialismus vor 1914, Die soziologischen Grundlagen der Aussenpolitik europäischer Grossmächte vor dem Ersten Weltkrieg* (2 Vols. München 1963, 2nd edition) (First edition 1935, extensively revised in 1963).

[46] Hans Rosenberg, *Grosse Depression und Bismarckzeit* (Berlin 1967).

[47] Helmut Böhme, *Deutschlands Weg zur Grossmacht, Studien zum Verhältnis von Wirtschaft und Staat während der Reichsgründungszeit 1848-1881* (Köln 1966).

[48] Hans-Ulrich Wehler, *Bismarck und der Imperialismus* (Köln 1969).

[49] Dirk Stegmann, *Die Erben Bismarcks, Parteien und Verbände in der Spätphase des Wilhelminischen Deutschlands* (Köln 1970).

[50] Peter-Christian Witt, *Die Finanzpolitik des Deutschen Reiches von 1903-1913* (Lübeck 1970).

[51] Klaus Saul, *Staat, Industrie, Arbeiterbewegung im Kaiserreich 1903-1914* (Hamburg 1974).

[52] Volker Berghahn, *Der Tirpitz-Plan* (Düsseldorf 1971).

the principal lines of debate have been concerned with the periods during and preceding WW I, and they have centred around the following questions: 1. *Mitteleuropa,* meaning the expansion of Germany, mainly at the expense of Belgium and Poland, but also including parts of France and a special relationship with Austria-Hungary; 2. the concept of *Mittelafrika,* the completion of the half-hearted colonial policy of Bismarck; and 3. direct ambition for annexations which in the later stages of WW I (after the Russian Revolution) included an attempt to partition Russia.

Despite Fischer's second book – *Krieg der Illusionen* (1969)[53] – discussing the developments of internal politics following the Morocco Crisis of 1911 and elaborating further on the argument contained in the most disputed two chapters of his first book, – the debate on the relationship between internal structures and expansionist concepts in so far as the Bismarck period was concerned, was to a greater extent dominated by Wehler's *Bismarck und der Imperialismus.* This was due firstly to the development of the debate on methodology between social sciences and history in general, but especially to the debate on "imperialism." Wehler contributed directly to this debate, focussing once more on the works of Eckart Kehr and Rosenberg; he was much concerned with the concepts of "formal" and "informal" imperialism, formulated by Gallagher and Robinson, whereas Fischer had used a more positivistic approach in order to attack the national-liberal school where it hurt most: by using new documents.

Wehler in a sense was summing up the debate – concentrating on, and perhaps exaggerating, the aspect of social imperialism. Once more, this book was attacked from all sides, even by the GDR-Marxists since they mistrusted a theory of imperialism which lacked a monopoly stage.[54] At all events, an attempt to amalgamate Marxian and Weberian methodologies was not deemed acceptable. On the other hand, those representatives of the German school stressing the importance of foreign policy could not accept a bias that emphasized the priority of internal politics.[55] Finally, those involved in colonial history, especially of the period after 1903, could not accept Wehler's strong emphasis on the connections between the great Depression and formal colonialism, since it

[53] Fritz Fischer, *Der Krieg der Illusionen* (Düsseldorf 1969).

[54] Manfred Nuszbaum, "Ökonomie, Politik und Kolonialpolitik. Bemerkungen zu Hans-Ulrich Wehler, Bismarck und der Imperialismus," *Jahrbuch für Wirtschaftsgeschichte* (1972), 3, p. 215 ff.

[55] Thomas Nipperdey, "Wehlers Kaiserreich. Eine kritische Auseinandersetzung", *Geschichte und Gesellschaft 1* (1975), pp. 539-560.

seemed unable to explain German expansionism in the boom period following 1896.[56] Fischer's two books have been followed by a wide range of critical and supportive works produced in both the GDR and West Germany, and to an even greater extent in the U.S.A. The main topics have been: the organisation of the industrial and expansionist lobby; the field of expansion, especially in the Balkans, in the Near East and in Poland; the finances of the system; and the internal political structure of the *Kaiserreich.* In his textbook *Das Deutsche Kaiserreich 1871-1918* (1973) (2nd edition 1975) Wehler has tried to sum up the debate.[57] Although the distances himself from Fischer's proposition that there was a very determined war-oriented German policy preceding WW I, (and in existence at least as early as the Morocco Crisis of 1911), the debate on both groups of topics can be easily followed by using his annotated bibliography. Wehler's *Kaiserreich* has subsequently provoked a counterattack from West German historians in articles published in various periodicals, including *Geschichte und Gesellschaft,* of which Wehler himself is an editor. These historians deny the predominance of internal politics in foreign policy and expansion; they doubt the validity of the argument postulating a permanent crisis in the *Kaiserreich;* and they deny that there was any special German emphasis on imperialism on the grounds that parallel developments existed in other European states. The weakness of this attack as at present constituted is that it fails to deal directly with the evidence accumulated so far and that it tends to misrepresent the main line of the arguments. In addition, it has not yet led to the production of an adequate alternative body of research. If one compares this very intensive research on the *Kaiserreich* (both that conducted in West Germany and the GDR, and that engaged in by non-German scholars) with the historiography on the period of British liberal imperialism following 1906, and the "late Victorian" debate, it appears that the latter – for all its intensity – has not reached the degree of synthesis of the various factors involved in historical developments, that has been achieved in the German discussion. The contribution of GDR scholars to this debate has been both very important and challenging, and it should not be underestimated, in view of the discussion in West Germany.

[56] Peter-Christian Witt, "Innenpolitik und Imperialismus in der Vorgeschichte des Ersten Weltkrieges" in: *Liberalismus und imperialistischer Staat,* ed. by Karl Holl a.o. (Göttingen 1975), pp. 7-34.

[57] Hans-Ulrich Wehler, *Das Deutsche Kaiserreich 1871-1918* (Göttingen 1973, 2nd edition 1975).

An important early summary of it is that produced by Fritz Klein (et al.) *Deutschland im Ersten Weltkrieg* (3 vols. Berlin 1968/70).[58]

It seems that the debate on expansionism before 1918 has not stimulated research on the interwar-period along similar lines. B.J. Wendt's book: 1938 *Appeasement, wirtschaftliche Rezession und Mitteleuropa* (1966)[59] and Claus Hildebrand's *Vom Reich zum Weltreich, Hitler und die koloniale Frage 1919-1945* (1969)[60] suggest some degree of continuity as shown by the titles. In terms of subsequent research on internal developments and studies of economic pressure-groups, this continuity has been maintained. But, basically, there is virtually no methodological kinship with either Fischer or Wehler, in so far as foreign relations are concerned, and two readers on the topic exemplify this: Manfred Funke[61] (Editor): *Hitler-Deutschland und die Mächte, Materialien zur Aussenpolitik des Dritten Reiches* (1976) and Forndran etc.[62] (Editor): *Innen- und Aussenpolitik unter nationalsozialistischer Bedrohung* (1977). It is rather surprising that discussion of the period between 1918-1945 omits the wider framework of European expansion and the later stages of "imperialism," because the re-organisation of Europe's colonial empires, and of Japan's position in the Pacific etc., were the basic events that prepared the post-War development of what was to become the Third World. But this perception seems to have escaped the attention of West German historians, speaking generally, despite such exceptions as Albertini, whose *Dekolonisation* covered the period between 1919 and 1960, or that of Immanuel Geiss's *Panafrikanismus,* which analysed the continuity of intellectual and political development among the Blacks of the Atlantic World.[63] Of course those who wrote outside the framework of European policy – in effect becoming regionalists,

[58] The GDR production is very important. For an early summary see: Fritz Klein a.o., *Deutschland im 1. Weltkrieg* (1968/70, 3 Vols.).

[59] Bernd-Jürgen Wendt, *1938: Appeasement, wirtschaftliche Rezession und Mitteleuropa* (Frankfurt 1966).

[60] Klaus Hildebrand, *Vom Reich zum Weltreich, Hitler und die koloniale Frage 1919-1945* (München 1969).

[61] Titles concerned with the debate on continuity are: Andreas Hillgruber, *Kontinuität und Diskontinuität in der deutschen Aussenpolitik von Bismarck bis Hitler* (Düsseldorf 1969); Karl Hildebrand, *Deutsche Aussenpolitik 1933-1945* (Stuttgart 1973, 2nd edition). For further titles see notes to Wehler's *Kaiserreich,* Chapter III/9. A reader: Manfred Funk, *Hitler Deutschland und die Mächte, Materialien zur Aussenpolitik des Dritten Reiches* (Düsseldorf 1976).

[62] Ehrhard Forndran a.o., *Innen- und Aussenpolitik unter nationalsozialistischer Bedrohung* (1977).

[63] Immanuel Geiss, *Panafrikanismus* (Düsseldorf 1969).

on India say, (Rothermund),[64] or on Africa (Ansprenger),[65] – reacted differently, but they did so outside the framework of European Expansion.

IV. THE SOCIAL-SCIENCE DEBATE ON THE MODES OF PRODUCTION AND ON THE DEVELOPMENT OF A WORLD MARKET

Of course, the debate on the Third World affected German language writing. But historical aspects entered it only indirectly, and only then because both of the main questions – the development of underdevelopment, and the stages of modes of production – (both of which have, for the most part, been articulated by marxist political economists of widely different backgrounds) – eventually threw up historical questions.

Three developments have contributed to the debate.

1. In the GDR, since the inception of the Markov-group, disputation has developed around the question of the modes of production although it has tended to focus largely on its merely European dimension. However, the beginning of international discussion concerning underdevelopment has spread this interest in periodisation to other regions. Even if the African sections of books written about colonial policies, have tended to perpetrate outdated and undifferentiated clichés on the political economy of precolonial societies, the discussion of the "Asiatic mode of production" has developed a much more sophisticated body of theory. The *Jahrbuch für Wirtschaftsgeschichte* devoted part of a volume to the theme in 1967. In particular the *Vorbemerkungen* of Elisabeth Welskop (Akademie der Wissenschaften, Berlin)[66] and *Zu den Problemen der asiatischen Produktionsweise,* reprinted in West Germany, have created a very stimulating framework, implying a need both for greater nuance, and a departure from the schematic application of the concept of modes of production. Most important, it has called for concrete historical research on the specific circumstances influencing the formation of different modes of production. The consequence of this approach has been a direct shift of attention towards regional studies, e.g. Walter Rusch's *Klassen und Staat in*

[64] Dietmar Rothermund, *Die politische Willensbildung in Indien 1900-1960* (Wiesbaden 1965).

[65] Franz Ansprenger, *Politik in schwarzen Afrika* (1961).

[66] *Jahrbuch für Wirtschaftsgeschichte* (1967) "Zur Problemen der asiatischen Produktionsweise", Elisabeth Charlotte Welskopf, Vorbemerkungen, pp. 165-180. Other authors: E. Varga, G. Lewin, B. Töpfer, T. Büttner.

Buganda vor der Kolonialzeit (East Berlin 1975)[67] which in order to assess the nature of the Buganda state had to reconsider the *Produktionsverhältnisse* in the context of the above mentioned general debate.

2. Another important stream of discussion – which in the initial stage of building a conceptual framework, has led to an attempt to integrate history into the continuing debate on the social sciences – has developed out of the theoretical discussion around the structure of the modern world market, and around theories on foreign trade. Whereas an international debate discovered the theoretical implications of underdevelopment in the fifties, when Prebisch, Singer, Myrdal, Nurkse, Kindleberger and other economists began to dispute the issue, a broad response to these developments only occurred in German-language writing under the stimuli of the recession of 1966/67, of the neomarxist revival, and of the students' movements. Within West German writing, therefore, the first centre for this reassessment became the *Freie Universität* of Berlin.

However, once again, the initial revival of theoretical debate on the structures of the modern world market has come from GDR economists, one of whom, Günther Kohlmey, made an influential and general contribution to it in the form of a discussion on Marx's theories of foreign trade.[68] In his work he has attempted to integrate the theoretical implications deriving from a currently Western dominated world market with the existence of relationships generated by the socialistic system, and in doing so he reformulated the concepts of unequal exchange.

In Berlin and West Germany, political economists – for the most part influenced by the recession of 1966/67 (which encouraged socialist expectations of an imminent crisis of modern capitalism) – have participated intensively in the debate. Closely associated with one another – often in the form of cooperative ventures – Altvater,[69] Neusüss[70] and Blanke;[71] Orbon,[72] Ahlers,[73] Westhof[74] and Busch,[75]

[67] see 32.

[68] Gunther Kohlmey, "Bemerkungen zur Theorie der komparativen Vorteile im Auszenhandel," in: G. Kohlmey, ed. *Aussenwirtschaft und Wachstum, theoretische Probleme des ökonomischen Wachstums im Sozialismus und Kapitalismus,* Vol. 3, Berlin 1968, and other articles. See comments and further bibliographical notes in Wolfgang Bärtschi and Hanns-Dieter Jacobsen, *Kritische Einführung in die Aussenhandelstheorie* (Rowohlt, Reinbek 1976), pp. 54.

[69] Elmar Altvater, *Die Weltwährungskrise* (Frankfurt 1969).

[70] Christel Neusüss, *Imperialismus und Weltmarktbewegung des Kapitals* (Erlangen 1972).

[71] B. Blanke, C. Neusüss, and E. Altvater, "Kapitalistischer Weltmarkt und Weltwährungskrise," in: *Probleme des Klassenkampfes,* 1 (November 1971).

Schöller,[76] Seelow,[77] created in the early seventies a broad approach to questions concerning the structure of the world-market: thus to the monetary system, to the theory of imperialism, and to a reformulation of the nature of the precapitalistic mode of production. This approach was aimed at formulating very general laws on the development of capitalism. In directly attempting to reinterpret Marx's position, they examined the "logic of capital" and the *Bewegungsformen des Kapitals* on the very broadest theoretical basis. It is not the scope of this paper to go into the economic and theoretical aspects of the debate. A good but very critical overview can be read in W. Bärtschi and H.-D. Jacobson, *Kritische Einführung in die Aussenhandelstheorie*[78] who also comment on Kohlmey. But in the course of this debate – which occured both in the GDR and in West Germany and West-Berlin – the special problems surrounding the question of precapitalist modes of production and of the genesis of the world market (which has been reduced by Western neo-Marxists to the theory of the Western world market) have generated a historical dimension.

In the GDR the practical problems of formulating appropriate strategies towards developing countries stimulated the search for adequate categories for "countries developing on the non-capitalist road." A good summary of these discussions, and of GDR contributions to it, can be found in the published papers of the *Proceedings of the Third International Conference of Africanist Marxists of Socialist countries* held in Varna, Bulgaria (1971).[79] In a paper contributed by Rathmann and Schilling (Rathmann has researched on German expansionism in South-East Europe and Turkey before 1918) the new political realities of the Third World and the position of the forces of the Western world market within it, stimulated the

[72] Ahlers, Donner, Kreuzer, Orbon, and Westhoff, *Die vorkapitalistischen Produktionsweisen* (Erlangen 1973).

[73] Ingolf Ahlers, *Kolonialismus und Bewegungs formen des Handelskapitals* (Berlin 1974).

[74] See 72.

[75] Klaus Busch, *Die multinationalen Konzerne, Zur Analyse der Weltmarktbewegung des Kapitals,* Edition Suhrkamp (Frankfurt 1974).

[76] Wolfgang Schöller, "Werttransfer und Unterentwicklung," in: *Probleme des Klassenkampfs,* 3 (1973) 6.

[77] Busch, Schöller and Seelow, *Weltmarkt und Weltwährungskrise* (Bremen 1971).

[78] Wolfgang Bärtschi and Hanns-Dieter Jacobsen, *Kritische Einführung in die Aussenhandelstheorie* (Rowohlt, Reinbek 1976).

[79] "Developing countries on the non-capitalist road", *Proceedings of the third international conference of Africanist Marxists of Socialist Countries* (Varna, September 1971, Sofia 1974).

authors to write a sophisticated assessment of the political nature of the social powers within the third world. The question was, how revolutionary change could be achieved in spite of the dominating role of the West on the world market. After the failure of the Third World bourgeoisie, "under the influence of world-socialism, representatives of petty-bourgeois circles, and, more particularly, revolutionary-democratic forces within the intelligentsia, will seize the reins of power and advocate change that ultimately may lead to socialism."[80]

At a first glance, this type of thinking may be thought to be irrelevant to research into the history of expansion, but by implication – and the first contributions demonstrated the point – it has generated a new sensitivity to the structures and historical heritage particular to specific social groups. Within the framework of the Leninist approach, it has stimulated scepticism concerning the inevitability of politico-economic processes in the Third World, changes which in traditional terms could only "lead to socialism." Indirectly, it is an answer challenging western neo-Marxist views on the question of inevitability and on the overwhelming power of the Western world market. Moreover, despite strong interest in problems of unequal exchange, the treatment of the concept of a "non-capitalist road" repeats the Leninist step from the economic structure to power. For these reasons it is worthwhile to keep in touch with future scholarship along those lines.

German language neo-Marxist and Marxist influenced works, especially those by political scientists, have been concerned to integrate the historical dimension in the course of their discussions; at least they have demanded it, and, in responding to the historiography of overseas expansion, they have attempted it. Four fields have been opened to historical reinterpretation: through analysis of the precapitalist mode of production and its transformation through European expansion (correlating with the penetration of the world by the capitalist mode of production – a dialectical process between regional historical developments and the logic of capital development) a new interest has focussed upon regional structures (for instance on the population of Latin America before and during the Colonial Period, or on the structural changes of the Ibo in Nigeria during the period of slave-trading (Ahlers)). The structure of Europe is regarded as decisively determined by the nature of its relations with the colonial world and with the world

[80] Lothar Rathmann, *Stossrichtung Nahost, 1914-1918* (Berlin 1963), p. 41.

market (Orbon,[81] Ahlers,[82] Krippendorf,[83] Elsenhans[84]). The theoretical question of the nature of imperialism has been directed towards the reinterpretation of the world market, at least as it existed since Bretton-Woods if not since the Great Depression of 1929 (Altvater, Neusüss, Busch). And the debate on non-capitalist roads of development for Third World countries (an aspect of discussions stimulated by the issue of development-aid and by Unctad) has revived interest in the history of Brazil and of Japan, and in economic thinkers like Friedrich List (Senghaas).[85]

General syntheses have been attempted on the history of European expansion from the beginning. The coincidence of parallel developments is very striking. Only after Ekkehardt Krippendorf had published his *Internationales System als Geschichte*[86] did he discover Immanuel Wallerstein's first volume on the "Modern-World-System." He even avoided too close a cooperation with Hartmut Elsenhans, who has also attempted a similar general history, putting the organization of labour into the center of his analysis. In a sense, the West German time-lag of about fifteen years behind Western historiography, and of about five years behind that of the GDR, seems to have been bridged in many areas of discussion.[87]

The fostering of historical research in order to deal with this level of general theory seems to have become an urgent necessity. However, historians have remained reluctant to attempt a general integration of accumulated knowledge, and have thus created such a climate of self-isolation that the more system-oriented social scientists have at last begun to take the initiative and to build up their own programmes for the teaching of history.

[81] See 72.

[82] See 73.

[83] Ekkehardt Krippendorf, *Internationales System als Geschichte* (Frankfurt 1975).

[84] Hartmut Elsenhans – who wrote a systematic analysis of *Frankreichs Algerienkrieg 1954-1962, Entkolonisierungsversuch einer kapitalistischen Metropole, zum Zusammenbruch der Kolonialreiche* (München 1974) – prepared a similar general analysis of the history of the Worldmarket, see: note 1 of Ekkehardt Krippendorf's review essay: "Die Entstehung des internationalen Systems," in *Neue politische Literatur* (1977), 1, p. 36.

[85] Dieter Senghaas, *Weltwirtschaftsordnung und Entwicklungspolitik, Plädoyer für Dissoziation,* Edition Suhrkamp (Frankfurt 1977).

[86] See 83.

[87] See 84. Krippendorf is stressing parallel intellectual developments on the theme of the history of the worldmarket in his review on Immanuel Wallerstein, *The Modern World-System* (1974); Ellen Brun and Jaques Hersh, *Der Kapitalismus im Weltsystem* (Frankfurt 1975); Max Savelle, *Empires to Nations: Expansion in America 1713-1824* (London 1974); Perry Anderson, *Passages from Antiquity to Feudalism* (London 1974); and Perry Anderson, *Lineages of the Absolutist State* (London 1974).

9. BELGIAN HISTORIOGRAPHY SINCE 1945

by

J. STENGERS

Our investigation does not cover the whole of the subject. It is confined to those works concerned with the history of Belgian colonization in the Congo, or, in short, to what the Belgians used to call 'our colonial history.' It is in this area, more than any other, that the development of the historiography, since 1945, has been most remarkable.

The Congo, now Zaïre, became independent in 1960, and it is around this date that we must articulate our discussion: it is a matter of fact that 1960 is as much a turning point in the historiography as it is in the history of the country itself.

I. THE DEVELOPMENT OF THE HISTORIOGRAPHY

But what characterized the development of the historiography prior to 1960? In the first place, it showed certain indisputable signs of dynamism, not least in the active institutional support given to historical scholarship. On the topmost rank we may cite the *Institut Royal Colonial Belge* (which became in December 1954 the *Académie Royale des Sciences coloniales,* and, then, in December 1959, the *Académie Royale des Sciences d'Outre-Mer*). Its Historical Commission sponsored, or at least patronized, numerous publications, and the Academy edited such reports as the *Biographie Coloniale* and the *Atlas général du Congo* in which history is allowed a substantial role. Five large volumes of the *Biographie Coloniale Belge* appeared between 1948 and 1958, and while the contents are not all of the same quality – far from it – these collaborative works symbolize a time of considerable enthusiasm. Private companies reflected this trend and published 'reports' retracing their history. Many of these "reports" came from the pen of the enthusiastic and able René-Jules Cornet,[1] whose name is

[1] See the works concerning the *Comité Spécial du Katanga* (1950; in collaboration with C. Terlinden amd M. Walraet); the *C.F.L., la Compagnie des*

particularly representative of this period. Apart from such company histories, it was Cornet's books, dedicated essentially to the Belgian "enterprise" in Africa, which brought the most success: *Katanga. Le Katanga avant les Belges et l'expédition Bia-Francqui-Cornet,* in 1943 (3rd edition in 1946); *La Bataille du Rail. La construction du chemin de fer de Matadi au Stanley Pool,* in 1947 (4th edition, 1958); *Terre Katangaise* in 1950; *Maniema* in 1952.[2]

Underlying this historiography was a tranquil if merely implicit sense of triumph. Colonial expansion hardly posed problems of conscience: it appeared inevitable. Men were convinced of its beneficient aims. Belgians – and historians among them no less than the rest – had the conviction of bearing civilization to backward peoples. How could they doubt it when in the Congo itself, the only Congolese voices to be heard were those of the *évolués,* who, in thanking the colonizers for their kindly deeds, faithfully echoed the latter's image of themselves.

"What was happening here (before the arrival of the Europeans)?" a Léopoldville *évolué* asked in an article of 1949. "Idolatry and superstition were rampant. Ignorance was passed on from father to son. Hygiene was unknown. Epidemics were rife. Cannibalism was a daily occurrence. Hunger was the lot of many regions, due to unproductive methods of husbandry. Only tracks served as means of communication. If we must recognize the existence of a few good customs, it is equally necessary to admit that the lack of a well-organized legal code caused innumerable conflicts and interminable internecine wars, since rights could best be defended by use of force. In short, we were backward – overwhelmed by all the evils of nature and isolated from world civilization. At last came the Belgians, applying all their energies, genius and tenacity for the purpose of transforming this previously unknown and impenetrable land into a proud and grateful country, the rapid development of which has been the admiration of the entire world."[3]

Chemins de fer du Congo supérieur aux Grands Lacs africains (1952); the *Comité National du Kivu* (1953); the *Union Minière du Haut-Katanga (1956)*; the *Forminière (1956); the Société Générale Métallurgique de Hoboken* – a metropolitan company the activities of which closely connect it to the *Union Minière* (1958); and the *Banque du Congo Belge* (1959). Among histories written by other authors, we cite for particular note that of the *Compagnie du Chemin de fer du Bas Congo au Katanga* (1956); anonymous, but attributed to J. Bolle.

[2] On René-Jules Cornet (1899-1976), see our obituary in the *Bulletin de l'Académie Royale des Sciences d'Outre-Mer,* 1977, no. 1 (*Annuaire 1977*).

[3] Antoine J. Omari, 'Le rôle civilisateur de Léopold II' in *La Voix du Congolais* (Léopoldville), December 1949, pp. 461-462. Antoine Omari was "a

Devoted to the idea of civilizing the Congo, the Belgians were also convinced that they had the future before them for a task that had no foreseeable end. Comfortable in this vision, colonization seemed to them a continuous process for several generations, at least. Such words as "colony" and "colonial" seemed to possess a completely natural meaning, at that time, the Belgians being in fact the last to abandon them. The ministry entrusted with the affairs to the Congo remained the "Ministry of the Colonies" right up to 1958. It was necessary to await the December of 1959 – as we have seen – before the *Académie des Sciences Coloniales* altered its name. In 1960, just at the moment when the Congo gained its independence, the University of Bruxelles (not, however, an especially conservative institution) still possessed a "*licence en sciences coloniales*," in which was included a course in "*politique indigène*." Because of the extraordinary shortness of the interval during which the process of decolonization was prepared and achieved, this climate of serene confidence in the future persisted, as we have seen, right up to the eve of independence, reassuring historians who worked within its perspective, of the certainty of a long-term harmonious colonial development.

Characteristically, the history they wrote was written from a European point of view. The African appeared most often as the appendage of the European, who in contrast was the principal actor. Little attention was given to the manner in which Africans themselves regarded that process of change to which they had been subjected. Nevertheless, this overview of the characteristics of Belgian historiography prior to 1960 necessarily masks exceptions. Thus a historian and missionary, Father Ceulemans, produced in 1959 a first rate book on *La Question arabe et le Congo (1883-1892)* in which the Arab point of view was taken as much into consideration as that of the European; in fact this work is a little pro-Arab in its sentiments.

On the other hand, one notes that even before 1960 there were dynamic developments in what has come to be called "ethno-history," and these gave rise to several scholarly works. These works, however, were essentially anthropological, and no real connection was worked out between ethno-history and colonial history. They were completely different sectors.

Finally, it is necessary to emphasize that colonial history generally

prominent figure among the Congolese elite of Léopoldville." He was to play a political role of considerable importance after independence (see on him C. Young, *Politics in the Congo* (Princeton, 1965), pp. 82 and 404-405 and B. Verhaegen, *Rébellions au Congo,* Vol. II, 1969, pp. 130, 140-142, 248-249 and 263-264).

aspired to accepted standards of scientific objectivity, perhaps incompletely so, but satisfactorily nevertheless. This was not without effort, however, since it had been necessary to traverse a great distance in order to reach this point. The title of a work prepared in 1931, *A nos héros coloniaux morts pour la civilisation,* indicates particularly unambiguously what had long been the tone of the writing on the colonial past. It was an epoque when this past was almost obligatorily labelled "epic," when the colonial veteran – whenever his name was evoked – had necessarily to be described as "brave," while those unworthy foreigners who dared to criticise the regime of Leopold II had to be attacked vigorously.

These ritual formulae – and above all the spirit which they represented – have since given way rather dramatically before the pressures exerted by university educated historians, who, naturally enough, have introduced the rules of the profession which they had learned at university. When one reads a thesis prepared in 1959 (by Miss R. Slade) *English Speaking Missions in the Congo Independent State (1878-1908)* it is history in the full sense of the word, where there is no longer any suggestion of an heroic idiom. It will undoubtedly be said that this is simply because it is a University of London thesis, but the works of Belgian universities can also be cited. Slade's work, it should be stressed, was published in the reports of the *Académie Royale des Sciences coloniales.*

Can we therefore assume from this, that such a development signifies the ubiquitous triumph of the scientific spirit even before 1960? It would be ridiculous to claim it. Colonial circles did not fail to give historians "good advice." It would be explained to them that "not all truths should be uttered aloud," that there were some aspects of the past over which it would be better to throw a veil. Drawing close, for a second or two, they might plead in the name of patriotism: the enemies of colonialism are numerous, they lie in wait for our minor lapses; do not deliver them the weapons with which they will fight us. Or, another argument: do not forget, they say, that Africans are beginning to read what we write; do not tell them anything that might destroy their confidence in us, or even turn them against us. Certain of us were not immune to such counseling. Above all, it could result in blockages. A man inspired to publicize abuses committed below the equator under European direction, Father Boelaert, twice saw the *Académie des Sciences coloniales,* of which he was a member, refuse to publish his papers; they were deposited in the archives of the Academy.[4]

[4] Cf. *Bulletin de l'Académie Royale des Sciences coloniales,* 1959, pp. 508-

Moreover, while mentioning the question of objectivity, one should speak only of progress, in so far as scientific works produced in the metropolis were concerned. But in the Congo itself, aside from those works which were the products of a university education, beginning in 1954,[5] one still encountered a history written for the use of Africans, which, at bottom, was apologetic. Thus one year and nine months before independence, the *Etat Major de la Force Publique* edited two parts of a History of the Congo, meant for future non-commissioned officers of the *Force Publique,* attending the latter's schools, which were generally speaking excellent.[6] Its professed assumption was that history "reveals how the Belgians, by acts of heroism, managed to create this immense territory." The battle against "formidable slave hunters" was their greatest title to glory. "In three years of sacrifice, perseverance and steadfast endurance, they brilliantly completed the most humanitarian campaign of the century, liberating the decimated and exploited peoples of this part of Africa." The "establishment of the country" has permitted the organization of a state "which must be cited as an example to the entire world." "A civilizing mission," "economic development," "the progressive uplift of the moral, material and social welfare of its peoples": it all fosters the vision of the great enterprise of Leopold II.[7] Such history serves merely to bring out cries of "Long live Belgium," "Long live the King." But most remarkable of all is the fact that right up to the eve of independence, it was precisely such cries which were drawn from the throats of

510 (session of 16th March 1959) and 844 (session of 13th July 1959). In both cases the decision was the result of lively discussion; it was taken by a vote in which the author of these lines found himself each time in the minority. Father Boelaert, one may note, had other chances of publication than by the Academy; for example, he gave a rather terrifying article, "Ntange," to the review *Aequatoria* (published in Coquilhatville, now Mbandaka), 1952, nos. 2 and 3.

[5] The date of opening of the University of Lovanium (Léopoldville). The *Université Officielle du Congo* was founded two years later at Elizabethville.

[6] Vol. I, *L'Afrique et le Congo jusqu'à la création de l'Etat Indépendant du Congo* (Léopoldville, 1st June 1959); Vol. II, *L'Etat Indépendant du Congo (1885-1908)* (Léopoldville, 1st October 1959).

[7] Volume I, pp. 10-11. In volume II – devoted to the history of the *Etat Indépendant du Congo* – and which consists of 145 pages, the problem of the abuses of the Leopoldian regime is treated in the following terms on the last page: "The criticisms emitted in the course of defamatory campaigns undertaken by jealous foreigners, were shown to amount to nothing by the commissions of enquiry sent by Leopold II to the Congo. Certainly, any enterprise must result in one or two mistakes and that of Leopold II has not escaped from this. But one can also say that the enterprise was both remarkable and prodigious, and that its weak points were negligible" (Volume II, p. 145).

the Congolese évolués. Patrice Lumumba, himself, had intoned them when turning to the historical past.[8]

II. THE SHOCK OF 1960

Given such an ideological landscape, the shock of 1960 overturned everything. This shock was not merely the result of independence, but even more a result of the troubles and disruptions experienced afterwards by the Congo, and especially due to the increasing concert of accusations which seemed – in the eyes of those Belgians accustomed only to hearing praise of their colonial enterprise – to be rising against them in the world at that moment.

After 1960, nothing would be quite the same as it had been. From the outset there would not be the same dynamism, disenchantment having destroyed the resiliency upon which it depended. Some colonial periodicals which had once published historical articles, disappeared.[9] The activity of an institution such as the *Académie des Sciences d'Outre-Mer* rapidly decelerated. Its *Biographie* (necessarily re-baptised as the *Biographie Belge d'Outre-Mer* – the adjective "colonial" no longer being permissible) was no longer able to maintain the same turn-over; after the 5th volume of 1958, it was necessary to wait until 1968 for the appearance of Volume VI, and 1973 for the first part of Volume VII. The general public no longer had a taste for books dealing with an epoque of colonization; that adventure seemed to have ended rather badly. Colonial companies no longer had any reason to evoke their past: frequently they withdrew from the Congo. One sentiment was current almost everywhere: forget the Congo. A friend confided to me in 1973 that in continuing to utter the word "Congo" in the offices of the *Union Minière* – the old and powerful *Union Minière du Haut-*

[8] "With a most sincere and humanitarian idealism, Belgium came to our aid, and with the support of vigorous native troops she eventually chased away the enemy (i.e. the slavers); she checked the spread of disease (i.e. sleeping sickness), instructed us, banned those of our customs that to some extent were inhuman, made us free, happy, vigorous, civilized. . . . All really human and rational men must express their gratitude and bow with respect before this grandiose task, realized in this country at the expense of incalculable material and human sacrifice" (Patrice Lumumba, *Le Congo, terre d'avenir, est-il menacé*) (1961, pp. 20-21; this work, drafted in 1956, and which he had wanted to publish, was not edited until after his death; the ideas that he developed there were those which he had expressed a number of times in public around the years 1954-56).

[9] The excellent review *Zaïre* for instance ceased to appear in 1961. It was necessary to wait until 1968 in order to see to those who had directed it launch a new periodical, also of very high quality, but possessing a largely new orientation, as the title indicates: *Cultures et développement.*

Katanga – one risked causing, so it seemed, as much of a shock as if one had uttered "*le mot de Cambronne.*"

Let us be wary, however, of painting too black a picture. Despite slowing down, research and publication continued. At the *Académie des Sciences d'Outre-Mer,* the Historical Commission did not for a moment lay down its arms. In 1965 and 1976, it published two important collective works: *L'Expansion belge sous Léopold Ier (1831-1865). Recueil d'études,* and *La Conférence de Géographie de 1876. Recueil d'études.* The Museum of Central Africa, at Tervuren, also sponsored publications, notably those of its keeper of the history section, M. Marcel Luwel.[10] A man like René-Jules Cornet, who had characterized the triumphalist phase of colonial historiography, was undoubtedly one of those most traumatized by events, but in a series of new books he sought to describe the most striking aspects of the Belgian enterprise in Africa; thus he evoked Belgian successes in the field of agronomy (*Les Phares verts,* 1965) and in medicine (*Bwana Munganga. Hommes en blanc en Afrique noire,* 1971). But some historians, who – like the author of these lines – could not be identified with those involved with the colonial venture, and whose sympathies in any case lay essentially in the metropolitan side of colonial history (and Leopold II, for example, certainly represented that side since he had never set foot in the Congo) – had hardly reason to concoct a defence against upheavals stemming from overseas.

If decolonization had demoralized certain people, and especially the elderly, it is nevertheless necessary to note that it had also a very positive side. It generated new enthusiasm among younger generations, and these new tendencies gave rise to an abundance of studies devoted for the most part to the 'emancipation' of the Congo, and to the first year of independence. These are studies harnessed both to history and to political science. We shall not refer in detail to the numerous foreigners, mostly Americans and English, also caught up in the subject, but among Belgian authors we cite, in particular, the names of Paule Bouvier, Michel de Schrevel, Paul-Henri Gendebien, and Jules Gérard-Libois,[11] and, above all

[10] See especially his book on *Sir Francis de Winton, Administrateur Général du Congo (1884-1886)* (Tervuren, 1964).

[11] P. Bouvier, *L'Accession du Congo belge à l'indépendance* (1965); M. de Schrevel, *Les Forces politiques de la décolonisation congolaise jusqu'à la veille de l'indépendance* (Louvain, 1970); P.H. Gendebien, *L'Intervention des Nations Unies au Congo (1960-1964)* (Paris-La Haye, 1967). (Mr. Gendebien has since turned towards politics and has become the president of one of the principal Belgian parties, the *Rassemblement Wallon*); J. Gerard-Libois, *Sécession au*

Benoît Verhaegen, who has given us a model of history written while still "hot," in his remarkable work on the *Rébellions au Congo.*[12] In this work, Verhaegen combines an original theoretical framework with a very concrete approach to the recent past. His principal theoretical contribution is his book *Introduction à l'Histoire immédiate* (1974), a work that is striking for its personal commitment. "*Histoire immédiate*" such as conceived by Verhaegen, is not history written immediately after the event, but employs a method which aims at maximum identification between the historian and the actors of history – between subject and object of knowledge – in a manner that assures that such knowledge will possess, so far as possible, a quality that is "immédiate."[13] Verhaegen elaborated his theory whilst in contact with Africa, its peoples and its political leaders; we thus see how complete and radical has been the reaction against the old history of colonization.

We have suggested above – while referring to recent studies of Congolese decolonization and independence – that they were works of political science as much as of history; but it is necessary to add quite bluntly, that in certain cases it is a question of works of politics. Such a label is applicable, for example, to the numerous well-documented, but strongly committed publications of the Brussels lawyer, Jules Chomé. Clearly the study of the recent past had become so bound up with politics at this juncture, that one of Chomé's books – devoted to the subject of General Mobutu – had important political consequences, provoking a serious crisis in relationships between Belgium and Zaïre and resulting in Zaïre's renunciation of its treaty of *amitié privilégiée* with Belgium.[14]

Katanga, 1963. We have ourselves attempted a brief analysis of the phenomenon of decolonization in a chapter of the *Histoire de la Belgique contemporaine* (1914-1970), 1974.

[12] 2 volumes, 1966-69. If one requires a synthesis: B. Verhaegen, "Les Rébellions populaires au Congo en 1964," *Cahiers d'études africaines,* no. 26 (1967).

[13] *Introduction à l'histoire immédiate,* passim, and especially pp. 69 and 188-189.

[14] The work of Jules Chomé, *L'Ascension de Mobutu. Du sergent Désiré Joseph au général Sese Seko,* was published in Paris by Maspero, in January 1974. But its sale was forbidden within France, by virtue of a clause in French law concerning the press, which permits the Ministry of the Interior to forbid all writing "derived from abroad" (see *Le Monde* of 31 January 1971). This very rarely applied clause was already commandeered three years before in order to forbid another anti-Mobutist work, that of Cleophas Kamitatu, *La grande mystification du Congo-Kinshasa. Les crimes de Mobutu,* also published by Maspero, (see especially the letter of François Maspero in *Le Monde* of 3rd July 1971). Fortified by the success he had obtained in France General

What, in large measure, had most compensated the slackening interest in Belgium, in so far as the history of colonization was concerned, was not so much the study of decolonization as such, as the development of historical research in the Congo itself. This development is connected with the foundation of the new Congolese universities; thus at *Lovanium University,* founded in 1954, specialized historical study commenced only in 1966-67; at Elisabethville, (now Lubumbashi) at the *Université Officielle du Congo,* founded in 1956, the history department opened in 1962; finally, in 1971, following the fusion of all universities under the aegis of the *Université Nationale de Zaïre* (UNAZA), historical studies became concentrated entirely at Lubumbashi, fed, however, by professors and teachers, drawn for the most part from Lovanium.[15] The work of the history department at Lovanium, and subsequently from the end of 1971, of that of the UNAZA at Lubumbashi, has been remarkable. We can speak without qualification, this time, of dynamism. The initial phase had been prepared by European teachers, and especially by Belgians, a particularly important role in animating this development being played by Profs. J.L. Vellut[16] and B. Jewsiewicki. Only in 1976 did Africanization result in the majority of places falling to Zaïrian professors. Some dozens of dissertations, doctoral theses (produced in numerous cases by doctoral candidates sent to European and American Universities after qualification in Zaïre) and publications like the series of *Etudes d'Histoire africaine,* demonstrate the kind of work that has been accomplished.[17] It is essential to emphasize, moreover, that the spirit behind this work has been strictly scientific, and, secondly, that it was founded upon systematic archival research. The utilization of archives kept in Zaïre itself dates precisely from this time.

Mobutu also wanted Belgium to forbid the distribution of Jules Chomé's book. But our law on the liberty of the press made such intervention by the Belgian government impossible. General Mobutu was violently upset by this, and it became an important element in the grave deterioration of Belgian-Zaïrian relations during 1974.

[15] On all of this see Ndaywel E Nziem, "La Formation des historiens africains à la Faculté des Lettres au Zaïre (1963-1975)," *Likundoli* (Lubumbashi), Series C, I (1976), 2, pp. 1-42, and B. Verhaegen, "L'Histoire au Zaïre, enseignement, recherches, publications," *Revue Belge d'histoire contemporaine,* VIII (1977).

[16] See notably his very useful *Guide de l'étudiant en histoire du Zaïre* (Kinshasa-Lubumbashi, 1974), which besides its practical side, contains views on certain of those problems with which we are here concerned.

[17] 7 volumes, Kinshasa (later Lubumbashi), 1970-1975. See also, from 1974 onwards, the periodical publications collected under the title of *Likundoli* (Lubumbashi; in part printed and in part cyclostyled).

The history of colonization, however, has only partially benefitted from this effort. The concerns of young Zaïrian historians have primarily led them, naturally enough, into studying the history of their own country, for its own sake, and towards the study of its different peoples. If they have sought a source of inspiration from the Belgian side, they must surely have felt themselves closer to a Jan Vansina than to one or another specialist in colonial history.[18] Yet the archives at their disposal, – archives practically all derived from colonial authorities, missions, and companies – contain materials which tend, for the most part, to favour the writing of what is precisely just such a colonial history. We shall not dispute the style or subject matter of this work; rather we shall confine ourselves to saluting contributions of high quality, from Lovanium and from Lubumbashi.

Not only did the shock of 1960 disturb the dynamism of research in Belgium; it also upset the basic conviction of certain of those who had devoted themselves to research. Previously, there were no doubts concerning the legitimacy and beneficial character of colonization; then the cracks began to appear. Remarks would be heard which before 1960 would have seemed outrageous. "Colonization, in spite of its results, and the very noble intentions of certain of those involved, appears to me in its entirety to be a serious crime – a sin against the spirit." Anyone saying that before 1960 would have been immediately classed as a dangerous revolutionary. In 1972 these words were uttered in the august context of the *Palais de Justice* in Brussels, and by a person as undisquieting as the president of the Conference of Young Barristers.[19]

In the Congo, needless to say, the revision of received ideas has been even more radical. Henceforth, Belgium would be called upon "to help Zaïre mend the irreparable damage caused by her colonial occupation," and "to redeem a fraction of the ineradicable misdeeds

[18] Jan Vansina, who has acquired an international reputation as an Africanist through his numerous works on oral tradition, on the Kuba, on the kingdoms of the Savanna, etc., taught for a long while at the University of Wisconsin, in Madison. Appointed professor at the Katholieke Universiteit Leuven (K.U.L.), he stayed there only a short while before returning to Madison in 1975. The fact that the K.U.L. did not deploy sufficient effort to keep a man of such value caused a scandal amongst Africanists. One can see in this a sign, to some extent, of the loss of interest in Central Africa among certain Belgian circles.

[19] Speech of Mr. Adrien Wolters at the session on the reopening of the *Jeune Barreau de Bruxelles,* on 17 November 1972, in the *Journal des Tribunaux,* 18 November 1972.

of colonization."[20] While Belgians claimed that they had opened their colony to civilization, Zaïrians replied "We had no need to be opened to your civilization – we had our own!"[21] In Zaïre, as elsewhere in Africa, colonization is denounced as an evil, or, to employ a more exact formula, as *the* evil.

Are we maintaining that this is all a question of moral judgement, of good and evil, and that moral judgement is alien to history? One can say it, in effect, and in our view, one must say it! But like it or not, it is the manner in which one writes history, that is here in question: the historian would not use the same tone for cases which, at bottom, he feels are "bad," as he would for those which he considers "good." He would not treat the history of the extermination of the Jews in the same way as the life of Saint Francis of Assisi. The Western historian no longer knows how to speak of the colonial past.

What he does know – and this is another new element – is that he cannot speak of the colonized in the same way as he did in earlier times. On the contrary he is required to treat them as full-fledged participants in the history of colonialism. Finally, he has to make as adequate a provision for the point of view of the colonized as he would for that of the colonist. The clap of thunder – so far as the Belgians were concerned, in this respect – was the speech of Patrice Lumumba on 30 June 1960.

On that day, the Congo gained its independence. At the independence ceremonies held at Léopoldville, the first to be heard was the Belgian king. In his speech, Baudouin expressed for the last time – just at the moment when the Belgian flag was being pulled down – the pure colonial tradition of Belgium, including all that went to embody its spirit of self-righteous satisfaction. The king said:

> The independence of the Congo constitutes the end of an enterprise conceived by the genius of King Leopold II. He undertook it with tenacious courage, and it was subsequently continued with perseverence by Belgium. . . . . During the past 80 years Belgium has sent the best of its sons to your land, first of all to deliver the Congo Basin from the odious slave trade, which had decimated its peoples; afterwards to unite the different tribes – which formerly had been enemies of one another – so as to build together the largest of the independent states of Africa; finally, so as to call the different regions of the Congo to a happier kind of life. . . . .
>
> When Leopold II undertook this great work – today finding its crowning achievement – he did not present himself as a conqueror before you, but as a

[20] Bondo Nsama, "Coopération belgo-zaïroise: nouveau point de départ," editorial of the newspaper *Salongo*, of Kinshasa, 26 September 1975.

[21] *500 Visages du Zaïre*, edited by the *Bureau du Président de la République du Zaïre*, (Kinshasa, 1975), p. 125.

civilizer. The Congo has been endowed with railways, roads, sea lanes, and air ways, which, in bringing your peoples into contact with one another, have stimulated unity and have opened your country to the wider dimension of the world. A medical service requiring years to perfect, has been patiently organized, delivering you from manifold dangerous diseases. Numerous remarkably useful hospitals have been constructed. Agriculture has been improved and modernized. Large towns have been built, and across the whole country there has been remarkable progress in conditions of housing and hygiene. Industrial enterprise has converted the natural riches of the earth to a new value. There has been considerable expansion in economic activity – augmenting the well-being of your peoples. . . . Due to mission schools – like those later to be created by the state – basic education has been extended, and an intellectual elite has begun to emerge by means of which your universities may rapidly grow. . . .

We are happy therefore, to have given the Congo – in face of the greatest difficulties – those elements indispensable for the structure of a country that has started on the march along the path of development.[22]

This image of the past – "How good we have been!" "What fine things we did!" – was followed by an unexpected response: that of Patrice Lumumba. It was not arranged in the programme that the Prime Minister should take the floor; the only speaker announced was the President of the new Republic, Joseph Kasa-Vubu. However, Patrice Lumumba shot up to the rostrum, in order to evoke a very different past. He cried out:

So far as our lot was concerned during the 80 years of the colonialist regime, our wounds are still too fresh and painful to be forgotten.

We have exchanged exhausting labour for salaries that did not allow us even to assuage our hunger, to clothe ourselves properly, to lodge ourselves decently, not to raise our children as beloved ones ought to be raised. We had to submit, day and night, to sarcasm, insults, and beatings, simply because we were negroes. Who could forget that, to a black, one said "tu" – not of course as if to a friend, but because the honourable "vous" was reserved for whites.

We knew all the time that our lands were being despoiled in the name of texts claiming to be legal, which only, however, recognized the right of the strongest. . . . .

We were quite aware that the law of the state was never the same for a black as for a white, cruel and inhuman to the one, accommodating to the other.

We were well aware of the atrocious suffering meted out to transportees – exiled in their own country for political opinions and religious beliefs; their lot was truly worse than death itself.

We knew that in the towns there were magnificent houses for the whites and ramshackle straw huts for the blacks; that a black was admitted neither into cinemas, restaurants, nor shops, labelled with a sign inscribed 'Europeans only'; that a black travelled at the bottom of the ship or at the feet of the white in his luxury cabin.

[22] J. Gérard-Libois and B. Verhaegen, *Congo 1960,* 1, (1961), pp. 318-319.

> Who, finally, will forget the shooting which killed so many of our brothers, the dungeons into which those who would not submit to this oppressive and exploitative regime of "justice" were brutally thrown. All that, my brothers, . . . we have deeply suffered.
>
> But all this – all that I have described above – all of it, has now ended.[23]

Lumumba's speech provoked a scandal. King Baudouin threatened to put an end to his visit and to leave immediately for Brussels.[24] But even if they were marked by gross exaggeration, Lumumba's remarks have become as deeply inscribed upon the threshold of Belgian colonial history as has the traditional version; that history would never be the same again.

To integrate the African point of view into colonial history – their reactions and their roles – in brief, the African dimension of things – appears today as an imperious necessity. And yet this task has encountered numerous obstacles with the result that it has scarcely even been roughed out, as yet.

Such obstacles are encountered in different forms. We cite the few that are undoubtedly the most important.

Firstly, what kind of people did the colonizer meet in Central Africa? The traditional version represents them as "bellicose and cannibalistic savages."[25] But we have reacted against these sombre colours for quite some time now. The principal precursor in this respect, was, undoubtedly, E.D. Morel, the leader of the Congo Reform Association in his *History of the Congo Reform Movement,* a work which, however, remained unpublished until 1968.[26] Morel – having deflated the importance generally attributed to internecine warfare and cannibalism – gave an almost idyllic description of

[23] *Ibid.,* Vol. I, p. 323. Also in *La pensée politique de Patrice Lumumba,* published by J. van Lierde (Paris, 1963), pp. 198-199.

[24] On the same afternoon, Lumumba had to agree to deliver a short speech in which he "clarified his ideas" and which the Belgians considered as an "apology." He said in it: "At the moment when the Congo is attaining independence, the entire government wishes to render a solemn homage to the King of the Belgians and to the noble people whom he represents for the enterprise accomplished in three quarters of a century . . . it is to the Belgians that we owe these magnificent deeds, which today causes the independent Congo and its government to be proud." (J. Gérard-Libois and B. Verhaegen, *op. cit.,* Vol. I, pp. 325-326; *La Pensée politique de Patrice Lumumba, op. cit.,* p. 202). These words which had been demanded from Lumumba, had been thrown onto paper by the Belgian Prime Minister, Mr. Gaston Eyskens, "There you are," said Lumumba, "*J'aurai eu mon nègre!*" (interview by Mr. Fernand Herman in the weekly *Knack,* 10 September 1975, p. 24).

[25] A. van Gele, 'Les origines de notre colonie,' *Congo* (April 1926), p. 544.

[26] Published by R. Louis and J. Stengers (Oxford, 1968).

fine-looking, active, intelligent peoples, already well-advanced in the domains of agriculture, crafts and trade.[27] Recent work has tended to lay its greatest emphasis upon the commerce practiced prior to the arrival of the Europeans, and this has entailed the emergence of a quite specific historiographic style: one pins up everything that reveals the existence of long-distance trade – the latter considered as a clear sign of civilization. It is not too much of a caricature of this mode of writing to say that description of the peoples of Central Africa has passed "from man-eaters to man-traders."

Is this problem simply one of harmonizing the different characteristics of the portrait? That would already be a serious problem after all, because in this portrait, as in all historical description, there are no objective criteria for distinguishing between major and minor traits. But the stakes in this debate are rather more serious and fundamental. The version of the "primitive savagery" of "barbaric communities," or of their 'fall from grace'[28] assumes that only European intervention – that is to say, only colonization – possessed a capacity to raise up the African peoples from the abyss. However, the greater clarity now thrown upon the characters of pre-colonial economic activity – or, as writes a young Zaïrian historian, "the vision of an Africa in motion, dynamic, organized according to its own characteristics, and capable of responding to new forces"[29] – leads us towards the contrary view, that colonization had hindered a development that Africans would have been perfectly capable of realizing themselves – in fact they had already begun it. Today, this last idea has become dear to Africans.[30]

[27] Ibid., pp. 11-15 and 16 ff. See also my critical notes published alongside the edition of the text, pp. 257-258.

[28] Letter from Leopold II to the agents of the *Etat Indépendant du Congo* of 16 June 1897, A. Lycops and G. Touchard, *Recueil usuel de la législation de l'Etat Indépendant du Congo,* II (1903), pp. 637-638. "Primitive savagery" and "fall from grace" are rather contradictory expressions, but colonial discourse is little concerned with such contradiction.

[29] Mumbanza mwa Bawele na Nyabakombi Ensobato, "La Politique locale africaine à la fin du dix-neuvième siècle et la colonisation européenne," *Zaïre-Afrique* (Kinshasa), August-September 1975, p. 427.

[30] If one is concerned with the time just before the eve of colonization, one may read, in the *500 visages du Zaïre,* an attempt to reconstruct the potentialities that then existed: "A certain transfer of technology . . . would have sufficiently levelled the technological gap (between Europe and Zaïre) while at the same time respecting the aspirations of our soul. With our wealth we should have been able to pay for it, ourselves. There was no need to colonize us for that." (op. cit., p. 140).

So far as this problem is concerned, we would say the same as what we previously said concerning the relevance of moral judgements about colonization; – it is not within the scope of a historian; the latter ought not to concern himself with the "ifs" of the past. But, as in the case of moral judgements, the repercussions of this debate upon the historian's practice are inevitable. However subjective are one's criteria for deciding on what may be 'important' or not, in the description of a society, it is normally necessary to recognize the importance of those traits that enable us to divine a sense of its underlying evolution – that is to say, to recognize the importance of that which has had, or will have, consequences. What characteristics of Congolese societies really speak of the future at the moment of European occupation? The debate is certainly fundamental but up to the present it has remained both very superficial and essentially polemical.

III. IMAGES OF THE BLACKS

Another debate which has failed to advance, and which thus remains problematic, centres on a further African aspect which requires to be integrated within colonial history: that of the mentality, psychology, and aptitudes of the men upon whom the colonizer established his power. But all that we have as evidence on this point is that produced by the conqueror himself – evidence, which must, of course, be treated cautiously, because of the imprint of assumptions and stereotypes upon it. But how do we extract a factual observation from this gangue of prejudice. Let us take, for example, the classic assumption of the white man, that "blacks are lazy and indolent," or as Leopold II declared (who nevertheless had never been there), "at bottom they are lazy and indifferent."[31] These sentiments have been repeated time and again, since the beginnings of colonization, and in all tones of voice. When it is a question of exploiting the natives, one says it with a particularly emphatic brutality. "All whites operating in the Congo find it necessary to *force* the negro to work. The necessity of this is inevitable and all the lamentations in the world will not prevail against it. The metropolitan colonizers, who deplore this state of things, are implicitly proclaiming the inviolable right of the Black to the most absolute sloth." The colonial journal, which expressed itself in this way, in

[31] Remarks by Leopold II to missionaries leaving for the Congo, cited in *Le Patriote* (Bruxelles), 20 January 1905.

1901, was attempting to justify the compulsory harvesting of rubber trees.[32] But aside from those involved in the organization of slavery, there was a large body of opinion which, whilst sympathetic to blacks, nevertheless judged them in all essentials little differently. It was not a slave trader but a missionary, who, in 1943, praised in anticipation the merits of "those who will discover the secret of making the Black work with joy and interest in his village. I say 'make work' because he will do nothing whatsoever by himself."[33] Nor was it a slave trader who publicly explained the necessity of plucking the black from his "idyllic sloth." It was Governor-General Ryckmans, in his speech of 1939, to the Council of Government. "By himself the Black will not take the right path. He may be able to plant palms, but he will not do so. We may give him seed, but he will not sow it in the soil. We are ready to educate him in husbandry, but he is not disposed to listen to our lessons. If he must be saved, he will only be saved by us. It rests for us to take him by the hand. What he needs is a boss who will tell him: "Take your hoe" – then he will take his hoe, "Work in the field" – and then he will work in the field. . . ."[34]

Today, the indignant African who reads such texts is profoundly shocked by them. Yet it is not so much a question of indignation as of perceiving clearly the role that incomprehension and prejudice on the one hand, and an authentically percipient observation, on the other, each had to play in them. This question must carry the more weight because it is precisely such prejudice that has frequently inspired the conqueror's policies. Compulsory cultivation for example, (which has profoundly marked the history of the Belgian Congo – what we used to call "educative cultivation"!) and measures relative to it, very largely found their *raison d'être* in the vision of the African which we have located in Ryckmans.

What is in question, therefore, is the rationality behind certain, sometimes major, aspects of colonial policies. It is a major debate, and one which is unlikely ever to be closed. But at the present moment one has not yet even elaborated a method which would permit us seriously to approach it.

[32] *Gazette coloniale* (Bruxelles), 10 November 1901.

[33] Letter of Father Bruno Geldhof written from Manono on 15 May 1943; reproduced in B. Jewsiewicki, *Agriculture itinérante et économie capitaliste. Histoire des essais de modernisation de l'agriculture africaine au Zaïre à l'époque coloniale,* II (Lubumbashi, 1975) (cyclostyled), Annexes p. 30. On Father Geldhof, see the obituary in the *Biographie Coloniale Belge,* V (1958), col. 337-338.

[34] P. Ryckmans, *Etapes et Jalons* (1946), p. 139.

There are certain people, one must note, that put the problem aside, by failing to attribute to the African any specific psychology. They thus fall into a trap which one American author (enumerating the "fallacies to which the historian is subject") calls "the fallacy of the universal man."[35] One puts the African on exactly the same footing as the European, when projecting into him the same psychological comportment, and the same system of motivations. One thus escapes from all possible reproaches of racism; the fear of appearing racist, which determines this attitude, is very evident. Works written under its influence have an air of unreality. They are certainly not racist, but whatever the authors themselves might think, with respect to this impeccable comportment before the African, they remain fundamentally Euro-centric, since they tailor the African to the pattern of the European. Between this unreality and the prejudices of earlier times, it will be necessary to find the correct way; it has not yet been found.

IV. THE PROBLEM OF WRITING NATIONAL HISTORY

Another delicate problem: what was the degree to which the African accepted European domination? The colonizer has beguiled himself for a long time with the idea that he had obtained the full support of his wards for his rule. This idea, today, rouses the young Zaïrian historians to indignation; they have the conviction almost on principle, that their fathers had never accepted the colonial yoke. To prop up their views they evoke, with evident predilection, the revolts of colonial times. The Zaïrian historian, one can write without irony, adores these revolts.[36] But in what measure do they express a real attitude of resistance, and in what measure do these facts, not very numerous in themselves, justify generalization? In this domain also, studies remain insufficient.

Let us return, finally, to the speech of King Baudouin of 30 June 1960 and to the reply of Patrice Lumumba. It is no longer possible – since the day of that memorable shock – for anyone to continue following the gospel of colonization according to the Belgian King. Nor is it possible to follow solely Patrice Lumumba. Moreover, all

[35] D.H. Fischer, *Historians' Fallacies* (New York, 1970), p. 203.

[36] See for example the work devoted to the Pende Revolt of 1931: cf. Sikitile Gize, "Les racines de la révolte pende de 1931," *Etude d'histoire africaine,* V (Lubumbashi, 1973), pp. 99-153 and "Les causes principales de la révolte pende en 1931," *Likundoli,* series C, I (1976), 2, pp. 181-200, and in *Zaïre-Afrique* (Kinshasa), November 1976 (with references to previous works).

history of colonialism worthy of the name, in erasing exaggerations and errors from one version or another, must combine these two readings of the colonial past. But according to what dosage? On what is it necessary to put the most emphasis? On the dignity of man or on results of a material order? On bread or liberty? The problem is not confined to the history of colonialism. It is one of universal history, and its solution must always be a subjective one. There is no hope, whatever, that the kind of subjectivity, to which European historians are generally victim, can ever be identical, on this point, with that affecting African historians. It is necessary to resign oneself to works dosed in different manners.

It must be added, however, that to "resign oneself" is not the most suitable phrase for describing this problem: divergencies are signs of health since they illustrate the liberty of the spirit. One awaits the moment, after all, when one shall be able to confront the old colonial history with a history conceived in a perspective which is clearly different, and which will be a real history of Zaïre. The dialogue which will install itself between colonial history and the history of Zaïre is likely to be very fruitful. So much the better if the history of Zaïre is nationalist: the dialogue will be the more passionately joined. But we are not yet there. A great history of Zaïre corresponding to the spiritual demands of a large independent country has yet to be written.

The programme for such a history – one created, naturally enough, in a nationalist spirit – has already been outlined. This was done on a notable occasion at the first seminar bringing Zaïrian historians together, and held at Lubumbashi in February 1974. The vice rector of the *Université Nationale du Zaïre* was particularly lyrical in his inaugural speech. He declaimed:

> The history of our people has henceforth been freed, and taken up by the sons of this country. . . .
>
> This is why, Zaïrian historians, the moment has come to repudiate once and for all, that missionary history – one can even call it missionarist (given that one may be permitted this neologism) – that history written by the old ideologues, a history that presumes that our ancestors were nothing more than vulgar, heathen fodder for conversion, heathens whose signs and symbols of the past were only fetishes, sorcery, and a worship of the dead.
>
> Zaïrian historians!
>
> The time has come to put an end, once and for all, to these old legends, spread during colonial times by colonialists who liked to maintain that, before their arrival (– they who quite shamelessly portray themselves as *the* Civilizers), our ancestors could do little more than die of hunger, of sleeping sickness, of interminable wars, and so on. They are liers. They lied, hoping that we would always remain the simple naive children that they believed they had met. Deceivers! They deceived us in the belief that it was possible to deceive a people for ever. Impossible!

Zaïrian historians!

Repudiate it all, remorselessly. Put an end to this swindle. Hunt and smash these degrading legends. The moment has come. Do not teach our children, any longer, that a certain monarch, with flowing beard, acted as the great humanitarian, the great anti-slaver, whilst passing in silence over all the mutilations, whippings, summary executions, and maledictions that this rule made weigh on our forebears' shoulders. The red rubber tree was a scourge. . . .

Zaïrian historians!

Tell our children about the simple but glorious history of our fathers' resistance. Recount the lofty deeds of Kasongo Nyembo; describe the incessant battles of Mwami Kabare of the Bashi; acclaim the bravery of our Azande fathers; tell the story of the patriotism of our Tetela brothers. These patriots were cast into the filth and into ridicule by those who fought against their gallant stand; they were called rebels and mutineers, but mutineers against whom? Can a man mutiny against his exploiter? Against his oppressor? The new textbook of the history of our country must rehabilitate these heroes for ever.

Tell! Tell it all! Tell of the glorious history of our elders who resisted invasion and were ashamed of being enslaved . . . Tell our children that many centuries before the colonial interval (an "interval," because it was only a parenthesis, in effect, during the long history of our societies), our fathers had established a form of peaceful coexistence between Bantoos, Sudano-Nilotics, and Batwa, and that each social group was integrated into society in terms of its specific vocation. . . .

Zaïrian historians!

Help us to revive the past, so that our people will henceforth be conscious of it.[37]

No history of the country has yet been written according to such a programme. A work published at Kinshasa in 1972 carried the title of History of Zaïre, but as the subtitle made clear it was in fact a study of the Belgian Ministry of the Colonies from 1908 to 1940.[38] Another History of Zaïre, written by Mr. Tshimanga in 1976, promised more.[39] It was published under the patronage of the Department of National Education, which had, according to

[37] Speech made by the Citizen Vice-Rector Koli Elombe Motukoa, *Commissaire du Peuple,* on the occasion of the opening of the first *Séminaire national des historiens zaïrois* (Lubumbashi, of 5th-8th February, 1974) (cyclostyled). According to certain information, the speech of the Vice Rector had been drafted by M. Pilipili Kagabo, Assistant Professor in the History Department of the University, who would later be appointed Assistant Secretary General of the Zaïrian Historical Society constituted after the Seminar of February 1974. On the development of this last see *Habari, Bulletin d'information de l'Université Nationale du Zaïre, Campus de Lubumbashi* (March 1974).

[38] Lutumba-Lu-Vily Na Wundu, *Histoire du Zaïre. L'Administration centrale du Ministère belge des Colonies (1908-1940). Structure et fonctionnement* (Kinshasa, 1972).

[39] Dr. Tshimanga Wa Tshibangu, *Histoire du Zaïre* (Bukavu, 1976).

its own preface, "encouraged and followed, pace by pace, the production of this book." The work is serious – the author has a Toulouse University diploma, where he has done a *doctorat de 3e cycle*[40] – but it is disappointing, being much closer to the colonial vulgate, than one would have expected of a history of Zaïre supposed to be enfused by a new flow of blood – an astonishing thing, when one remembers the above remarks.[41] This is not the book which will stimulate a fertile confrontation with colonial history. This confrontation cannot take place on the level of a new order of knowledge except in so far as particular themes are concerned. If we lay aside the products of ethnohistory, one of the themes which has been most fully treated from the perspective of the history of the country itself, is that discussed in an excellent doctoral work of Mr. Mulambu, *Le Régime des cultures obligatoires et le radicalisme rural au Zaïre (1917-1960).*[42] This is a promising example of what we can expect from the new Zaïrian historiography.

Finally one can also argue that colonial history – despite the shock of 1960 – remains in the current of what, in a general sense, already appeared before 1960. This is the aim of attaining a serious, scientific level. Decolonization has been valuable, not least in shedding colonial history of the advice and earnest entreaties of those who wanted it to respect certain taboos. The old taboos have disappeared. But are they not being replaced? It was found wrong that in 1959 Father Boelaert had so forthrightly published details of the brutality of certain colonists. Now there are certain persons who fear to bruise the honour of the colonized. We are asked not to evoke their past in a manner that would be humiliating for them. The idea has not altered: "Not all truths ought to be told." Resistance must continue from those historians who are conscious of the responsibilities of their profession.

[40] His doctorat was on the subject of *La France et la Conférence antiesclavagiste de Bruxelles* (1971). Mr. Tshimanga has prepared an article: "Léopold II face à la France au sujet de la création des droits d'entrée dans le bassin conventionnel du Congo: 1890 et 1892," *Etudes d'histoire africaine,* VI (Lubumbashi, 1974), pp. 169-203.

[41] As a touchstone, we can turn to the manner in which he treats the problem of the abuses of the Leopoldian regime, which is particularly significant, even leaving aside the whole question of nationalism. It is the object of only a few rather vague lines (see pp. 50, 59 and 60).

[42] Thesis presented to the *Université de Bruxelles,* 1974. Currently it is only accessible in a condensed form: Mulambu Mvuluya, "Cultures obligatoires et colonisation dans l'ex-Congo belge," *Cahiers du Cedaf,* nos. 6-7 (1974).

Generally speaking, one has to conclude that a new post-1960 history of Belgian colonialism has not yet acquired a clear physionomy. It is searching for it. It is still at an early stage of its development. But periods of gestation are amongst the most passionately lived.

10. EUROPEAN EXPANSION: NORDIC HISTORIOGRAPHY AFTER 1945

by

NIELS STEENSGAARD

The Nordic countries, in spite of their peripheral position, participated formally and actively in European expansion, creating trading colonies, acquiring colonies etc. On the other hand, the participation in European expansion was never of such magnitude that it became a major political, economic or moral issue such as in most other West European countries, and problems of colonial politics have only for short periods played a great role in the internal debate in the Nordic countries.

The Nordic contributions to the study of European expansion are correspondingly modest, though of course the expansionist aspects of our national histories or, to put it adversely, the Nordic contributions to the expansion of Europe, had been the subject of a number of studies. It may be added that the history of European expansion in its largest sense has been studied also from another starting point than that of national history. Contemporary historians and social scientists in a small language area must take up international themes in their research and teaching in order to counter the threat of provincialism. Significantly, the history curriculae at the Nordic universities to a varying degree include international and non-European history.

It follows that the field is not easily surveyed or regimented into a few schools of thought. Without any pretension to exhaust the topic, I shall in the following draw attention to some of the more interesting fields of study. My main themes will be colonial history, history of emigration and what somewhat vaguely may be called international studies.

I. COLONIAL HISTORY

The Greenland settlement and the Vinland voyages are conventionally included in the history of European expansion, and Nordic historians and archaeologists have contributed notably to a literature, which, in the words of Samuel Eliot Morison includes "scores of books and articles by assorted oddballs."[1] Fortunately there are also several excellent books and articles on the subject, based upon the large but difficult and fragmentary evidence of archaeological remains, diplomas and the Norse sagas.[2]

There can be no doubt that the Norsemen actually visited North America, and the problem of the location of Vinland seems to have been finally solved by the Norwegian Helge Ingstad.[3] The Vinland of the Sagas was in all probability the site L'Anse aux Meadows at the Northern tip of New Foundland. The Scandinavian pride has been satisfied so far, the viking voyages to America are authentic, but at the same time it must be admitted, that they did not leave much trace in world history. Though the Norse in the 11th century technically were able to cross the North Atlantic and even to return to the same spot year after year, no permanent settlement was established, and the geographical knowledge and navigational skill remained isolated from the general European trend. Even if the so-called Vinland map had been genuine, the general impression had been much the same. Since the publication of the Vinland map, however, the prevailing opinion among Scandinavian specialists has been that the Vinland map was too good to be believed.[4] Of course, this does not exclude the possibility that Columbus had some knowledge of the North Atlantic, but the admirable activities of the Norsemen have hardly played a major role in the history of definite discovery.

The Norse colonization of parts of Greenland from the 10th to the 15th century is certainly more interesting. Judging from the archaeological evidence it was possible to keep an amount of livestock, which is unthinkable under present conditions. During the high middle ages the colony enjoyed a modest prosperity as the northernmost province of the Catholic Church under its own bishop and with perhaps as much as 6000 inhabitants. Climatic

[1] Samuel Eliot Morison, *The European Discovery of North America: The Northern Voyages 500-1600* (New York 1971) p. 72.

[2] A useful guide is the annual publication *BONIS: Bibliography of Old Norse-Icelandic Studies* (Copenhagen 1963-).

[3] Helge Ingstad, *Land under the Pole Star* (New York 1966); id., *Western Way to Vinland* (New York 1969).

[4] Ib R. Kejlbo, "Claudius Clavus and the Vinland Map" *The American-Scandinavian Review* vol. 54 (1966); id., "Vinlandskortet og Claudius Clavus" *Kulturgeografi* No. 106 (1968); Finn Gad, "Vinlandskortet" (Danish) *Historisk Tidsskrift* 12. rk. vol. 2 (1966).

conditions deteriorated, however, and after the 14th century crisis, which hit Norway very hard, communications with Norway broke off. Whether the last Norsemen on Greenland were killed by the eskimo, perished in an attempt to evacuate the settlement or just faded away, we shall never know. The graves of the last period tell their sad and unmistakable story of undernourishment and disease; when contact was reopened in the late 16th century, no human trace of the settlements remained.

The history of the Norse settlements and of the early migrations of the eskimo has been pieced together from fragmentary written and archaeological evidence. From the 17th and especially from the 18th century onwards the documentary evidence is abundant.[5] Quite a large literature exists on the history of Greenland,[6] but it is only within the last decade that a proper history of Greenland has been or rather is being written.[7] It is to be hoped that Finn Gad will continue his *Grønlands Historie,* which so far carries the story on till 1808 and which combines sound, if somewhat traditional, historical scholarship with a solid knowledge of Greenland's nature and people. The materials for the study of the history of Greenland in the 19th and 20th centuries are very rich, quite a number of studies have been published but the present trend in Greenland and Eskimo studies is towards the social sciences rather than history.

In the age of European expansion proper, i.e. in the mercantilist period, Denmark – Norway and to a lesser extent Sweden – joined the general West-European scramble for a share in the overseas trade and the acquisition of trading and plantation colonies. The standard work on the Danish expansion is the eight volume *Vore Gamle*

[5] Louis Bobé (ed.), *Diplomatarium Groenlandicum 1492-1814: Aktstykker og Breve til Oplysning om Grønlands Besejling, Kolonisation og Missionering = Meddelelser om Grønland* 55:3 (Copenhagen 1936); Sune Dalgaard (ed.), *Grønland. Gengivelser af aktstykker og breve fra det 16. til det 20. århundrede = Fra Rigsarkivets samlinger* IV (Copenhagen 1960).

[6] Unfortunately no recent bibliography is available. Card index in the Royal Library in Copenhagen. See also the periodical *Meddelelser om Grønland,* General Index for vols. 1-150 (Copenhagen 1969) and Povl Balle, *Avisit atuagagssiatdlo kalatdlisut agdlagsimavfiat* (Index of Greenlandic Newspapers and Periodica) (Minerva Microfilm a/s Copenhagen 1969).

[7] Finn Gad, *The History of Greenland.* The two first volumes covering the period until 1782 available in English (London 1970 and 1973). The third volume *Grønlands Historie 1782-1808* so far available in Danish only (Copenhagen 1976). Part of the remaining period is covered by P.P. Svejstrup & Sune Dalgaard, *Det danske Styre af Grønland 1825-1850 = Meddelelser om Grønland* 145:1 (Copenhagen 1945).

Tropekolonier (Our Old Tropical Colonies).[8] It is a collection of monographs on the Danish settlements on the Gold Coast, in India and in the West Indies throughout their history as Danish possessions. It is a solid work and well written, its authors are among the best Danish historians of their generation. In some ways *Vore Gamle Tropekolonier* is too good without being good enough. It was planned and written in the years immediately following the German occupation of Denmark, but if the publishers anticipated a piece of nationalist propaganda, they were disappointed. All the volumes are based on meticulous research, and the Danish effort is seen in its proper small scale perspective. On the other hand, the authors were not in a position to utilize the new trends and findings in the study of the relations between Europe and the rest of the world which have become so prominent in the 1950's and 60's. So, even if *Vore Gamle Tropekolonier* is an excellent standard work on the history of Danish expansion, much remains to be done to reconsider the evidence in the context of the European expansion, as we now see it.

The Danish tropical "empire" included possessions in India, on the Gold Coast and in the West Indies (The Virgin Islands). Research into colonial history has not been very intense neither before nor after the publication of *Vore Gamle Tropekolonier.* Some of the fields where interesting work has been done are the history of the Danish sugar trade and sugar production,[9] the history of the Danish East India Company and East India trade,[10] the Guinea plantations[11]

[8] Johannes Brøndsted (ed.), *Vore gamle Tropekolonier.* Vol. I, J.O. Bro-Jørgensen, *Dansk Vestindien indtil 1755, Kolonisation og Kompagnistyre;* Vol. II, Jens Vibæk, *Dansk Vestindien 1755-1848,* Vestindiens Storhedstid; vol. III, Fridlev Skrubbeltrang, *Dansk Vestindien 1848-1880, Politiske Brydninger og social Uro;* Vol. IV, Georg Nørregaard, *Dansk Vestindien 1880-1917, Reformforsøg og Salgsforhandlinger;* vol. V, Gunnar Olsen, *Dansk Ostindien 1616-1732, De ostindiske Kompagniers handel på Indien;* vol. VI, Kamma Struwe, *Dansk Ostindien 1732-1776, Tranquebar under Kompagnistyre;* vol. VII, Aage Rasch, *Dansk Ostindien 1777-1845, Storhedstid og Hensygnen;* vol. VIII, Georg Nørregaard, *Guldkysten, De danske Etablissementer i Guinea* (2d. ed. Copenhagen 1966).

[9] P.P. Sveistrup & R. Willerslev, *Den danske Sukkerhandels og Sukkerproduktions Historie* (1945).

[10] R. Willerslev, "Danmarks første Aktieselskab" (Denmark's first joint stock company) (Danish) *Historisk Tidsskrift* 10. rk. vol. 6; Kristof Glamann, "The Danish Asiatic Company 1732-1772" *Scandinavian Economic History Review* vol. VIII (1960); Aage Rasch & P.P. Sveistrup, *Asiatisk Kompagni i den florissante Periode 1772-1792* (1948); Ole Feldbæk, "The Danish Trade in Bengal 1777-1808" *Scandinavian Economic History Review* vol. XII (1964); Ole Feldbæk, *India Trade under Danish Flag 1772-1808 = Scandinavian Institute of Asian Studies Monograph Series* No. 2 (Copenhagen 1969).

[11] Henrik Jeppesen "Danish Plantations on the Gold Coast" *Geografisk Tidsskrift* Vol. 65 (1966).

and the slave trade.[12] The even smaller Swedish "empire" has been studied by among others Waller, Hildebrand and Ekman.[13]

An interesting recent initiative is the research into the history, society and economy of the former Danish West Indies undertaken by 21 students at the University of Copenhagen under the guidance of Ove Hornby and Ole Justesen from the Institute of Economic History.[14] The preliminary report published by the institute contains promising results and further publications are to be hoped for from this group.

II. EMIGRATION

The Scandinavian tropical "empires" had dwindled into insignificance a long time before the sale of the Virgin Islands in 1917 put a final and ignominious end to this episode. Greenland remained a Danish colony and eventually became part of Denmark, but led a very separate existence until the middle of the 20th century. The Nordic countries did not directly participate in the 19th century scramble for colonies, but contributed largely to the exploration of the Arctic and Antarctic regions.

The main contribution, however, of the Nordic countries to European 19th century expansion probably was the emigration. It has been estimated that 2,5 million people emigrated from the Nordic countries between 1840 and 1915. This may be roughly 5% of total European emigration in this period, while the Nordic population in the same period hardly accounted for more than 3% of total European population.[15]

[12] Sv. E. Green-Pedersen, "The Scope and Structure of the Danish Negro Slave Trade" *Scandinavian Economic History Review* vol. XIX (1971) and "Teologi og Negerslaveri" *Festskrift til Povl Bagge* (Copenhagen 1972).

[13] Ingegerd Hildebrand, *Den svenska kolonin S:t Barthélemy och Västindiske kompaniet fram till 1796* (Lund 1951); Sture Waller, "Det svenska förvärvet av S:t Barthélemy. Huvuddragen av de svensk-franska förhandlingarna och parternas syften" (The Swedish acquisition of St. Barthélemy. Main lines in the Swedish-French negotiations and the aims of the parties) (Swedish) *Historisk Tidskrift* vol. 73 (1953); Ernst Ekman, "St. Barthélemy and the French Revolution" *Caribbean Studies* III (1964).

[14] Ove Hornby & Ole Justesen (ed.s) *Studier i de danskvestindiske øers histoire 1665-1976 = Memorandum fra Institut for Økonomisk Historie ved Københavns Universitet* no. 4 (1976).

[15] *Emigrationen fra Norden indtil 1. Verdenskrig.* (Report presented to the Nordic Historical Congress in Copenhagen, 1971) p. 12 ff.

19th century sources for the study of Nordic emigration are quite abundant and offer themselves readily to quantitative treatment. In all the Nordic countries comprehensive studies of emigration have been carried through within the last generation yielding much information, not only on emigration properly, but also on more general aspects of social history and non-European history. It is not possible here to summarize this very large literature,[16] but special attention should be paid to the Sweden and America project in Uppsala, a team project which has resulted in several publications. While some members of the project to a rising extent have concentrated on internal migration and on the methodological issues involved,[17] others have studied problems which are highly relevant to the history of European expansion in a wider sense.[18]

[16] The report referred to in note 15 above has been summarized and reviewed in English in *Scandinavian Economic History Review* vol. XX (1972). *The Scandinavian Journal of History* vol. 3:2 (1978) was a special issue on the theme of emigration in 1978. The most important Danish, Finnish and Norwegian monographs are Kristian Hvidt, *Flugten til Amerika eller drivkræfter i masseudvandringen fra Danmark 1868-1914* (Aarhus 1971), also in English: *Flight to America: The Social Background of 300,000 Emigrants* (New York 1975); Reino Kero, *Migration from Finland to North America in the Years between the United States Civil War and the First World War* (Turku 1974); Olavi Koivukangas, *Scandinavian Immigration and Settlement in Australia before World War II* (Turku 1974); Ingrid Semmingsen, *Veien mot Vest* 2 vols. (1942-50); id., "Norwegian Emigration in the 19th Century" *Scandinavian Economic History Review* vol. VIII (1960).

[17] Some of the more important results are summarized in Harald Runblom & Hans Norman (ed.s), *From Sweden to America* (Uppsala 1976). For questions of method see Birgitta Odén "Ekonomiska emigrationsmodeller och historisk forskning," *Scandia* vol. 37 (1971); Sune Åkerman, "Theories and Methods of Migration Research" in Harald Runblom & Hans Norman (eds.), *op. cit.;* and the discussion in *Scandinavian Economic History Review* vol. XXIV (1976).

[18] E.g. Sten Carlsson, *Skandinaviska politiker i Minnesota 1882-1900* (Uppsala 1970); Ulf Beijbom *Swedes in Chicago. A Demographic and Social Study of the 1846-1880 Immigration* (Växsjö 1971); Sture Lindmark, *Swedish America 1914-1932. Studies in Ethnicity with Emphasis on Illinois and Minnesota* (Uppsala 1971); also from the same group, though with a different emphasis, Harald Runblom, *Svenska företag i Latinamerika, etableringsmönster och förhandlingstaktik 1900-1940* (Swedish enterprises in Latin America: Patterns of Establishment and Tactics of Negotiation) (Uppsala 1971).

III. INTERNATIONAL STUDIES

Colonial history and emigration history may be said to be part of the national histories of the Nordic countries. To these studies which take their point of departure in our own past, a number of studies should be added which take their point of departure in a non-Nordic context. It must be emphasized, however, that probably very few gems lie hidden in the Nordic languages. Nordic historians have become used to publishing in better known languages, most often English, if they consider their work of international interest.

The field is difficult to survey, however. The publications fall outside the scope of the national historical bibliographies, and Nordic specialists in expansion or non-European history often maintain closer contacts with colleagues abroad than with each other, in spite of the efforts of the Scandinavian institutes, because the language area is too small to create a self-contained milieu. Nevertheless, concentration or specialisation around certain universities may be discerned. In Copenhagen the traditional interest in the history of international trade has been carried overseas by Kristof Glamann and myself.[19] Other Copenhagen historians like Sune Dalgård, Ole Feldbæk and Ole Lange work primarily with Danish sources, but always within an international framework which makes their work of considerable interest from the point of view of the history of European expansion.[20] The history of

[19] Kristof Glamann, *Dutch-Asiatic Trade 1620-1740* (Copenhagen and the Hague 1958); id., "The Dutch East India Company Trade in Japanese Copper," *Scandinavian Economic History Review* vol. I (1953); Niels Steensgaard, *Carracks, Caravans and Companies = Scandinavian Institute of Asian Studies Monograph Series* No. 17 (Copenhagen 1973) reissued under the title *The Asian Trade Revolution of the Seventeenth Century: The East India Companies and the Decline of the Caravan Trade* (Chicago and London 1974) id., "European Shipping to Asia 1497-1700," *Scandinavian Economic History Review* vol. XVIII (1970); id., "Consuls and Nations in the Levant from 1570 to 1620," *Scandinavian Economic History Review* vol. XV (1967).

[20] Ole Feldbæk, *op. cit.* note 10 above; id., *Dansk neutralitetspolitik under krigen 1778-83* (Copenhagen 1971) id; "Caracas-spekulationen 1782-83. Dansk neutralitetsudnyttelse under den amerikanske frihedskrig," (Danish) *Historisk Tidsskrift* 12. rk. Bd. 6 (1972); Sune Dalgaard, *Dansk-Norsk Hvalfangst 1615-1660* (Copenhagen 1962); id., "Danish Enterprise and Mauritius Ebony 1621-24," *Scandinavian Economic History Review* vol. IV (1956); Ole Lange, "Denmark in China 1839-65: A Pawn in a British Game. An Interim Account of Danish Economic and Diplomatic Activity," *Scandinavian Economic History Review* vol. XIX (1971); id., "Mysterious Mr. Dunn," *Festskrift til Povl Bagge* (Copenhagen 1972).

Africa and of European missionary activities in Africa has especially attracted the attention of Swedish historians.[21] Also Latin American studies are more developed in Sweden than in the other Nordic countries, especially, Magnus Mörner will be internationally known for his publications on Latin American history.[22] Copenhagen University has a strong tradition in Orientalist studies, but research into the period of European expansion is more dispersed. So far South Asia has attracted most attention[23] but some of the research in progress aims at South East Asian and East Asian areas. As for the Pacific, the studies of the Norwegian author and explorer, Thor Heyerdahl, are presumably well-known. Less spectacular, but perhaps more relevant to the theme of European expansion, is the work done by a number of scholars, mostly Danish, in the fields

[21] Åke Holmberg, *African Tribes and European Agencies: Colonialism and Humanitarianism in British South and East Africa 1870-1895* (Göteborg 1966); Sigbert Axelson, *Culture Confrontation in Lower Congo* (1970); David Lagergren, *Mission and State in the Congo* (1970); Stiv Jacobsson, *Am I not a Man and a Brother? British Missions and the Abolition of the Slave Trade and Slavery in West Africa and the West Indies 1736-1838* (1972); Lars Sundsröm, *The Trade of Guinea* (1975). See also Anna-Britta Wallenius (comp.), *Africana-Scandinavica 1960-1968*: Books on Africa Published in Denmark, Finland, Norway and Sweden. A Selected Bibliography (Uppsala 1971); id., *Africana Suecana 1945-1965*: An Analytical Approach to Swedish Printed Material on Africa (Uppsala 1975). The *Scandinavian Journal of History* vol. 4:1 was a special issue on the study of African History in Scandinavia.

[22] Among Mörner's numerous works one may mention Magnus Mörner, *The Political and Economic Activities of the Jesuits in the La Plata Region. The Hapsburg Era* (Stockholm 1953); id., *La corona espanola y los foráneos en los pueblos de indios de América* (Stockholm 1970); id., "La reorganización imperial en Hispanoamérica," *Ibero-romanskt* IV:1 (Stockholm 1969). See also *The Study of Latin American History and Society in Scandinavia = Scandinavian Studies on Latin America* vol. I and Miguel Benito, *Latinamerika i svensk bibliografi 1959-1969* (Stockholm 1971).

[23] E.g. Sten Åke Nilsson, *Europeisk arkitektur i Indie 1750-1850* (Lund 1967); Benedicte Hjejle, "Slavery and Agricultural Bondage in South India in the Nineteenth Century," *Scandinavian Economic History Review* vol. XV (1967); G. Djurfeldt and S. Lindberg, *Behind Poverty: The Social Formation in a Tamil Village = Scandinavian Institute of Asian Studies Monograph Series No. 22;* id., *Pills against Poverty: A Study of the Introduction of Western Medicine in a Tamil Village = Scandinavian Institute of Asian Studies Monograph Series* No. 23 (Lund & London 1975); Björn Hettne, "Penetration och mobilisering i det koloniale Mysore," (Swedish) *Historisk Tidskrift* vol. 96 (1976). A monograph by Björn Hettne, *The Political Economy of Indirect Rule: Mysore 1881-1917,* is scheduled for publication in the Scandinavian Institute of Asian Studies Monograph Series in 1977. Jorma Ahvenainen, *The Question of German Information Services in the Far East before the First World War = Scripta Historica* II (Oulu 1969).

of cultural geography, social anthropology, history of religion etc. on the Pacific islands Bellona and Rennell.[24]

IV. REGIONAL CENTRES FOR RESEARCH AND INFORMATION

As indicated above, the size of the countries and the language area create a practical problem for the development of a research milieu. Only a few of the Nordic universities can afford more than one or a few specialists in the history of European expansion and non-European history in their history departments. To counter this problem and to make the most of limited resources, Nordic research into non-European history, language, culture and society is surveyed and co-ordinated by the three regional institutes, for Asian studies in Copenhagen, for Latin American studies in Stockholm and for African studies in Uppsala. These three institutes currently issue newsletters, bibliographies and lists of scholars engaged in relevant research projects.[25]

[24] See Caroline Ralston, *Pacific Research in Scandinavia = Scandinavian Institute of Asian Studies, Special Publications* No. 4 (Copenhagen 1972).

[25] Asia: Centralinstituttet for Nordisk Asiensforskning (CINA), Kejsergade 2, DK-1155 Copenhagen, Denmark. *Latin America*: Latinamerikainstitutet, Odengatan 61, Fack S-102 30 Stockholm, Sweden. *Africa*: Nordiska Afrika-institutet, Sysslomansgatan 7, Box 2126 S-750 02 Uppsala, Sweden.

Attention should finally be drawn to the useful publication *Excerpta Historica Nordica,* which has been published bi-annually since 1950. It includes titles and to some extent summaries of books and articles published by Nordic historians on topics of comparative or non-Nordic interest.

PART IV

A VISION FROM THE OTHER SIDE

11. JAPANESE HISTORIOGRAPHY AND EUROPEAN SOURCES

by

LEONARD BLUSSÉ

I. INTRODUCTION

Nearly all contributions to this volume deal with the work of Western historians concerning European overseas expansion, based for the most part on European sources. It is striking that even in the case of Christopher Bayly's essay on India – the only one that deals extensively with the work of non-European historians – all such studies have been written in a European language.

In this paper on Japan and the West the roles will partly be reversed, not because, as Percival Lowell has observed, "the Japanese speak backwards, read backwards and write backwards" but rather because I shall be speaking of Japanese historiography drawn from Western sources.[1] I intend to focus this essay on a school of Japanese historians who, through skillful and original use of Dutch source materials, have exercised a profound influence on Japanese historiography concerned with the encounter between Japan and the West in the beginning of the 17th century, an encounter which resulted in the so-called closure of Japan, *sakoku*. The structure of this school with its strong vertical ties between teacher and student is a characteristic inherited from Japan's long educational tradition. Hence I shall devote a large part of this essay to a reconstruction of the intellectual lineage (*keitō*) of this school in order to show how the ties between the authors of the works on *sakoku* came into being.

By reconstructing the ways in which foreign (in this case Dutch) materials came to be known to Japanese historians and were utilized by them to explain the Tokugawa governments's epochal policy to halt Western expansion, I hope to provide a point of reference for historians in other Asian and African countries who are also currently struggling to come to terms with the problems which Western ex-

[1] Cited in: Hearn, Lafcadio, *Japan, An Interpretation.* (Tokyo: Tuttle 1971[11]) p. 7.

pansion poses for the writing of a national history, not to speak of the challenge to balance the use of their own and Western sources.

The paper is composed as follows. First, in order to appraise the difficult political conditions in which the school took shape, I shall comment briefly on the effect of the divergent political backgrounds before and after the war on Japanese historiography concerning Western and Japanese expansion in general. Second, I shall make a few remarks on the position of the Dutch in early Tokugawa Japan, and on the Dutch source materials from this period, which have been preserved in the *Algemeen Rijksarchief,* the Hague. After this introduction I shall discuss the collection of source materials and the emergence and development of the school with a special emphasis on the two historians who through their pioneering work before World War II laid a firm base for the post-war research on the basis of Dutch materials. In the last part of this paper, I will assess the impact of the school on the historiography of the encounter between early modern Japan and the West, the so-called *sakoku* studies.

II. HISTORIOGRAPHY ON EXPANSION BEFORE AND AFTER THE WAR

According to Numata Jirō in his book *Japan and the West (Nihon to Seiyō),* Japanese historians are in a unique position: because Japan was not reduced to a colony in the 17th century and because it neither suffered under a colonial government nor from military aggression in the 19th century, the Japanese can (theoretically) regard Western expansion in a cool and objective way.[2] Paradoxically, however, the study of expansion history in general has enjoyed little popularity since the war. The term expansion even has an offensive connotation in Japan today. This is due to two factors. First, in the eyes of the average Japanese, Western expansion into Asia has in the past forced his country on one occasion to close itself off and on another occasion to expand rashly in a way leading to disaster. Second, both the concept of "a necessary expansion overseas," which played such an important role in pre-war politics and the disastrous outcome of these policies have not yet been forgotten, or rather, they have not yet properly been digested.

In pre-war times Japanese historians were not interested in

[2] Numata Jirō, ed., Nihon to Seiyō (Japan and the West) in Tōzai Bunmei no Kōryū (East-West Cultural Exchange) series. Vol. 6, (Tokyo: Heibonsha, 1971) p. 11.

Western expansion as such but rather treated it in connection with Japanese history itself. Although they showed great interest in the methods and mechanisms of the English, French and Dutch colonial administrative models at the time when Japan had incorporated Taiwan and was nibbling into Korea, they did not seem particularly interested in the underlying motives of the West in its expansion.

Initially, Japan's expansion into Taiwan and Korea was explained away by politicians as necessary in "the search for defensible frontiers," but in the 1920s the concept of imperial self-sufficiency was developed. As the annexation of more and more territories seemed necessary in order to reach this state of self-sufficiency, a religio-political concept of "missionary expansion" to the West and South was created during the thirties as a legitimation for these aggressive policies. Consequently the expansionist policy of the army was made impregnable to all criticism by the sanction of "political religion," after the re-establishment of the Emperor as a "Heaven-sent ruler" in 1935. As Reischauer has succinctly put it: . . . "since the emperor, rather than law or an abstract ethic, was the ultimate ground both of morality and of political legitimacy, the imperial mission of the emperor's army could hardly be found morally wrong. Expansion did not need to be justified as long as it was successful.[3]

The gradual adoption of a non-negotiable terminology clipped the wings of all creative historical scholarship in expansion: while Western expansion into Asia was labelled in terms of *shinryaku* and *seiha* (invasion and hegemony), Japan's own aspirations were veiled in terms as *kaigai hatten* (overseas development) within the friendly context of a *Daitōa Kyōeiken* (Greater Asian Co-prosperity Sphere). As an example of the kind of discrepancy that this juggling with terms *vis à vis* Japanese and Western expansion led to, the title of the Japanese translation of E.S. de Klerck's *A History of the Netherlands East Indies* might be quoted. The book was published in 1939 under the title *Ran-in Shinryaku-shi* (A History of the Invasion of the Dutch Indies).

Even comic strips for children illustrated the moral rightness of Japan's advance into Asia: the military adventures of a little black dog named *Norakuro* in "piggy-land" symbolised Japan's forceful expansion into Northern China, while the solitary and eventful life of a Mickey Mouse-like creature called *Bōken Dankichi* among the distant "natives" reflected the way of life of thousands of

[3] Fairbank, J.K., Reischauer, E.O., and Craig, A.M., *East Asia, The Modern Transformation* (London, 1965), p. 565.

Japanese shopkeepers, salesmen, bicycle-repairmen and photographers who made a living in Southeast Asia.[4]

These stray remarks on terminology may suffice to give us an impression of how writings on expansion in the pre-war period were to an increasing degree subjected to the reigning nationalist ideology, and often deliberately used as its weapon.

Those historians who did not adjust to the reigning ideology, its terminology and its historical theory, the so-called *Kōkoku shikan,* (imperial views of history) had to face the prosecutions of censorship as the case of Yanaihara Tadao illustrates. This specialist in matters of modern colonialism produced several critical works on Japan's imperialist policies in Manchuria and Taiwan. This critical stand led to his dismissal from his teaching position at Tokyo University in 1935 and to the proscription of his books. Professor Minobe Tatsukichi, a leading authority on constitutional law, who saw the throne as "an organ of the government" was charged by the army in the same year with *lèse-majesté.* He was dealt with in the same way as Yanaihara. Thereafter, the emperor was referred to as "the bodily representative of Heaven on Earth," a step with far-reaching consequences, as the world has seen.

The hitherto relatively large freedom of expression of Japanese academic life was now considerably constrained. This tightening censorship did not fail to touch even the historiography of early Japanese and European expansion, which I will discuss below. Studies on Japanese and European expansion during the 16th and 17th centuries came to be used as an instrument to legitimize the expansion of Imperial Japan. The reasoning was that as the Japanese had engaged in overseas expansion in Asia at an earlier date than the European maritime powers, they were perfectly entitled to receive their slice of the cake in Asia during the 20th century. "The rise of Japan in the seventeenth and eighteenth centuries as the great power in Asiatic waters, a rise which might have been comparable to that of Great Britain in European waters, would have been an accomplished historical fact if Japan had not secluded herself in 1639" remarks Kuno Yoshi in 1940.[5] In other words the isolationist policies of the Tokugawa leaders had bungled Japan's chances for a great future in Asia. A rather innocent collection of radio speeches by the then director of the Historiographical Institute of Tokyo University, Itazawa Takeo, entitled *Mukashi no Nanyō to Nihon* (Southeast Asia and Japan in former times, i.e. the 17th

[4] See: Hirano Kenichirō, "Nihon no Ajia gaikō" (Japan's Asian Foreign Relations), *Ajia no naka no Nihon* (Japan in Asia). (Tokyo, 1975), pp. 221-228.

[5] Kunō Yoshi, S., *Japanese Expansion on the Asiatic Continent* (Berkeley, 1940), II, p. 97.

century) was published by the Broadcasting Company in 1939 with the following text, clearly not by the writer himself, on its cover: "... (Southeast Asia) was before *sakoku* the sphere of the activities of the Yamoto race ... we can go so far as to say that our policy to proceed to the South takes place in the spirit of reclaiming our lost territories ... Shedding bitter tears the writer traces the evidence, and exposes the mechanism of invasion by the West Europeans into Southeast Asia and their atrocious attitude toward Asia, and proposes that capable men practicing "the Japanese way of life" should be planted together with the gumtree (over there) ...."[6]

The outcome of the disastrous Pacific war left Japan a foreign occupied country, shrunken to its main islands and denuded of all its overseas possessions. In this context the long period of crisis undergone by the study of expansion history after the war on account of its pre-war ties with nationalistic writings and the aggressive ideology of the militaristic government is hardly surprising.

The recent upsurge of interest among historians in Japan's 20th century imperialism in East and Southeast Asia is due to the strong impulse that has come from American research in this field. It goes without saying that this American research should be seen within the context of the worldwide reappraisals of imperialism during the nineteen sixties. It is true that during the 1950's Japanese Marxist historians had written about Japan's expansion; however they refused to treat the subject as such, but rather as no more than one of the inevitable results of pre-war Japanese-brand fascism.

This reserve may also be discerned in post-war research on earlier expansion. Tanaka Takeo, today's expert on Japan's overseas trade and expansion in medieval times and on the history of the *wakō*, the pirate-traders who together with Chinese counterparts ravaged the China coast from the 14th until the 17th century, has remarked that most works produced during the 1930's are of small interest because of their nationalist tenor.[7] There has been little continuity in this field, especially because most pre-war writers refrained from publishing on the subject thereafter. Murakami Naojirō and Iwao Seiichi, who both worked during the pre-war period at Taihoku Imperial University on Taiwan, form striking exceptions. Engaged in teaching and research about Japanese and Western expansion in the 16th and 17th centuries, they not only used Asian but also European and especially Dutch sources. Their use of foreign source materials, which indicate a different approach, and their independent

[6] Itazawa Takeo, *Mukashi no Nanyō to Nihon*. Rajio shinsho series, vol. 24. (Tokyo, 1939).

[7] Tanaka Takeo. *Chūsei kaigai kōshōshi no kenkyū* (Studies on Overseas Relations during the Middle Ages). (Tokyo, 1959), p. 259.

political viewpoint seen to have enabled them to carry out their work without any nationalist bias in a time when virtually none of their contemporaries could escape it. Perhaps another factor which helped was their relatively great distance at Taihoku University from the Japanese metropolis: the atmosphere there was relatively free. Thus they laid the foundations for a field of study that has grown into full majority during the post-war years: the history of overseas relations of early modern Japan. In the following paragraph the reasons why Dutch materials figure so prominently among the Western sources for this period will be discussed.

III. JAPAN AND THE NETHERLANDS

The Netherlands have, in one way or another, maintained continuous relations with Japan for the last 350 years, about 225 years longer than any other Western nation. It is generally acknowledged that Western science and culture were introduced into Japan during its period of seclusion (1639-1853) via Dutch writings. The task of reviewing the historiography of Holland's – or rather the Dutch East India Company's – role as pedlar of European culture in Japan, I shall leave to the cultural historian.[8]

The crucial role that the Dutch East India Cy or "Vereenigde Oost-Indische Compagnie" (V.O.C.) played in bringing about the seclusion policy of 17th century Japan, as we shall see later, is less well known outside Japan. Much attention has been given by Japanese historians to the motivating forces that gave birth to the *kaikin* or maritime prohibitions that were issued by the Tokugawa government. These political steps obviously have had enormous consequences upon Japanese culture and its internal and external policies up to this century. Theories have even arisen to explain Japan's "lack of a scientific mind" and "its blind run down the path of military expansion" in the 20th century in terms of these isolationist policies.

After having gained supreme power through his victory at Sekigahara in 1600, Tokugawa Ieyasu carried out a program of political reunification and economic integration based on the land survey of his predecessor Toyotomi Hideyoshi. These measures led to the emergence of a feudal system peculiar to Tokugawa Japan, the *Bakuhan Taisei.* During the same period a program of dynamic expansion overseas sent Japanese ships with government passes to nineteen ports along the coast of Southeast Asia. Two decades later this expansion was curtailed to such an extent by the

[8] See: *Acceptance of Western Cultures in Japan, from the sixteenth to the mid-nineteenth century.* (Tokyo: Centre for East Asian Studies, 1964).

above mentioned maritime prohibitions, better known as *sakoku-rei,* that Japan virtually became a "closed country," the so-called *sakoku.*

While these developments were taking place in Japan and abroad, the first V.O.C. ships came to Japan. Permission to establish a trade factory in Hirado was obtained from Tokugawa Ieyasu and a bitter rivalry between Portuguese, Spanish, English and Dutch traders ensued in the following years. By 1639 all but the Dutch had been excluded from the Japanese market. Considering these facts, it will be easily understood why the records of the V.O.C., which played an increasingly important political and economic role through the occupation of nearby Formosa (1624) and through the ability to supply the Japanese market with practically everything needed by the end of the 1630s, contain a wealth of information on economical and political issues in Japan and on the coastal regions of East Asia at the time.

The keen interest which historians in Japan have shown with regard to the causes leading to the closing of the country has resulted over the years in the origination of a small but influential school of historians. These scholars seek to incorporate the data they gain from V.O.C. documents like *Koopmansboeken, Daghregisters, Resolutiën* and *Generale Missiven* into the writing of "the history of overseas relations in early modern Japan," a field which embraces such contrasting areas as Japan's expansion and seclusion in connection with European expansion.[9]

IV. HISTORICAL METHODS AND COLLECTION OF MATERIALS

A few years after the Meiji restoration (1868) several government-sponsored historiographical projects were initiated which were obviously meant to emphasize the legitimacy of the new government. Numata Jirō has described in an essay on the historian Shigeno Yasutsugu how the Western form of historiography, incorporating causal treatment of events within a chronological arrangement, did not fail to impress the Japanese historians who were engaged in those projects, as it seemed more systematic and comprehensive than the traditional annalistic Chinese form of historiography. Shigeno wrote: "Unlike Japanese and Chinese histories, which confine themselves to factual statement, Western histories inquire into causes and consider effects, provide detailed accounts of their subjects and vivid pictures of conditions of the

[9] *Accountbooks, Journals, Resolutions* by the Council of the Japan Factory and the *General Missives,* which were regularly sent by the Governor General in Batavia to the directors of the V.O.C. in the Republic.

time with which they are concerned. There can be no doubt that their form and method embody many points of value to us."[10]

This interest in Western research methods was by no means confined to the historical disciplines but was a phenomenon that could be perceived in all fields of learning. Mori Arinori, then minister of education, laid in 1885-6 the basis for the new education system, with its dichotomy of practical and higher learning. Trying to work out a system by which education was to be used for social control by indoctrinating the *plebs,* and the support of the state by training officials for the government elite, he established a dual system: at the bottom "a compulsory sector heavily indoctrinated in the spirit of morality and nationalism" and at the top "a university sector for the elite in an atmosphere of the greatest possible academic freedom and critical rationalism."[11] As a result a change swept through university education: study programs were fundamentally modified and new departments of learning were introduced.

Within this framework of reorganisation, the 26-year-old German historian Ludwig Riess, a disciple of Ranke, was invited to come to Japan and teach at the newly established department of history in the college of literature of Tokyo Imperial University in 1887. He was "to give instructions in the regular methods of historical research employed in the West, especially those of Germany."[12] Thus Riess paradoxically was to develop new approaches for the study of the history of one of "Die Völker des ewigen Stillstandes." In 1889 he submitted a memorandum "in which he explained the necessity of such ancillary disciplines as diplomatics and the collection of sources, and further explaining the necessity of learning the European techniques in these disciplines." Please take special note here that Riess' intellectual roots were apparent in these proposals: on one hand Ranke's belief in the *Primat der Aussenpolitik,* the doctrine that a country's foreign relations determine the nature of its internal policies, and on the other hand the passion for archives which is so characteristic of the German historical tradition.

The belief in the primacy of foreign policy involves "the thesis that external affairs are the decisive factor in the march of events, and that therefore they must form the essential framework of our

[10] Numata Jirō, "Shigeno Yasutsugu and the Modern Tokyo Tradition of Historical Writing," Beasly, W.G. and Pulleyblank, E.G. (eds.), *Historians of China and Japan* (London, 1961), p. 277.

[11] See: Passin, Herbert, *Society and Education in Japan* (New York, 1965).

[12] Numata (1961), p. 278.

general history."[13] It is understandable that such theories were warmly welcomed in early Meiji Japan which after its forced opening was entangled by unequal treaties with the European powers, and was striving for equal status within the family of nations.

Justification for the opening of the country by the American fleet in 1853 was not only a Japanese problem but also a Western one, and consequently it was also Riess' problem. Thus Ranke's theories with their heavy emphasis on foreign relations, apparently so eminently appropriate for all involved, were enthusiastically put into practice. This ultimately resulted in some very detrimental effects on the interpretation of *sakoku* as we shall see later. Studying the period prior to the opening of the country Riess was automatically led into the direction of the study of the "closed country." It is in this connection that he specially mentioned among the foreign sources that should be copied and collected forthwith the archives of the former Dutch trading posts in Hirado and Nagasaki, materials which had been shipped to Holland only twenty years before. Riess' proposals led in the following year to an agreement with the *Algemeen Rijksarchief* in The Hague, where documents concerning Japan were to be copied and sent to Japan. Unfortunately the project soon came to a halt because of the lack of funds.[14]

Still the point about the necessity of the collection of source materials had been made. It was realised that rather than commissioning a few scholars to collect materials and write a history on a certain subject, as had been the custom, a specific institute had to be established, which would have the task, through selecting, compiling and editing historical source materials, of making materials accessible to all scholars. In 1895 the *Shiryō Hensan Gakari,* the predecessor of today's Historiographical Institute was set up. In the framework of the activities of this institution a new impetus was given to the collecting of Dutch material by the initiation in 1899 of a gigantic source publication project: the *Dai Nippon Shiryō* (Chronological Sourcebooks of Japanese History) a compilation of documents which is still in progress. So far, 239 volumes and a total of 220,000 pages have been published. A student of Riess, Mikami Sanji, was appointed chief of the publication project, and it was decided that important foreign documents should be included in the publication.

13 Butterfield, Herbert, *Man on his Past* (Cambridge, 1969), p. 117.

14 Numata Jirō, "Zaigai mikan Nihon kankei shiryō shūshū jigyō no enkaku ni tsuite." On the history of the collection of unpublished foreign source materials concerning Japan, *Nihon Rekishi,* vol. 186, pp. 49-56.

The gifted linguist and historian Murakami Naojirō, also a student of Riess, was sent in 1899 for a three-year period to Europe to collect materials for the section of the project dealing with the early Edo period. This could only lead to a hasty collection of materials, but upon a closer examination it turns out that he proved quite successful in selecting the most important ones. Thereafter, nothing more was added for nearly two decades. It was not until 1921 that the Japanese government received a proposal from Mikami Sanji, by then one of the directors of the Historiographical Institute of Tokyo University. In it he recommended that a new long-term project be undertaken for the acquisition of virtually all foreign documents relating to Japan. Priority was to be given to the copying of Dutch materials. His project was approved and an agreement was concluded in the following year with the Rijksarchief in The Hague to hand-copy all existent *daghregisters* of the Dutch trade factories in Japan. Although this work was faithfully carried out from 1923 onwards, only fifty of the 250 years of *daghregisters* had been copied when the work came to an abrupt halt on account of the outbreak of the Second World War.

In 1955 a new mass copying project, this time using microfilms, was begun through the good offices of UNESCO, which involved not only Holland, but also countries like France, England, the U.S., and the Vatican. Upon completion the Historiographical Institute of the University of Tokyo published in 1964 a number of catalogues including the inventory of historical documents in Holland relating to Japan.[15] This marked the actual culmination of Mikami's efforts.

Hence Riess' original recommendations concerning the collection of foreign materials have been well followed up. The fact that two of his students played an important role in the collection of sources brings us to the discussion of his intellectual inheritance.

Riess no monjin, Riess and his Students[16]

During his sixteen years tenure at Tokyo University Riess exercised a profound influence on the development of the history of international relations and of international trade history, with which we are concerned here. At first glance such great influence

[15] *Historical Documents Relating to Japan in Foreign Countries: An Inventory of Microfilm Acquisitions in the Library of the Historiographical Institute*, vol. I to V, (Tokyo: University of Tokyo, 1964).

[16] I should like to thank prof. Nakamura Takashi for explaining to me the ins and outs of the "Riess family tree."

from a foreigner may seem surprising, but it becomes understandable if we consider the development of historical studies during the Meiji period in general.

Historical subjects which had never been taken into consideration as worthwhile subjects for study, were now taken up. Neglected fields like foreign relations or overseas trade were not bound any longer with the fetters of the Confucian ideology of the Tokugawa government, i.e. they were not exclusively seen thereafter as merely comprising part of the tributary system. Riess was not only the first to realize the importance of collecting (foreign) materials for these studies, but he also laid down guidelines as to how these subjects should be studied. Although we now remember him chiefly for a few monographs he produced on early trade relations, written as models for his students, he also gave the impetus to compiling materials for the writing of histories of commercial towns.[17]

A concomitant development which tended to strengthen Riess' influence in this field was the fact that several universities followed Tokyo University's example and created their own history departments. By the time these chairs were installed Riess had just trained his first generation of historians. Chairs at Kyoto and Keiō university were occupied by his students. Soon his methods were being taught at both these universities, in addition to the University of Tokyo. A short pedigree of Riess *monjin* (students) will not only show us the impact of his teaching but will also illustrate how long term continuity depends on factors like strong vertical ties between teacher and students, a relatively independent attitude towards government policies, and a well-planned collection of source materials that are accessible to everybody. At Tokyo University all these factors were present to a certain extent. This may explain why only this university has enjoyed an unbroken interest in foreign and especially in Dutch studies.

Kyoto University

Uchida Ginzō was the first to occupy the chair of history at Kyoto University in 1907. He had graduated from Tokyo University, where he had followed Riess' courses in 1896. Foreign

[17] Riess, L. "History of the English Factory at Hirado," *Transactions of the Asiatic Society of Japan,* vol. 26 (1898), pp. 1-114.
Riess, L., "Geschichte der Insel Formosa", *Mitteilungen der Deutschen Gesellschaft für Natur- und Völkerkunde Ostasiens,* vol. LIX (1897) pp. 406-447.
For a recent study on Riess and his work see: Kanai, Madoka, *Jimbun kagakuhen* (Humanities vol.) of the "Oyatoi gaijin" (Foreign Advisers) series, (Tokyo: Kashima Shuppan, 1977), pp. 107-197.

languages were still taught by foreigners at the time, and, like many students of this period, he was quite proficient in English and French and was thus able to compare Japanese and foreign documents with ease. Although he died at the comparatively young age of 47, he left an impressive collection of studies concerning Japan's external relations in the 17th century and *sakoku.*[18] His doctor's thesis concerned the import and export of Japanese silver and gold in the same period.

Miura Hiroyuki (1871-1931), a colleague of Uchida, also received training from Riess. A compiler of historical materials on the principal port of medieval Japan, Sakai, he wrote a history of this city.[19] This study has remained a model for all urban histories which have followed. Kobata Atsushi, one of his students, took part as an assistant in the compilation of his work. Kobata is well-known in the West as an authority on the financial history of 17th and 18th century East Asia. Although he did not himself follow Uchida Ginzō's teaching on this subject, he nonetheless seems to have been influenced by his writings. A fourth scholar in the Riess tradition was Yano Niichi.[20] Having graduated under Riess in 1899, he taught Asian history (Tōyō shi) at Kyoto University. He is particularly well remembered in the field of trade history for the account that he wrote in the monumental city history of Nagasaki of the trade between Japan and other Asian countries. After the retirement of Miura and Yanō, interest at Kyoto University in Japan's overseas relations diminished and research was more concerned with Japan itself. Asao Naohiro, whom we shall meet as one of the recent influential writers on *sakoku,* was a product of this later trend.

Keiō University

Kōda Shigetomo was appointed professor of history at Keiō University upon the opening of a history department in 1910. He had graduated under Riess in 1896, compiled source materials for the history of Osaka from 1901 until 1909 and taught two years at Kyoto university before he accepted the chair at Keiō. A collector and bibliophile, he built up an outstanding private library of rare books concerning Dutch-Japanese relations and "the Christian Century in Japan." On these subjects he has written several well-known books. Kōda ordered from the archives in The Hague a

[18] Uchida Ginzō, *Kinsei no Nihon* (Early Modern Japan) (Tokyo, 1919).
[19] Miura Hiroyuki (ed.), *Sakai-shi shi,* 8 vols., (Osaka, 1929-1931).
[20] Yano Niichi, *Nagasaki-shi shi; Tsūkō bōeki hen, Tōyō shokoku bu.* (Nagasaki, 1938).

colossal amount of photostats at his own expense. Since all these materials remained in his private collection, they must have made other historians highly envious. Unfortunately Kōda published only one monograph on the basis of these sources before his death.[21] Well-known scholars of early Japanese Christianity (like Yoshida Kogorō and Hayashi Motoi, whom we shall meet later) were his students in this field. None of Kōda's students, however, has continued his "Dutch Studies." Thus at Kyoto as well as Keiō University the study of Dutch sources withered away after the first generation.

Tokyo University

The secret of the healthy state of Dutch studies at Tokyo University is easily explained. Compilation, translation and annotation of Dutch materials at the Historiographical Institute have gone hand in glove with continuity in teaching. On these two levels Murakami Naojirō and Iwao Seiichi respectively have played important roles. It therefore seems fitting to relate the development of the Tokyo branch in connection with the careers of these two scholars.

The Scholar-Translator

Murakami Naojirō (1868-1966) was engaged during the first decades of the century at the Historiographical Institute, compiling materials for the *Dai Nippon Shiryō,* as we have seen. Although during this period he taught only for short and intermittent periods he did inspire a few able and enthusiastic followers, among whom Iwao Seiichi and Itazawa Takeo were the most prominent. Then from 1926 until his retirement in 1935 Murakami taught full time *Nanyō shi* (Southeast Asian History) at the newly established Taihoku Imperial University in Taiwan. Of the students from this period, Nakamura Takashi, today the best known historian on the Dutch colonial period of Taiwan, should be mentioned. After his retirement from Taihoku University Murakami was consecutively president of three universities, among them Sophia University. Consequently the main contribution of this historian has not been so much in teaching as in administration and above all the compilation, translation and annotation of foreign language materials. Well versed in English, German, Dutch, French, Spanish, Portuguese, Italian and Latin, he edited the Dutch materials with which we are concerned here; moreover, his first translations mainly dealt with

[21] Kōda Shigetomo, *Nichiō tsūkōshi* (A History of European-Japanese Relations). (Tokyo, 1942); a collection of his university lectures.

English materials. His role in the development of the studies on the "Christian Century" can hardly be overestimated, but this lies outside the scope of this paper. At any rate, aiming to make valuable Dutch documents accessible to his colleagues, he annotated and translated several diaries of the Dutch trading post on Deshima (ranging from 1641 until 1654) and published them in 1938 as *Deshima Rankan Nisshi* (revised edition 1957).[22] Furthermore he translated all those parts of the daily records of Batavia which deal with Japan, Taiwan and the China coast from 1619 until 1661 (the loss of Taiwan). This collection was partly published in 1937, but the complete and revised edition in three volumes that was edited by Nakamura Takashi appeared after his death only two years ago.[23] During his long life-span Murakami laid the foundation of the research at Tokyo University on Dutch materials. His success in establishing a group of scholars who can work with Dutch source materials was due to his extraordinary gift for languages, while his unfailing stimulation and shaping – even bullying – of students and collaborators made up for the relatively short period during which he actually taught. "His *exprès* letters brought daily by the postman were like orders from an old general shouting at his whole army," Nakamura Takashi dryly remarks.[24]

In true Murakami tradition, Mrs. Nagazumi Yōko, a student of Iwao, published in 1969 her four-volume translation of eight diaries which had been kept at the trade factory at Hirado from 1627 until 1641.[25] Thus all Dutch diaries from the period between 1627 and 1654 have now been translated into Japanese. As we shall see in the last part of this paper these translations have produced new evidence which has radically altered the ideas concerning *sakoku* studies. Recently the Historiographical Institute has initiated a new ambitious source publication project. Over the next hundred years or so (given the rate at which they are edited now), all diaries of the Dutch trade factory from 1627 until the opening of the country in 1854 will be published in Dutch and Japanese. For reasons, unknown to me, the editors have decided to start at 1627 again, so that for the time being exactly the same diaries which Murakami and Nagazumi

[22] Murakami Naojirō, *Nagasaki Oranda shōkan no nikki.* Diaries of the Dutch Factory in Nagasaki. 3 vols., (Tokyo, 1956-8).

[23] Murakami Naojirō and Nakamura Takashi, *Batavia-jō Nisshi* (The Diaries of Batavia Castle), 3. vols. Tōyō bunko series no. 170, 205, 271 (Tokyo 1970-5).

[24] See (23), vol. 3, p. 437.

[25] Nagazumi, Yōko, *Hirado Oranda shōkan no nikki* (The Journals of the Dutch Factory in Hirado) (Tokyo, 1969-70).

have already edited are being published.[26] One more valuable source publication project in the process of publication is the *Oranda Fūsetsugaki,* a Collection of the "World News" presented annually by the Dutch Factory at Deshima to the Tokugawa Shogunate from 1641 until 1857.[27] Other translations which have been made since the war include those of François Caron's *Mighty Kingdom of Japan* and Schaep's Journal of his imprisonment in Japan.[28] Some additional remarks should be made about the character of these translations and the use that is being made of them. Japanese historians are not only interested in the activities of the V.O.C. as described in the company's documents, but also, and even to a greater degree, in the wealth of information about their own country which can be found in these documents. Matters which were taken for granted by the Japanese and did not seem worth noting down were carefully recorded by their Dutch contemporaries. The translator-annotator therefore takes great care in identifying the strangely transcribed geographical and personal names that figure so predominantly in the V.O.C. documents concerning Japan. The result is that reports which were originally meant to inform the superiors in Batavia and Amsterdam about every facet of the company in East Asia have now been considerably widened in scope and have become integrated into the historiography of Eastern Asia. Thus a voluminous collection of materials has been made available to all those Japanese historians who work on the early Edo period but cannot read Dutch. To show how scholars who can read Dutch source materials have put them to use, here a short survey of Iwao Seiichi's career as a historian and teacher may serve as an example.

The Scholar-Teacher

After three years of research in Europe, the greater part of which had been spent in the Rijksarchief in the Hague, Iwao Seiichi

[26] *Oranda shōkan-chō nikki* (Diaries kept by the Heads of the Dutch Factory in Japan). Nihon kankei kaigai shiryō (Historical Documents in Foreign Languages concerning Japan) series, 3 vols. in Japanese and 3 vols. in Dutch, covering the period 1633-39 (Tokyo: Tokyo University, 1974-77).

[27] *Oranda fūsetsukagi shūsei.* (A Collection of the "World News," presented annually by the Dutch Factory at Deshima to the Tokogawa Shogunate, 1641-1857), vol. 1. Japanese text under the supervision of dr. S. Iwao, edited by Hōsei Rankagu kenkyū-kai (Tokyo: The Japan-Netherlands Institute, 1976).

[28] Kōda Shigetomo, *Nihon daiōkokushi* (The Mighty Kingdom of Japan). Tōyō Bunko series, no. 90 (Tokyo, 1967).

Nagazumi Yōko, *Nambu hyochaku-ki* (The journal of the Dutch skipper Cornelis Schaep, who drifted ashore at Yamada-ura in Nambu) (Tokyo: Kirishitan Bunka Kenkyūkai, 1974).

succeeded Murakami in 1935 at Taihoku Imperial University. He continued basically the direction of research and teaching along the lines that had been set out by his predecessor: the study of the historical relations between Japan and Southeast Asia, and the study of Formosan local history with an emphasis on Formosa under the Dutch. In the framework of this research an agreement was reached with the *Rijksarchief* regarding the copying of all important seventeenth century source materials concerning Formosa. When the German invasion of Holland in 1940 brought this undertaking to a halt, some three thousand folios had already been handcopied. Only recently the work on the publication of the Journals of Zeelandia Castle, the main settlement of the V.O.C. on Formosa, has been again undertaken, this time as an international cooperation project between historians from Taiwan, Japan and the Netherlands.[29]

Iwao's primary occupation however, was neither the editing nor translating of Dutch source materials, but rather the elaboration of new concepts on the overseas relations of early modern Japan on the basis of the materials that he had collected during his *tour d'archives* in Europe. Although he has complained in the foreword of one of his books that it was not easy to write after December 1941 when airplanes were continuously raiding the sky above his study in Taihoku, this distraction does not seem to have kept him from finding a new orientation in research, one which has exercised a profound influence on the *sakoku*-studies after the war.[30]

Iwao's work was highly innovative. From 1936 until 1937 he published a series of articles called "The rise of the Japanese settlements in Southeast Asia," which were published in book form in 1940.[31] In this study he describes how Japanese emigration in the last decades of the 16th and the beginning of the 17th century to various overseas ports around the South-China Sea resulted in the established of Japanese colonies called *Nihon Machi*, "Japan towns." Little research had previously been done on these commercial settlements – primarily because historical material was virtually lacking in Japan. On the basis of Iberian, English and especially Dutch documents originating from the European merchants and

[29] The first volume covering the period 1629-1645 is to be published in 1980 as part of the *Rijksgeschiedkundige Publicatiën* (big series). For further details see *Itinerario*, Bulletin of the Leiden Centre for the History of European expansion, 1978 – 1, pp. 3-7.

[30] Iwao Seiichi, *Nanyō Nihon-machi no kenkyū*. A study of the "Japan-towns" in Southeast Asia (Tokyo, 1966), p. 1.

[31] *Ibid.* (Tokyo: Minami Ajia Bunka Kenkyūjo, 1940).

trade companies, which competed with the Japanese traders in this area, he was able to put together from a jigsaw puzzle of information a work which offered new insights into the growth, size, population, administration, economic and political activities of these overseas settlements in Cochin China, Cambodia, Siam and Luzon.

Iwao's activities were by no means an isolated one-man effort. At his side two other "second generation" disciples in the Riess tradition were involved in closely related research. Kobata Atsushi, originating from the Kyoto branch, published during the war several now classic studies on Japanese trade with China and Ryūkyū during the Muromachi period, while Yanai Kenji was involved in research on Japanese-Philippine relations in the early modern period.[32]

Japan's surrender in 1945 interrupted all research in these directions at Taihoku Imperial University. The Japanese staff of the university, now rebaptised "National Taiwan University," were repatriated and scattered all over Japan. The severely straitened circumstances during the immediate postwar period and the simple pursuit of the necessities of life as a result of this left little time for research for scholars. Iwao however was most fortunate in that he was allowed by the Chinese authorities in Taiwan to take his research notes home at a time when other repatriates had to leave all their private possessions behind. Because of this he was able to pursue his studies, while others, like Yanai, who had been forced to leave his notes behind, had to start anew.

In 1948 Iwao succeeded Itazawa Takeo to the chair of Japanese history at Tokyo University. Itazawa, whom I have mentioned as a student of Murakami and director of the Historiographical Institute, had been appointed professor at Tokyo University shortly before the war. It is obvious that he ran the risk of being used for propagandistic purposes in this exposed function. As a matter of fact his writings were coloured by these circumstances and consequently he went into a self-chosen seclusion after the war until he was called back and started teaching at Hōsei University in the 1950s. In

[32] Kobata Atsushi, *Chūsei Nisshi Bōekishi no Kenkyū* (A Study of the History of Sino-Japanese Intercourse and Trade) (Tokyo, 1941).
Kobata Atsushi, *Chūsei Nantō Tsūko Bōekishi no Kenkyū* (A Study of the History of Intercourse and Trade with the Southern Islands during the Middle Ages (Tokyo, 1939). This book has been partly translated into English: Kobata, A. and Matsuda, M., *Ryukyuan Relations with Korea and South Sea Countries* (Kyoto, 1969).
Yanai Kenji, "Manila no Parian ni tsuite" (Concerning the Parian of Manila), *Taihoku Teikoku Daigaku Bunseigakubu, Shigakuka Nenpō,* No. 5 (1936).

this capacity Itazawa was most prolific in the field of *Rangaku,* the school of Dutch learning during the Tokugawa period.[33]

After his appointment at Tokyo University, Iwao formed a research group with, among others, staff members of the Historiographical Institute like Numata Jirō, some ten to fifteen people in all. This group, the *Nichīran Kōshōshi Kenkyūkai,* has been meeting once a month ever since that time. Traditionally, one or more members of the staff of the Dutch Embassy in Tokyo are also present, and as one diplomat somewhat ruefully admitted, most of them leave Japan at the end of their tour of duty with a considerably broadened knowledge of 17th and 18th century Dutch. During these meetings papers are presented and translation projects are undertaken. Of the latter, the complete translation of the Deshima diaries from 1800 to 1854 (the year of the opening of the country) should receive particular notice. Well-known historians like Kanai Madoka, Katō Eiichi, Morioka Yoshiko, Shōji Mitsuo, Nagazumi Yōko, Yamawaki Teijirō, to name just a few, have all been trained within this tradition.

Since his retirement from Tokyo University in 1963, Iwao has continued teaching at Hōsei University. In 1975 he founded, together with Ogata Tomio, a *rangaku* scholar, the *Nichiran Gakkai* (Japan-Netherlands Institute) a research centre of Dutch-Japanese cultural relations.[34] Among other activities this centre publishes monographs like the above-mentioned *Oranda Fūsetsu Gaki Shūsei* and is now preparing a *bibliographie raisonnée* in English on all Japanese studies concerning Dutch-Japanese relations, which hopefully will fill in the gaps in this essay in the near future. Through Iwao's teaching and the activities of the research group that he is directing, a new generation of scholars has come to the fore. Although I restrict myself to reviewing the impact that these historians have exercised on *sakoku* studies, it should be pointed out that they are publishing on vastly diverging subjects such as *Rangaku,* the Dutch East India Company, Overseas Chinese, *Bakuhan*-studies and Indonesian history.[35]

Having studied the growth of the Tokyo school on the basis of the activities of its two protagonists it is now time to assess the impact that they have exercised on *Sakoku* studies.

[33] Itazawa Takeo, *Nichiran Bunka Kōshōshi no Kenkyū* (Study of the Dutch-Japanese Cultural Relations) (Tokyo, 1959).

[34] For further information write to the secretary of the Nichiran Gakkai, 3-28-1, Yushima, Bunkyō-ku, Tokyo, 113, Japan.

[35] Nagazumi Akira, *Oranda Higashi Indo Gaisha* (The Dutch East India Company) (Tokyo, 1971).

Sakoku Studies

As Katō Eiichi has already given a survey of the development of Japanese studies on *sakoku,* I shall limit myself to a few general remarks before I proceed to show the influence exercised by the group of researchers I have just mentioned and the materials they have made available.[36]

The term *sakoku,* "closed country," is said to be derived from the writings of the German doctor Engelbert Kaempfer who, after a stay of several years at Deshima, published his monumental *The history of Japan* in 1727. To this work he appended a short essay with the ponderous title, *An inquiry whether it be conducive for the good of the Japanese empire to keep it shut up, as it is now, and not to suffer its inhabitants to have any commerce with foreign nations either at home or abroad.* A Japanese Dutch interpreter in Nagasaki, Shizuki Tadao, translated that essay in 1801, calling it: "*Sakokuron*" (treatise on closing the country). This translation was secretly circulated and served as reading matter to those who advocated the overthrow of the Tokugawa regime and the reopening of the country (*kaikoku*). This was in fact a rather surprising turn of events since their conclusion ran directly counter to Kaempfer's own that Japan would be better off when it remained closed.

The introduction of Western historical research methods by Riess in the 1890s led, as we have seen, to the study of the history of Japan's foreign relations. In an age when theories about the necessity of diplomatic relations on equal footing, imperialism and "open door" policy in China were rife, the *sakoku* period seemed an anomaly. Consequently it became a major field of study, eventually serving in this age of westernization as the coatstand on which everything that seemed uniquely Japanese could be hung.

Iwao Seiichi has remarked that *sakoku* can be studied on three levels: the origins of *sakoku;* the essence of *sakoku;* and the effects and influence of *sakoku* (and on this last level we should say the whole of the Tokugawa period, and its influence on subsequent times).[37] This tripartite approach may facilitate our understanding of the different approaches by historians to the phenomenon.

Around the turn of the century historians, and among them Riess' outstanding student Uchida Ginzō, were directly struggling

[36] Katō Eiichi, "Development of Japanese Studies on Sakoku, closing the Country: a Survey," *Acta Asiatica,* vol. 22 (Tokyo: Tōhō Gakkai, 1972), pp. 84-103.

[37] Iwao Seiichi, "Sakoku" (The Closed Country), *Iwanami Kōza: Nihon Rekishi* series vol. X, Kinsei (early modern period) 2, (Tokyo, 1963), pp. 57-100.

with the aftereffects of *sakoku* on social, economic and political life. Although Uchida saw the closing of the country as the beginning of *Kinsei* (the early modern period) – the concept of *ewige Stillstand* had already been done away with fortunately – he was not able to make much headway into the study of the essential nature of the closure of Japan. He became hopelessly enmeshed in the debate over the merits and demerits of *sakoku,* as the studies and the *magnum opus* of his main antagonist, Tsuji Zennosuke, testify.[38] On the other hand, as children of Riess and of their time, they all agreed that the closing of the country was caused by external affairs i.e. European expansion. This of course was a remarkable shortcut to an explanation of the origins of *sakoku.* And although Katō Eiichi has remarked: "As a method of historical study it seems somewhat strange to deal with the advantage and disadvantage of a historical phenomenon" nevertheless these seemingly futile arguments led to the introduction of more scientific research methods.[39] All parties agreed that there were two main factors which had contributed to the initiation of the isolation policy:

1) the prohibition of the Christian religion;
2) the monopolisation of foreign trade by the Tokugawa government.

These conclusions resulted in studies in the fields of Christianity and trade history.

As for the study of the so-called "Christian century" (1540-1640) I shall be brief. Still smouldering suspicion concerning the aims of the Catholic Church in 17th century Japan – the result of 250 years of anti-Christian Tokugawa propaganda – and the highly exotic character of the subject in the eyes of Japanese led to a rather anecdotal treatment before the war, including references to the demonic policies of expansion by Spanish kings on the one hand, and to stories of Japanese martyrs being boiled in bubbling volcanic pools on the other. After the war this interest was gradually channeled into a more balanced view depicting Roman Catholicism in 17th century Japan as one of those religious movements, like the famous *Ikkō* Buddhist sect fifty years earlier, which was expected to bow down to the central government, and which was ultimately destroyed when it did not do so. Remarkable studies and syntheses on this subject in English, which to a certain extent also

[38] Uchida Ginzō, *Kinsei no Nihon* (Early Modern Japan) (Tokyo, 1919). Tsuji Zennosuke, *Kaigai kōtsū shiwa* (Talks on the History of Overseas Trade) (Tokyo, 1917, revised and expanded edition, 1930).
[39] Katō Eiichi (1972), p. 87.

reflect the development of Japanese research in this field, are those by C.R. Boxer and George Elison.[40]

In the field of trade history with which we are concerned, foreign materials are also of obvious help. The first thorough attempts to incorporate these sources were made at the end of the thirties by Iwao Seiichi, as we have seen, and by Okamoto Yoshitomo who, using Iberian materials, describes in an admirable study Japan's trade and cultural contacts with Portugal and Spain.[41]

Based on Okamoto and Iwao's studies and Murakami's translation of the diary of Batavia, Hayashi Motoi published several articles during the war years which opened up a bold new approach.[42] Struck by the important role that the *pancado,* (the bulk purchase system of silk) seemed to have played in the policies that led to the closing of the country, Hayashi played down the importance of Western expansion, which until then had seemed the major cause of the monopolisation of foreign trade and the prohibition of the Christian religion. Beginning in 1604, Portuguese silk imports were subjected to a monopolistic purchase system organised by the *Bakufu* along the same lines as those in Macao and Manila. Under the terms of this arrangement, the bulk of the annual cargo of silk delivered by the Portuguese was purchased by representatives of a guild of silk merchants from the three major cities, Sakai, Kyoto and Nagasaki, which were under the direct control of the *shogun.* The merchants of Osaka and Edo also joined the guild and from 1631 onwards the Chinese were subjected to the *pancado* too.

A series of progressively more restrictive measures slowly hampered the overseas Japanese merchants during the 1630's until, in 1635, navigation to overseas settlements was forbidden to the Japanese. This resulted in the withering away of those "Japan towns" which, deprived of their supply of manpower and trade from the mother country, could not survive.

Interesting in this regard are Iwao's remarks in his study about the Japan towns concerning the ties between the V.O.C. and these

[40] Boxer, C.R., *The Christian Century in Japan, 1549-1650* (Berkeley, Los Angeles, 1951); Elison George, *Deus Destroyed, The Image of Christianity in Early Modern Japan* (Harvard, 1973).

[41] Okamoto Yoshitomo, *Jūroku-seiki Nichiō kōtsūshi no kenkyū* (Studies in the History of Intercourse between Japan and Europe in the Sixteenth Century) (Tokyo, 1936).

[42] Hayashi Motoi, "Pancada ni tsuite" (Concerning the Pancada), *Shakai Keizai Shigaku,* vol. XIII, pp. 64-79 (1944).
Hayashi, Motoi, "Itowappu no tenkai; sakoku to shōgyō shihon" (The Development of the Pancada; Sakoku and Commercial Capital), *Rekishigaku Kenkyū* vol. 126 (1946), pp. 1-25.

settlements. He shows that the V.O.C. incorporated the Japanese in Indo-China into its trade network immediately after Japanese navigation was prohibited. When the establishment of the policy of *sakoku* was completed in 1639 through the exclusion of the Portuguese, the Dutch, as the only remaining European traders, were also subjected to the *pancado.*

It is a strange coincidence that Hayashi, in order to gain a clear insight into the functioning of the Japanese *pancado,* did research in the mechanism of the *pancado* system in Manila which had been studiously copied by the Japanese, while at the same time Van Leur extolled the remarkable and progressive nature of the Asian bureaucratic régime in comparison to its European counterpart, using the example of the *pancado,* in his eyes an Asian invention, to drive home his argument.[43]

Hayashi argued that a group of rich merchants close to the central government built up a monopoly by way of the *pancado* in the silk trade under the aegis of the government: they then proceeded to push their rivals, the overseas Japanese traders, out of business and finally subjected the European traders to their monopoly. Thus, according to Hayashi, *Sakoku* was arrived at through the machinations of a small group of merchants.

More than a decade went by, however, before Hayashi's view was challenged. The turmoil of the last war years and the material and spiritual crises hampering academic life in the immediate postwar years contributed to the formation of "Zeitgeist" in which lack of confidence in Japan's own cultural values was rife among intellectuals. One would be tempted to ask Tsunoda Ryūsaku, were he still alive, if he still supports the statement he made in 1949 "The conclusion of the war had given a new lease of freedom to Japanese historians and the rewriting of history had already started with speed. I also began to argue within myself that Japanese history should be rewritten, this time, not only as the offshoot of Chinese civilization but also as an integral part of the history of Western domination."[44] Although these remarks show the elation of the historians because the bonds of censorship had fallen away, they also indicate a startling lack of confidence in their own cultural background now that Japan was occupied by foreigners.

[43] Van Leur, J.C., *Indonesian Trade and Society* (The Hague, English edition, 1956) pp. 205-8.

[44] Tsunoda Ryūsaku, *Japan in the Chinese Dynastic Histories: Later Han through Ming Dynasties* (South Pasadena, 1951). See foreword.

This feeling of disappointment in Japan's cultural values was also reflected in Watsuji Tetsuro's *Sakoku: Nippon no higeki,* (*The Closed Country, Japan's Tragedy*), which appeared in 1950.[45] The author describes the expansion of Europe and Christianity from the Middle Ages onwards, showing how Japan, which was at the same time expanding into Asia, came into contact with Western culture, even accepting Christianity within its own frontiers by the 16th century. The "egotistical military rulers," however, ultimately prohibited the Christian religion and foreign intercourse in order to secure their own positions. In the last chapter of Watsuji's book, *sakoku* and its consequences are described. By forsaking her colonies and isolating her culture, Japan, he says, lost contact with foreign civilizations, Christianity, and the rational thought system of Europe. According to Watsuji, these factors all contributed to a lack of a scientifically oriented mind in the Japanese and the formation of irrational policies by the militarist clique in the preceding decades, characteristics which finally plunged Japan in World War II. Watsuji in all likelihood was trying to settle accounts with his country's recent history in what one Japanese commentator termed as "a Philippic against the *gunbatsu,* the military rulers." Although the book inspired comment from all sides of the intellectual community, it actually had little impact on *sakoku* studies *per se,* because it suggested no new approach.

By 1956 the research on the causes of *sakoku* had resumed and Hayashi Motoi's thesis based on the study of *pancado* was seriously challenged for the first time.

Criticism came from two sides: Nakata Yasunao proved, based on Japanese source material, that it was the officials surrounding the *Shōgun* who formulated the seclusion policies.[46] Rather than being able to manipulate these officials, merchants were themselves manipulated and were incorporated into the bureaucracy, so that the government was able to keep a tight grip on them. Nagazumi Yōko, a student of Iwao, on the basis of her translation of the Dutch Hirado diaries, proved that, had the *pancado* merchants driven the overseas traders out of business, they would have cut into their own businesss, since some of these traders were members of the *pancado,* and the *pancado* merchants invested in overseas

[45] Watsuji Tetsurō, *Sakoku: Nippon no higeki* (The Closed Country: Japan's Tragedy) (Tokyo, 1950). See also the penetrating review by Hubert Cieslik, *Monumenta Nipponica,* vol. VII, 1951, pp. 327-38.

[46] Nakata Yasunao, "Itowappu no seiritsu" (The Formation of the Pancada system), *Shichō,* vol. 61, pp. 19-39. See also his chapter on foreign relations in Numata Jirō, ed., *Nihon to Seiyō* (note 2), p. 112.

trade themselves.[47] She also showed that the Dutch were subjected to the *pancado* in 1641, after the seclusion, and not in 1636, before the seclusion, as Hayashi had stated. Although the problem as to what might have caused *sakoku* remained unsolved, the importance of economic data in Dutch sources was shown. Along these lines, V.O.C. documents turned out to be of great value and were extensively used during the sixties.

In 1958 Iwao Seiichi published his by-now classical study on the *shuinsen.*[48] These were the Japanese ships which sailed to foreign ports with *shuinjō,* (passes issued by the shogunate). Using Dutch, Portuguese, Spanish and Japanese source materials, he describes the origin of the "red-seal" ship system, the cargoes, the position held by this type of shipping within Japan's overseas trade, and the relationship between this trade and the *sakoku* policy. This study, together with his earlier work on the "Japan towns," thoroughly describes Japanese overseas trade expansion, and gives much quantitative materials from the V.O.C. sources. He shows that from 1601 until 1636, the volume of cargo carried by *shuinsen* considerably exceeded that of all foreign shipping taken together. He also remarks that during this period the *pancado* not only made it possible for the central government to have a finger in the pie of foreign trade, but also served to restrict Portuguese trade with Japan, thus offering to other nations an opportunity to expand their trade. This arrangement does not point at a fear of foreign expansion, but rather at an active policy to diversify foreign trade. In an article published in 1961 Iwao worked out the theoretical groundwork of the *sakoku* policies in greater detail, but he still arrived at the rather conventional thesis that the closing of the country was the result of administrative intervention aimed at giving the central government a firm grip on foreign intercourse, so that once and for all the Roman Catholic religion could be eliminated from Japan.[49] I call this a conventional thesis, as this theory still takes for granted the idea that Western expansion was the cause of the seclusion policy.

All the important publications that appeared during the sixties cannot be enumerated here so I shall have to restrict myself to those which I feel to be the most important ones.

[47] Nagazumi Yōki, "Itowappu shōnin no seikaku" (The Character of the Pancada Merchants), *Shigaku Zasshi,* vol. 66, pp. 28-38. Also see her interesting article in English: "Japan's Isolationist Policy as seen through Dutch Source Materials" *Acta Asiatica,* vol. 22 (1972), pp. 18-35.

[48] Iwao Seiichi, *Shuinsen Bōekishī no Kenkyū* (Study on the Trade history of the "Red-Seal" Ships) (Tokyo, 1958).

[49] Iwao Seiichi, see note 37.

Yanai Kenji, not only an expert on Japanese-Philippine relations, but also on the local history of Kyūshū where Catholicism gained its greatest following, wrote an article in 1968, in which he emphatically stated that although religion and foreign trade had always seemed to be the two main factors leading to the policy of seclusion, the prohibition of Catholicism, already forbidden by 1624, had little to do with these policies, as Christianity had been all but stamped out by 1639.[50] According to him, the explanation of *sakoku* should be found in foreign trade: "The attempt made by the *Bakufu* to secure a trade monopoly, especially the monopoly of silver export, led to the closing of the country." This theory emphasizes a Japanese initiative.

Following the lines of research set by Iwao, Yamawaki Teijirō examined the trade between Japan and China and the role played by the *pancado* in this intercourse.[51] Here also descriptive and quantitative Dutch material was in abundant supply, as the V.O.C. personnel in Hirado and Nagasaki had for decades jealously noted down all transactions between their rivals, the Chinese, and the Japanese.

Katō Eiichi set himself the task of analysing the entire set of account books kept by the Dutch trading post in Hirado over the crucial years preceding the seclusion in 1639.[52] From these account books he gained an extraordinary insight into the market situation within Japan in those years, and he was able to prove that there was a relationship between the changes that took place in foreign trade and the existence of market problems in Japan.

The combined work of Yamawaki and Katō was of great importance as it threw additional light on the role played by the traders from China and Holland, the only two nations which continued to have intercourse with Japan even after the last seclusion edict in 1639 had been issued. Although the data in these studies showed that market conditions within Japan were changing at that time, it still seemed difficult to arrive at an explanation of this phenomenon.

[50] Yanai Kenji, "Kan-ei sakoku ni tsuite no ichi kōsatsu" (An Inquiry into the closing of the country in the Kanei period), *Kyūshū Bunkashi Kenkyūjo Kiyō,* Vol. 13 (1968).

[51] Yamawaki Teijirō, *Kinsei Ni-Chū Bōekishi no Kenkyū* (Studies into Chinese-Japanese Trade in the Early Modern Period) (Tokyo, 1960).

[52] Katō Eiichi, *Tokyo Daigaku Shiryō Hensanjo hō,* vols. 3, 4, 5, 6 (1968-71). An English survey of these researches can be found in the special issue of *Acta Asiatica* (vol. 30, 1976) on the history of foreign trade in early modern Japan: "The Japan-Dutch Trade in the Formative Period of the Seclusion Policy – Particularly on the Raw Silk Trade by the Dutch Factory at Hirado, 1620-40," pp. 34-84.

It is here that historians of institutional history showed a new approach. Their publications during the nineteen sixties gave a considerably deeper insight into the mechanism of the *bakuhan taisei*, the feudal system which was in its formative stage during the years preceding *sakoku*.

According to them the dictates of the internal policy of the *bakufu* were the principal causes of Christianity's doom. Both Asao Naohiro, a member of this school, and Katō Eiichi, although working with different approaches, showed that the adjustments within the economic structure of Japan, as a result of the emergence of the *bakuhan taisei*, were of such a radical nature that foreign trade had to be reorganised.

In 1967 Iwao published his definitive study on *sakoku*.[53] This was a collection of brilliant essays on the different aspects of the early 17th century Japanese foreign trade and the role the V.O.C. had played in East Asian waters during the same period. He clearly showed that the institution of the seclusion policy was at the same time the institution of a trade monopoly for the V.O.C. Thus in his view the V.O.C. had played an active role in the final closure of Japan. Furthermore, he adjusted his theoretical groundwork as a result of discoveries, some of which had been made by himself, concerning the Japanese economic structure. He maintained that although the eradication of Christianity may have provided some motivation for closing the country, other aspects of an institutional nature should not be overlooked. These remarks however, did not go far enough in the eyes of the students of the *bakuhan taisei*, the historians of institutional history.

In 1974, Asao Naohiro published his own views on *sakoku*, although he states very clearly that he bases his opinions on the research done by Iwao and others into foreign sources.[54]

I feel that the intrinsic danger of the institutional approach is the emphasis on formal aspects (legalistic, constitutional and institutional) and often the neglect of informal aspects. Who were the men behind the decisions at the court, and what informal procedures

[53] Iwao Seiichi, *Sakoku*, Nihon no Rekishi (Japanese History) series 13, (Tokyo: Chūō Kōron-sha, 1966).

[54] Asao Naohiro, *Sakoku*, Nihon no Rekishi (Japanese History) series 17, (Tokyo: Shōgaku-kan, 1975). Unfortunately I was not able to integrate into my paper the excellent article of Ronald P. Toby, who has further elaborated Asao's point of view in the field of Japanese-Korean relations.
Toby, Ronald, P., "Reopening the Question of Sakoku: Diplomacy in the Legitimation of the Tokugawa Bakufu," *Journal of Japanese Studies* (1977), vol. 3-2, p. 332.

took place? Questions like these were first posed by Hayashi Motoi and later answered by Iwao and his students. This is the kind of research Asao has in mind when he says he is under great obligation to Iwao.

In his opening chapter Asao states that *sakoku* is a term of foreign invention and shows that since the term was introduced in Japan in the second half of the 19th century, the concept of foreign relations by the Tokugawa shogunate has seemed to be of a negative and passive nature. According to Asao, Japan's political situation during the past one hundred years has contributed to this state of mind. Now it is time, he says, to realize that there never was a closed country. The Tokugawa military government restored order in a country which had been torn apart by more than a hundred years of civil war. The *bakufu,* as the nucleus of the *bakuhan taisei,* instituted a system of inland trade and division of labor, a policy which placed the reins of government firmly in the hands of the *shōgun.* Foreign relations and foreign trade had to be adjusted to this policy. There was no place anymore for foreigners serving a lord other than the *shōgun.* The traditional focus of Japanese morality in *chū,* the loyalty owed to political authority, became even sharper during this period. It was through the extreme flexibility and the repeated exhibitions of loyalty to the *shōgun* shown by the V.O.C. in Japan, that the Dutch gained a place within the Japanese state system.

It should be pointed out that the relation with Holland must not be treated apart from those with Japan's other tributaries, Korea and Ryūkyū. These two countries, both acknowledging a Japanese suzerainty, also fitted into the Chinese state system. Thus a Japanese world order came into being along with the Chinese world order. The secret of 250 years of peaceful coexistence between these two world systems from the 1630's onwards should probably be explained by the fact that the buffer states Ryūkyū, Korea and Holland (through its V.O.C. settlement on Formosa) were accepted in both these world orders as tributary states. Spheres of political influence had peacefully converged. Holland's position as a European tributary became odd, being a geographically remote territory, only after it was no longer a neighbour of Japan through the loss of Formosa to Coxinga in 1661, a fact which has not yet been dealt with by the specialists in the field. Although these political measures may have given Japan – in the eyes of Western observers – a peculiar place within the family of nations from the 17th century until well into the 19th century, it was a perfectly normal one within the East Asian context. And so the *opperhooft* of Deshima travelled every year like a *daimyō* to the court in Edo to show his respects to the shōgun and to arrange his business through the presentation of gifts to the members of the Council. "Please do send us," wrote the Governor General in Batavia to the *Heeren Zeventien,* the V.O.C.-directorate, in Amsterdam, "the things they (the nobles of the Japanese court) ask for and all other rare objects you might find in Holland."[55] At this point, the history of expansion becomes the history of expense accounts.

Thus it may be stated that even if Western European expansion had not taken place at all in East Asia, measures towards the restriction of foreign intercourse would still have been carried out. It is evident, however, that European penetration, be it in the form of missionaries or traders, has directly influenced both the pace of the formative measures that shaped the political constellation of Tokugawa Japan and the manner in which they took place.

V. CONCLUSION

Fear of diplomatic isolation has been an ever-recurring theme in Japanese foreign policy since the country was opened up in 1853. This fear, be it right or wrong, has manifested itself through intermittent periods as either a kind of internationalism combined with openness to foreign ideas (early Meiji and postwar period), or a nationalistic retirement within itself in combination with aspirations to reach a state of self-sufficiency (early Shōwa). Objectively speaking, it is quite understandable that this fear of isolation should appear in a country that has stood uneasily between East and West over the last 125 years, and it is a notion that will not easily be dispelled.[56]

A circumstance reinforcing this state of mind in Japan's case has been that a series of political and economical measures taken by the first Tokugawa rulers in order to strengthen their sway over the country has been wrongly interpreted through methods and concepts derived from Ranke's diplomatic history. Diplomacy stands for the art and practice of negotiations between sovereign states. Diplomatic history as such consequently represents a European notion of foreign relations that has only emerged over the last few hundred years in the West, a notion which does not necessarily

[55] Coolhaas, W.Ph., *Generale Missiven,* vol. I ('s-Gravenhage, 1960), p. 602.

[56] See also Iriye's Akira remarks on the question of Japan's diplomatic isolation in "Japanese Imperialism and Aggression: Reconsideration II," *Journal of Asian Studies,* vol. XXIII (1964), p. 112.

apply to 17th century East Asia. An excessive emphasis on external affairs as decisive factors in the march of events led to the erroneous interpretation of the *bakufu* policies as constituting a closing up of the country under pressure of Western expansion. It has created a formidable, almost pathologic obsession among the Japanese, leading them to believe that, whenever things do not exactly work out as they would like them to, they are standing alone confronting the rest of the world. The contribution of scholars like Murakami and Iwao in supplying translations of Western (Dutch) source materials with their rich economic data, and, along with these, studies based on multi-archival research, has made it possible for historians of institutional history to write a true national history by dispelling the myth of an isolation created as a desperate act to counter the aggressive pressure of foreign expansion.

It is tempting to speculate whether or not this 180 degree turn in the assessment of "the closure" of Japan will eventually lead to a more detached vision of Japans's relationship with the rest of the world. After all, the country's famous – or infamous – 250 years of isolation turn out not to have been a reaction of last resort to foreign pressure, but rather a brand-new beginning, deliberately chosen, even if for short term reasons.

Riess' students mentioned in this paper

Ludwig Riess

Kyoto University

- Yano Niichi; Uchida Ginzō; Miura Hiroyuki
  - Kobata Atsushi
    - Asao Naohiro

Keiō University

- Koda Shigetomo
  - Hayashi Motoi

Tokyo University

- Murakami Naojirō
  - Nakamura Takashi (Taihoku University)
  - Iwao Seiichi
    - Kanai Madoka; Nagazumi Yōko; Nagazumi Akira; Yamawaki Teijiro; Katō Eiichi
  - Itazawa Takeo
    - Numata Jirō; Yanai Kenji

PART V

BIBLIOGRAPHY

12. POST-COLONIAL BIBLIOGRAPHY: SOME USEFUL TITLES

by

G.J. TELKAMP

To gain bibliographic access to pre-war expansion studies, we would have to rely on reference works dealing with national European histories, Oriental and other extra-European studies, but above all on general colonial bibliographies and catalogues which devoted some sections to historiography proper. After the Second World War and decolonisation, in Western Europe somewhat later than in the United States, in a long, painful, scarcely completed process, the old Oriental and related studies merged with the social sciences part of colonial studies into what gradually came under the common denominator of "area studies." In this multi- and interdisciplinary context expansion studies were continued, the more so because development theories and the growth of university education in Third World countries stimulated a renewed interest in the history of the so-called underdeveloped countries. This continuity of research explains the fact that a bibliographic approach to post-war expansion historiography should focus on reference tools dealing with the national histories of countries in three continents and include national or area studies bibliographies in addition to the colonial or overseas history sections in bibliographies covering the history of former colonial powers.

For obvious reasons it would be a bit superfluous or even pretentious to include in the bibliographic section of this rather bibliographic volume a list of "classic" or "relevant" titles of books or articles in the field of European expansion history. Therefore a selection has been made of reference books, mainly bibliographies and bibliographies of bibliographies, with the emphasis on fairly recent titles with a fairly large coverage of the relevant post-war literature. Some handbooks, review articles and historiographical introductions have been included. As appears from the titles and as is explained above many publications do not refer explicitly to colonial or expansion history or they do not exclusively cover historical studies. To whet the researcher's appetite a number of bibliographies have been added which point to specific aspects of European expansion, e.g. tools covering colonial *belles lettres* or biographies of nationalist leaders. This forms an arbitrary selection and a bibliography of bibliographies relevant to expansion history remains an unfulfilled wish of workers in our field of study. For, as a matter of fact, the definition of the scope of expansion studies may determine the kind of specialist bibliographic source one uses. This scope depends on the researcher's point of view of what expansion includes and on the special aspect he may fall in love with including the degree of interdisciplinarity which he wishes to pursue. To give a few examples: a student of colonial urban history would be advised to consult the *Urban History Yearbook* (though urban history is still a rather "western" theme within the historical discipline). Those studying the influence of Chinese art upon European painting as an example of "exotism" would – apart from Donald F. Lach's *Asia in the Making of Europe* – consult the appropriate bibliographies of (European) art history. Those interested in missionary history will be referred to the *Bibliografia Missionaria* which is annually published by the *Pontificia Biblioteca Missionaria* in Rome. And the students of Anglo-Indian literature or Multatuli might do good to use (current) bibliographies of English and Dutch literature. The theme of the history of European expansion and its reactions as well as its bibliographic coverage is continually expanding.

A SELECTIVE BIBLIOGRAPHY OF BIBLIOGRAPHICAL WORKS RELEVANT TO THE STUDY OF EUROPEAN EXPANSION

General Works

The American Historical Association's Guide to Historical Literature, ed. by George Frederick Howe (New York 1961).

Foreign Affairs Bibliography. A selected and annotated list of books on international relations (New York 1933–).

Halstead, John P., and Serafino Porcari. *Modern European Imperialism: a bibliography of books and articles 1815-1972* (Boston 1974). 2 Vols. Vol. 1. *General and British Empire.* Vol. 2. *French and other Empires; regions.*

Ragatz, Lowell Joseph. *A bibliography of articles, descriptive, historical and scientific, on colonies and other dependent territories, appearing in*

American geographical and kindred journals, 2nd enl. ed. 2 Vols. (Washington 1951) Vol. 1. Through 1934. Vol. 2. 1935 through 1950; comp. by Janet Evans Ragatz.

Ragatz, Lowell Joseph. *The Literature of European Imperialism, 1815-1939; a bibliography* (Washington 1944).

Bibliographies Covering Specific Aspects of European Expansion

Albion, R.G. *Naval and Maritime history; an annotated bibliography,* 4th rev. and exp. ed. (Mystic 1972).

Carlson, Andrew R. *German Foreign Policy, 1890-1914 and Colonial Policy to 1914: a handbook and annotated bibliography* (Metuchen 1970).

Carnell, Francis. *The Politics of the New States; a select annotated bibliography with special reference to the Commonwealth* (London 1961).

Coolhaas, W.Ph. *A Critical Survey of Studies on Dutch Colonial History* (The Hague 1960).

Emmer, Pieter C. "The History of the Dutch slave trade, a bibliographical survey." *Journal of Economic History 33* (1973) 3, September, 723-747.

Hogg, P.C. *The African Slave Trade and its Suppression; a classified and annotated bibliography* (London 1973).

Lohf, Kenneth A., and Eugene P. Sheehy. *Joseph Conrad at Mid-Century; editions and studies, 1895-1955* (Minneapolis 1957).

National Maritime Museum. Catalogue of the library. Vol. 1. *Voyages and Travel* (London 1968).

Ristow, W.W., and C.E. Le Gear. *A Guide to Historical Cartography; a selected, annotated list of references on the history of maps and map making* (Washington 1960).

British Colonial History, Empire and Commonwealth

Berkowitz, David S. *Bibliotheca bibliographica Brittanica, or, Bibliographies in British history.* Book 2. Part. 4. Guides to exploration, colonies, empire and Commonwealth history (Waltham 1969).

Biography catalogue of the library of the Royal Commonwealth Society (London 1961).

Cambridge History of the British Empire. 8 Vols. (Cambridge 1929-1959).

Catalogue of the Colonial Office Library, London. 15 Vols. (Boston 1964).

Curtin, Philip D. "The British Empire and Commonwealth in recent historiography." *American Historical Review 65* (1959), October, 72-91.

Flint, John E. (ed.). *Books on the British Empire and Commonwealth: a Guide for Students* (London 1968).

Gipson, C.H. *The British Empire before the American Revolution.* 13 Vols. (New York 1965-1968).

Harlow, Vincent T. *The Historiography of the British Empire and Commonwealth since 1945* (Uppsala 1960).

Hewitt, A.R. *Guide to Resources for Commonwealth history in London, Oxford and Cambridge* (London 1957).

Livingston, William S. (ed.). *Federalism in the Commonwealth, a bibliographical commentary* (London 1963).

Morrell, W.P. *British Overseas Expansion and the History of the Commonwealth: a select bibliography;* 3rd rev. ed. (London 1961).

Patchett, Keith, and Valerie Jenkins. *Bibliographical Guide to Law in the Commonwealth Caribbean* (Jamaica 1973).

Subject catalogue of the Royal Commonwealth Society. 7 Vols. (Boston 1971).

Winks, R.W. (ed.). *The Historiography of the British Empire-Commonwealth* (Durham and London 1966).

AFRICA

General

Asamani, J.O. *Index Africanus* (Stanford 1975).

Besterman, Theodore. *A World Bibliography of African Bibliographies.* rev. and brought up to date by J.D. Pearson (Oxford 1975).

Historiography

Current Themes in African Historical Studies; a selected bibliographical guide to resources for research in African history, ed. by Daniel G. Matthew (Westport 1970).

Emerging Themes of African History, proceedings of the International Congress of African Historians (Nairobi 1968).

Discoveries

Casada, James A. *Dr David Livingstone and Sir Henry Morton Stanley: an annotated bibliography* (Garland Publishing Inc. 1976).

Current bibliography

International African Bibliography; current books, articles and papers in African studies (London 1971–).

Handbooks

Colonialism in Africa, 1870-1960. 5 Vols. (London 1969-1975). Vol. 5. *A Bibliographical Guide to Colonialism in Sub-Saharan Africa,* by Peter Duignan and Lewis H. Gann. 1973.

The Cambridge History of Africa, general eds. J.D. Fage and Roland Anthony Oliver (Cambridge 1975–). 8 Vols. In progress.

German colonies

Bridgeman, Jon, and D.E. Clarke. *German Africa: a selected annotated bibliography* (Stanford 1965).

Italian colonies

L'Italia in Africa, serie storica (Roma 1958–).

British African Studies

Hammond, Dorothy, and Alta Jablow. *The Africa that never was: four Centuries of British Writing about Africa* (New York 1970).

French African Studies

Dinstel, Marion. *List of French doctoral dissertations on Africa, 1884-1961* (Boston 1966).

Soviet African Studies

Holdsworth, Mary. *Soviet African Studies 1918-1959; an annotated bibliography* (London 1961).

Africa South of the Sahara

Africa South of the Sahara; index to periodical literature, 1900-1970, comp. in the African section, General Reference and Bibliographic Division, Reference Department, Library of Congress. 4 Vols. (Boston 1971. 1st suppl. 1973).

Guide to Research and Reference Works on Sub-Saharan Africa, ed. by Peter Duignan; comp. by Helen F. Conover and Peter Duignan (Stanford 1971).

The Historian in Tropical Africa (London 1964).

Select Annotated Bibliography of Tropical Africa, comp. by the International African Institute under the direction of Daryll Forde (New York 1956. Repr. New York 1969).

Algeria

Dejeux, Jean. *Essai de Bibliographie Algérienne, 1er janvier 1954-30 juin 1962; Lecture d'une Guerre.* Cahiers nord-africains no 92 (1962).

Lawless, Richard I. *Algerian Bibliography: English Language Publications 1830-1973* (London and New York 1976).

Cameroon

De Lancey, Mark W., and Virginia H. De Lancey. *A Bibliography of Cameroon* (New York 1975).

East Africa

History of East Africa (Oxford 1963–). In progress.

Egypt

El-Benhawy, Mohamed Amin. *The Suez Canal; a descriptive bibliography* (Ph.D. The University of Michigan 1964).

Maunier, René. *Bibliographie économique, juridique et sociale de l'Egypte moderne (1798-1916)* (New York 1971).

Equatorial Guinea

Berman, Sanford. *Spanish Guinea: an annotated bibliography* (Washington 1961).

Ethiopia

Marcus, Harold G. *The Modern History of Ethiopia and the Horn of Africa; a select and annotated bibliography* (Stanford 1972).

Gambia

Gamble, David P. *Bibliography of the Gambia* (Bathurst 1967).

Ghana

Afre, S. *Ashanti Region of Ghana: an annotated bibliography from earliest times to 1973* (Boston 1975).

Johnson, Albert Frederick. *A bibliography of Ghana, 1930-1961* (Accra 1964).

Ivory Coast

Janvier, Geneviève, *Bibliographie de la Côte d'Ivoire.* Vol. 2. Sciences de l'homme (Abidjan 1973).

Kenya

Webster, John B., Shirin G. Kassam, Robert S. Peckham, and Barbara A. Skapa. *Bibliography on Kenya* (Syracuse 1967).

Lybia

Hill, Roy W. *A Bibliography of Lybia* (Durham 1959).

Mali

Brasseur, Paule. *Bibliographie générale du Mali (Anciens Soudan français et Haut-Sénégal-Niger)* (Dakar 1964).

Brasseur, Paule. *Bibliographie générale du Mali (1961-1970)* (Dakar 1976).

Brown, Edward F., Carol A. Fisher, and John B. Webster. *A Bibliography of Mali* (Syracuse 1965).

Morocco

Miège, Jean-Louis. *Le Maroc et l'Europe, 1830-1894*. Vol. 1. *Sources, bibliographie* (Paris 1961).

Nigeria

Aguolu, Christian Chukwunedu. *Nigeria: a comprehensive bibliography in the humanities and social sciences, 1900-1971* (Boston 1973).

North Africa

Blaudin de Thé, Bernard M.S. *Essai de bibliographie du Sahara français et des régions avoisinantes* (Alger 1959).

Rwanda + Burundi

Clément, Joseph R.A.M. *Essai de bibliographie du Ruanda-Urundi* (Usumbura 1959).

Sierra Leone

Williams, Geoffrey I. *A Bibliography of Sierra Leone, 1925-1967* (New York 1971).

South Africa

Jaarsveld, Floris A. van. *The Afrikaner's Interpretation of South African History* (Capetown 1964).

A Select Bibliography of South African history; a guide for historical research, ed. by C.F.J. Muller, F.J.A. van Jaarsveld and Theo van Wijk (Pretoria 1966). 1st suppl. 1974.

Musiker, Reuben. *Guide to South African Reference Books;* 4th ed. (Capetown 1965).

Nicholson, Gilliam. *German Settlers in South Africa; a bibliography* (Capetown 1962).

The Oxford History of South Africa ed. by Monica Wilson and Leonard Monteath Thompson. 2 Vols. (London 1969-1971).

Ushpol, Rowse. *Select Bibliography of South African Autobiographies* (Capetown 1958).

Verner, Beryl Anne. *Huguenots in South Africa; a bibliography* (Capetown 1967).

Southern Africa

Gross, Felix. *Bibliography for Rhodes of Africa* (London 1956).

Thompson, Leonard Monteath, Richard Elphick, and Inez Jarrick. *Southern African History before 1900: a select bibliography of articles, 2nd pr.* (Stanford 1972).

Zaire

Walraet, Marcel. *Bibliographie du Katanga.* 3 Vols. (Bruxelles 1954-1960).

ASIA. THE MIDDLE EAST AND THE PACIFIC

General

Besterman, Theodore. *A World Bibliography of Oriental Bibliographies,* rev. and brought up to date by J.D. Pearson (Oxford 1975).

Cumulative bibliography of Asian studies, 1941-1965. 8 Vols. (Boston 1969-1970).

Cumulative bibliography of Asian studies, 1966-1970. 6 Vols. (Boston 1972-1973).

Pearson, J.D. *Oriental and Asian bibliography* (London 1966).

Special bibliography

Trager, Frank N. *Furnivall of Burma: an annotated bibliography of John S. Furnivall* (New Haven 1963).

Islam

Sauvaget, Jean. *Introduction to the history of the Muslim East; a bibliographical guide;* based on the 2nd ed. as recast by Claude Cahen (Berkeley 1965).

Schwartz, Klaus. *Verzeichnis deutschsprachiger Hochschulschriften zum islamischen Orient (1885-1970). Deutschland – Oesterreich – Schweiz* (Freiburg im Breisgau 1971).

Australia

Crowley, Francis Keble. *South Australian History; a survey for research students* (Adelaide 1966).

Burma

Trager, Frank N. *Annotated Bibliography of Burma* (New Haven 1956).

China

Fairbank, John King, Masataka Banno, and Sumiko Yamamoto. *Japanese Studies of Modern China; a bibliographical guide to historical and social-science research on the 19th and 20th centuries* (Cambridge Mass. 1971).

Lust, John. *Index sinicus: a catalogue of articles relating to China in periodicals and other collective publications, 1920-1955,* comp. with the assistance of Werner Eichhorn (Cambridge 1964).

Yüan, T'ung-li. *China in Western Literature: a continuation of Cordier's Bibliotheca sinica* (New Haven 1958).

China/Japan

Beasly, William Gerald, and Edwin George Pulleyblank. *Historians of China and Japan* (London 1961).

India

The Cambridge History of India; ed. by E.J. Rapson a.o. Vol. 1, Vols. 3-6 and suppl. Vol. (Cambridge 1922-1953) (Repr. 1957-1964).

Datta, Kāli Kinkara. *A Survey of Recent Studies on Modern Indian History,* 2nd ed. (Calcutta 1963).

Grevāla, Jagatāra Simha. *Muslim Rule in India; the assessments of British Historians* (London 1970).

Gupta, Brijen Kishore. *India in English Fiction, 1800-1970; an annotated bibliography* (Metuchen 1973).

Historians and Historiography in Modern India, papers read at the 6th annual conference of the Institute of Historical Studies, held at Srinagar (Kashmir) in Oct. 1968, ed. by S.P. Sen. (Calcutta 1973).

Ladendorf, Janice M. *The Revolt in India 1857-58, an annotated bibliography of English language materials* (Zug 1966).

Mohandas Karamchand Gandhi; a bibliography; a project of the Indian Council of Social Science Research (New Delhi 1974).

Morris, Morris D., and B. Stein. "The economic history of India: a bibliographical essay". *Journal of economic history 21* (1961), June, 179-207.

Nīlakanthạ Śāstrī, K.A. *Sources of Indian history with special References to South India* (London 1964).

Scholberg, Henry Caesar. *Bibliographie des Français dans l'Inde; avec la collaboration d'Emmanuel Divien* (Pondicherry 1973).

Sharma, Jagdish Saran. *Indian National Congress; a descriptive bibliography of India's struggle for freedom* (Delhi 1959).

Sharma, Jagdish Saran. *Mahatma Gandhi; a descriptive bibliography.* (Delhi 1955).

Spencer, Dorothy Mary. *Indian Fiction in English: an annotated bibliography* Philadelphia 1960).

India/Pakistan

Wilson, Patrick. *Government and Politics of India and Pakistan, 1885-1955: a bibliography of works in Western languages* (Berkeley 1956).

India/Pakistan/Sri Lanka

Philips, Cyril Henry. *Historians of India, Pakistan and Ceylon* (London 1961).

Indochina

Auvade, Robert. *Bibliographie critique des oeuvres parues sur l'Indochine française; un siècle d'histoire et d'enseignement* (Paris 1965).

Indonesia

Excerpta Indonesica (Leiden) no. 1– (1970–).

An Introduction to Indonesian Historiography, ed. by Soedjatmoko and Mohammad Ali, G.J. Resink a.o. (Ithaca 1965).

Tairas, J.N.B. *Indonesia: a bibliography of bibliographies* (New York 1975).

Iran

Sabā, Muhsin. *Bibliographie française de l'Iran; bibliographie méthodique et raisonnée des ouvrages français parus depuis 1560 jusqu'à nos jours;* 3e éd. rev. et augm. par Mohsen Saba (Tehran 1966).

Japan

Goedertier, Joseph M. *A Dictionary of Japanese history* (New York 1968).

Recent trends in Japanese historiography; bibliographical essays; Japan at the 13th International Congress of Historical Sciences in Moscow, 1970; ed. by the Japanese National Committee of Historical Sciences. 2 Vols. (Tokyo 1970).

Têng, Ssŭ-Yü. *Japanese Studies on Japan and the Far East; a short biographical and bibliographical introduction;* with the collaboration of Maruda Kenji and Kaneda Hiromitsu (Hong Kong 1961).

Malaysia

Tong Suit Chee. *Bibliography of Penang* (Pulau Pinang 1974).

Middle East

Lewis, Bernard, and P.M. Holt. *Historians of the Middle East* (London 1962).

Middle East and Islam; a bibliographical introduction; ed. by Derek Hopwood and Diana Grimwood-Jones (Zug 1972).

Oceania

Cammack, Floyd M., and S. Saito. *Pacific Island Bibliography* (New York 1962).

Matsuda, Mitsugu. *The Japanese in Hawaii, 1868-1967; a bibliography of the first hundred years* (Honolulu 1968).

O'Reilly, Patrick. *Bibliographie méthodique, analytique et critique de la Nouvelle-Calédonie* (Paris 1955).

O'Reilly, Patrick. *Bibliographie méthodique, analytique et critique des Nouvelles-Hébrides* (Paris 1958).

O'Reilly, Patrick, et Edouard Reitman. *Bibliographie de Tahiti et de la Polynésie française* (Paris 1967).

Philippines

Hart, Donn V. *An Annotated Bibliography of Philippine Bibliographies: 1965-1974* (Wyoming 1974).

Onorato, Michael P. *Philipine Bibliography (1899-1946)* (Santa Barbara 1968).

South Asia

Case, Margaret H. *South Asian History, 1750-1950; a guide to periodicals, dissertations and newspapers* (Princeton 1968).

Patterson, M.L.P., and R.B. Inden. *South Asia; an introductory bibliography* (Chicago 1962).

South East Asia

Hall, D.G.E. *Historians of South East Asia* (London 1961).

Morrison, Gayle. *A Guide to Books on Southeast Asian History (1961-1966)* Stephen N. Hay ed. (Santa Barbara 1969).

SarDesai, D.R., and B.D. SarDesai. *Theses and Dissertations on Southeast Asia; an international bibliography in social sciences, education, and fine arts* (Zug 1970).

Southeast Asian History; a bibliographic guide; ed. by Stephen N. Hay and Margaret H. Case (New York 1962).

Sri Lanka

Goonetileke, H.A.J. *A Bibliography of Ceylon; a systematic guide to the literature on the land, people, history and culture published in Western languages from the sixteenth century to the present day*, forew. by J.D. Pearson. 2 Vols. (Zug 1970). Suppl. Vol. (1976).

Turkey

Kornrumpf, Hans Jürgen. *Osmanische Bibliographie mit besonderer Berücksichtigung der Türkei in Europa*, unter Mitarb. von Jutta Kornrumpf (Leiden 1973).

Vietnam

Jumper, Roy. *Bibliography on the political and administrative history of Vietnam 1802-1962* (Saigon 1962).

Nguyền Thế-Anh. *Bibliographie critique sur les relations entre le Viet-Nam et l'Occident (ouvrages et articles en langues occidentales)* (Paris 1967).

AMERICAS

General studies

Bibliografía americanista española 1935-1963. (Sevilla 1964).

Dictionary catalogue of the history of the Americas, New York Public Library, Reference Department. 28 Vols. (Boston 1961).

Argentina

Fúrlong, Cardiff Guillermo, and Abel Rodolfo Geoghegan. *Bibliografía de la revolución de mayo, 1810-1828* (Buenos Aires 1960).

Brazil

Borba de Moraes, Rubens, and William Berrien. *Manual bibliográfico de estudos brasileiros* (Rio de Janeiro 1949).

Borba de Moraes, Rubens. *Bibliografia brasileira do período colonial; catálogo comentado das obras dos autores nascidos no Brasil e publicades antes de 1808* (Sao Paolo 1969).

Canada

Garigue, Philip. A Bibliographical Introduction to the Study of French Canada (Montreal 1956).

Story, Norah. *The Oxford Companion to Canadian History and Literature.* (Toronto 1973).

Thibault, Claude. *Bibliographia Canadiana* (Ontario 1973).

Caribbean

Comitas, Lambros. Caribbeana 1900-1965: *a topical bibliography* (Seattle 1968).

Development Towards Self-government in the Caribbean; a selective bibliography (The Hague 1955).

Marshall, Woodville K. "A review of historical writing on the Commonwealth Caribbean since c. 1940." *Social and Economic Studies 24* (1975) 3, September, 277-307.

Williams, Eric E. *British Historians and the West Indies* (London 1966).

Caribbean/Latin America

Bayitch, S.A. *Latin America and the Caribbean, a bibliographical guide to works in English* (Coral Gables 1967).

Cuba

Pérez Cabrera, José Manuel. *Historiografía de Cuba* (México 1962).

French Guiana

Abonnenc, E., J. Hurault, R. Saban et autres. *Bibliographie de la Guyane Française, tome 1: ouvrages et articles de la langue française concernant la Guyane et les territoires avoisinantes* (Paris 1957).

Haiti

Pressoir, Catts, Ernst Trouillot, et Hanock Trouillot. *Historiographie d'Haiti* (Mexico 1953).

Jamaica

Ingram, K.E. *Sources of Jamaican History 1655-1838; a bibliographical survey with particular reference to manuscript sources* (Zug 1976).

Latin America

Alcina Franch, José, and Josefina Palop Martínez. *América en la época de Carlos V; aportación a la bibliografía de este período desde 1900* (Madrid 1958).

Cline, H.F. (ed.). *Latin American History; essays on its study and teaching 1898-1965.* 2 Vols. (Austin 1965).

Dequenne, Jean. *Amérique latine; essai de bibliographie des ouvrages belges publiés sur l'Amérique latine, 1875-1962* (Bruxelles 1965).

Handbook of Latin American Studies; a guide to the material published on anthropology, archaeology, economics, geography, history, law and literature. Vol. 1-13 (Cambridge Mass. 1935-1947). Vol. 14– (Gainesville 1948–).

Latin America; a guide to the historical literature, Charles Griffin, ed.; J. Benedict Warren, assist. ed. (Austin 1971).

Gropp, Arthur E. *A Bibliography of Latin American Bibliographies Published in Periodicals.* 2 Vols. (Metuchen 1976).

Humphreys, Robin Arthur. *Latin American History: a guide to the literature in English* (London 1958).

Indice histórico español; bibliografía histórica de España e Hispano-America (Barcelona 1953–).

Mörner, Magnus. "The Spanish American hacienda: a survey of recent research and debate" *Hispanic American Historical Review 53* (1973), 183-216.

Wilder Weisman, E. "The history of art in Latin America, 1500-1800, some trends and challenges in the last decade." *Latin American Research Review 10* (1975) 1, 7-50.

Martinique

Jardel, Jean-Pierre, Maurice Nicolas, et Claude Relouzat. *Bibliographie de la Martinique* (Fort-de-France 1969).

Mexico

Hernandez Tapia, German. *Ensayo de una bibliografía de la intervención Europea en México en el siglo XIX, 1861-1867* (México 1962).

Ramos, Roberto. *Bibliografía de la historia de México* (México 1956).

Netherlands Antilles

Bibliografie van de Nederlandse Antillen (Amsterdam 1972).

North America

Fenton, William N., L.H. Butterfield, and Wilcomb E. Washburn. *American Indian and White Relations to 1830; needs and opportunities for study* (Chapel Hill and Williamsburg 1957).

Johnson, Thomas Herbert. *The Oxford Companion to American History,* in consultation with Harvey Wish (New York 1966).

Lanctôt, Gustave. *L'oeuvre de la France en Amérique du Nord; bibliographie sélective et critique* (Montréal 1951).

Puerto Rico

Vivó, P. *The Puerto Ricans: an annotated bibliography* (New York 1973).

Surinam

Bibliografie van Suriname. (Amsterdam 1974).

Price, Richard. *The Guiana Maroons; a historical and bibliographical introduction* (Baltimore 1976).

United States of America

America: History and Life; a guide to periodical literature (Santa Barbara 1964–).

Blacks in America; bibliographical essays; by James M. McPherson, Laurence B. Holland, James M. Banner Jr., and others (Garden City 1971).

The Negro in the United States; a working bibliography, compiled by Dorothy B. Porter (Ann Arbor 1969).

Smith, D.L. *Afro-American History: a bibliography* (Santa Barbara and Oxford 1974).

Smith, D.L. *Era of the American Revolution; a bibliography* (Santa Barbara 1975).

United States/Latin America

Trask, David F. *A Bibliography of United States – Latin American relations since 1810; a selected list of eleven thousand published references,* comp. and ed. by David F. Trask, Michael C. Meyer, and Roger R. Trask; 2nd pr. (Lincoln 1969).

NOTES ON THE CONTRIBUTORS

C.A. BAYLY is fellow and tutor of *St. Catharine's College, Cambridge.*
His publications include:
The Local Roots of Indian Politics. Allahabad 1880-1920 (Oxford 1975) and various articles on India dealing in particular with the history of towns and merchant communities.

H. BLEY (1935) is professor of modern history at the *University of Hannover.*
His publications include:
South-West Africa under German Rule 1894-1914 (Heinemann, London 1971), *Bebel und die Strategie der Kriegsverhütung 1904-1913* (Göttingen 1975) and various articles on African history and political developments.

L. BLUSSÉ (1946) is research fellow at the *Centre for the History of European Expansion, University of Leiden.*
His publications include:
"Western Impact on Chinese Communities in Western Java at the Beginning of the 17th Century," *Nampo Bunka* 1975 – 2: pp. 26-57, and various other articles dealing with the overseas Chinese within colonial society.
He is preparing a doctoral thesis on the Dutch colonisation of Taiwan during the first half of the 17th century.

H. BRUNSCHWIG (1904) is *Directeur d'études* at the *Ecole des Hautes Etudes.*
His publications include:
Mythes et réalités de l'impérialisme colonial français, 1871-1914. Paris 1960. (English translation: *French Colonialism, 1871-1914. Myths and Realities,* London 1966).
L'avènement de l'Afrique noire ["The Awakening of Black Africa"], Paris 1963.
Le partage de l'Afrique noire ["The partition of Black Africa"], Paris 1971.

P.C. EMMER (1944) is research fellow at the *Centre for the History of European Expansion, University of Leiden.*
His publications include:
Engeland, Nederland, Afrika en de Slavenhandel in de Negentiende Eeuw ["England, the Netherlands, Africa and the Slave Trade of the 19th Century"] Leiden 1974.

with Jean Mettas & Jean-Claude Nardin (eds.), La Traite des noirs par l'Atlantique; Nouvelles approches ["The Atlantic Slave Trade; New Approaches"] *Revue française d'histoire d'outre-mer,* LXII (1975).

A.G. HOPKINS (1938) is professor of economic history at the *University of Birmingham.*
His publications include:
An Economic History of West Africa, London & New York 1973. (Ed., with Clive Dewey) *The Imperial Impact: Studies in the Economic History of Africa and India,* London 1978.

J.L. MIÈGE (1923) is professor of history at the *Université de Provence* and Director of the *Institut d'Histoire des Pays d'Outre-Mer* at Aix-en-Provence.
His publications include:
Le Maroc et l'Europe ["Morocco and Europe"], Paris 1961-1964 (4 vols.).
L'impérialisme colonial italien de 1870 à nos jours ["Italian Colonial Imperialism since 1870"], Paris 1968.
Expansion européenne et décolonisation de 1870 à nos jours ["European Expansion and Decolonisation since 1870"], Paris 1973.

N. STEENSGAARD (1932) is professor of history at the *University of Copenhagen.*
His publications include:
Carracks, Caravans and Companies, Copenhagen 1973. (Amer. edition: *The Asian Trade Revolution of the Seventeenth Century. The East India Companies and the Decline of the Caravan Trade.* Chicago and London 1974).

J. STENGERS (1922) is professor at the *University of Brussels.*
His publications include:
Combien le Congo a-t-il coûté à la Belgique? ["How much did Congo cost to Belgium?"], Brussels 1957.
Belgique et Congo. L'Elaboration de la Charte Coloniale ["Belgium and Congo. The Drawing up of the Colonial Charter"], Brussels 1963.
Emigration et immigration en Belgique au XIXe et au XXe siècle ["Emigration and immigration in Belgium, 19th-20th centuries"], Brussels 1978.

G.J. TELKAMP (1947) is documentalist at the *Centre for the History of European Expansion, University of Leiden.* He compiles the *Current Annotated Bibliography of Dutch Expansion Studies.*

H.L. WESSELING (1937) is professor of contemporary history and director of the *Centre for the History of European Expansion, University of Leiden.*
His publications include:
Soldaat en Krijger. Franse opvattingen over leger en oorlog, 1905-1914 ["Soldier and Warrior. French Opinions on Army and War, 1905-1914"], Assen 1969.
(Ed.) *Expansion and Reaction,* The Hague 1978.

G.D. WINIUS (1928) is senior lecturer, *Department of History, University of Leiden.*

His publications include:

The Fatal History of Portuguese Ceylon; Transitions to Dutch Rule (Cambridge, Mass. 1971).

with B.W. Diffie, *Foundations of the Portuguese Empire, 1415-1580* (Minneapolis/Oxford 1977).

INDEX OF AUTHORS